GOOD-TASTING, GOOD-LOOKING, NUTRITIOUS, AND DIET-CONSCIOUS MEALS— ALL IN UNDER ONE HOUR!

From Champagne Cocktail to Chicken Velouté to Lemon Meringue Pie, this busy-dieter's cookbook will help you streamline your schedule while you streamline your figure—with 250 delicious recipes and all these special features:

- Calorie, protein, fat, carbohydrate, sodium, and cholesterol counts

- Make-ahead recipes to store in the freezer

- One-dish, no-cook, and single-serving recipes

- Party menus requiring minimal last-minute preparation

- Time-saving and dollar-stretching symbols to highlight especially quick and economical dishes

WEIGHT WATCHERS®
Fast & Fabulous
COOKBOOK

WEIGHT WATCHERS®
Fast & Fabulous
COOKBOOK

Ⓟ
A PLUME BOOK
NEW AMERICAN LIBRARY
NEW YORK AND SCARBOROUGH, ONTARIO

WEIGHT WATCHERS *is a registered trademark of*
Weight Watchers International, Inc.

Copyright © 1983 by Weight Watchers International, Inc.
All rights reserved. For information address
New American Library.

A hardcover edition was published by New American Library
and simultaneously in Canada by The New American Library
of Canada Limited.

 PLUME TRADEMARK REG. U.S. PAT. OFF. AND FOREIGN COUNTRIES
REG. TRADEMARK—MARCA REGISTRADA
HECHO EN HARRISONBURG, VA., U.S.A.

Designed by Julian Hamer
Cover photography and photo insert by Gus Francisco
Drawings by Marcy Gold

SIGNET, SIGNET CLASSIC, MENTOR, ONYX, PLUME,
MERIDIAN and NAL BOOKS are published *in the United
States* by NAL PENGUIN INC., 1633 Broadway, New York,
New York 10019, *in Canada* by The New American Library of
Canada Limited, 81 Mack Avenue, Scarborough, Ontario
M1L 1M8

LIBRARY OF CONGRESS CATALOGING IN PUBLICATION DATA
Main entry under title:
Weight Watchers fast and fabulous cookbook.
    Includes index.
    1. Reducing diets—Recipes.   I. Weight Watchers
International.
RM222.2.W3135   1984   641.5′635   83–12097
ISBN 0-453-01008-3
ISBN 0–452–25727–1 (pbk.)

First Plume Printing, September, 1985

        8   9   10   11   12   13   14

PRINTED IN THE UNITED STATES OF AMERICA

Contents

Acknowledgments

This book could never have been created without the combined inspiration, determination, and dedication of the chefs, home economists, editors, and secretarial staff of Weight Watchers International. For the numerous hours spent developing and testing recipes we thank Bianca Brown, Nina Procaccini, and Judi Rettmer. For the complicated task of researching, writing, and editing the manuscript our grateful appreciation goes to Patricia Barnett, Anne Hosansky, Harriet Pollock, Eileen Pregosin, and Elizabeth Resnick. And for the many hours of typing, and patience with the author's revisions, a large measure of thanks goes to Lucille Corsello, Isabel Fleisher, Lola Sher, and Gladys Werner.

Lelio G. Parducci, Ph.D.
VICE PRESIDENT
RESEARCH & DEVELOPMENT SERVICES

Introduction

Dear Reader,

I often think the most appropriate logo for our times would be the face of a clock, for these days most people lead frantically busy lives. The daily juggling acts of home/family/job/school have become more pressured than ever. Of course, this affects the amount of time and effort you can afford to put into the challenges of meal preparation. That's true not only for women, but also for men, who are pitching in to help more and more these days. Even youngsters want to know how to cook easy meals, so they can help out while Mom and Dad are working.

To help the busy cook prepare first-rate meals, recipes need to offer two main ingredients: ease of preparation and a relatively short cooking time. (Of course, the third essential "ingredient" is help in *slimming*, since a quick-and-easy dish shouldn't have to be paid for in pounds.)

All of these factors have been blended into the recipes in our *Fast & Fabulous Cookbook*. We have heard your requests for help and here's our answer: a cookbook that serves up dishes that are not only figure-conscious, but time-conscious too. *These dishes can be prepared in a minimum amount of time*—so easily even a novice can toss them off, and with such bewitching results that family and friends will be convinced you're a kitchen magician.

You'll find simple but savory recipes for almost any occasion you can dream up, recipes that not only call for *simple* cookery but, in some cases, for *no* cookery at all. There are tips for transforming routine family meals into surprising delights as well as suggestions for hosting without hassle, even at the last minute. Since we haven't forgotten the "live-aloners," there is a whole chapter on ways to treat *yourself* like a VIP. Sprinkled throughout are savvy economy tips and scores of suggestions for getting twice as much mileage from your efforts. Whether you live alone or are a family member, we believe you owe it to yourself to be free of unnecessary—and unnecessarily tempting—time in the kitchen.

For more than two decades, the Weight Watchers Organization has been dedicated to the belief that every human being has the right to a truly rewarding life-style, and that weight control is an important factor in being able to feel good about yourself. That's the philosophy that underlies our famous Food Plan, our self-management and exercise plans, and the group support offered in all our meetings, round the world. And that dedication is a major ingredient in every one of our best-selling cookbooks.

We are confident this book will be another valuable friend in your kitchen and these fast and fabulous dishes will add to your enjoyment of life.

> *Jean Nidetch*
> FOUNDER,
> WEIGHT WATCHERS INTERNATIONAL

Setting Up for Success

—◆◆◆—

ORGANIZING YOURSELF

If cooking is to be "fast and fabulous," the first ingredient has to be advance planning. The major difference between a cook who is hurried, harried, and exhausted and one who is enviably calm and cool is proper planning and organizing. Of course, experience helps, but unless you can afford to spend all day in the kitchen, organizing yourself really is the key to preparing fabulous dishes swiftly and easily.

Begin by taking stock of yourself. If you're weighed down by time-consuming kitchen routines, think about reshaping them along more workable lines. Efficient organization can save steps, time, and the wasteful effort of unnecessary searching and backtracking.

By putting the following valuable suggestions to work for you, you can become that dreamed-of individual: the organized cook.

Make sure you have all the ingredients you need. Check your food cupboard, refrigerator, and freezer to see what ingredients are on hand and what's missing. Then prepare a *written* list. Do your shopping in advance and give yourself ample time to purchase any hard-to-find items.

Schedule your time. Estimate how much time you need to prepare each step of the recipe and make certain that it coincides with your daily schedule (and your budget). If it does, prepare a written schedule; begin with the day and time the meal is to be served and work backward from there. Don't forget to include:

• Preparation time (a new recipe may take longer than one that is tried and true).
• Cooking time (include marinating and/or chilling).
• Any other time requirements (e.g., does the dish need time to sit before being carved or sliced).

Plan to fill any time gaps with jobs that don't have to be done at specific hours (e.g., setting the table). If you're cooking something that must be watched but doesn't require much effort, you can start preparing another part of the meal (or even part of another meal).

1

Save extra steps. Minimize trips to the refrigerator and/or freezer by taking out everything you need at one time. This saves extra steps and conserves energy—yours and the appliance's.

You can also save steps by using a tray or serving cart to transport food if the dining area isn't in or near the kitchen.

Minimize the mess. Instead of having to *escape* from the mess, *avoid* it as much as possible—and also save the hassle of having extra dishes to wash.

• When pouring foods such as coffee, sugar, salt, pepper, etc., into containers, do it over the sink and with the help of a funnel. (An easy way to clean a funnel is with a baby-bottle brush or a chopstick wrapped in a paper towel.)

• Sift flour onto wax paper or a paper plate rather than into a bowl.

• Pare vegetables and fruits over a paper towel for easy disposal.

• When preparing a recipe, set out ingredients on paperware or on wax paper.

• Use freezer-to-oven-to-table cookware whenever possible.

Learn little tricks of the trade. Develop a repertoire of time-saving techniques that clever cooks use. For example:

• Chop hard-cooked eggs with a pastry blender to ease your efforts.

• Cooking several vegetables at once doesn't have to mean a batch of saucepans. You can avoid having to juggle burners (and extra cleaning-up) by cooking all the vegetables in the same saucepan. Do this by placing each of the vegetables on a separate piece of foil. Season as desired and gather the foil into small bundles. Lower them into boiling water, starting with the ones that require the longest cooking time. (Or place the vegetable requiring the longest time *directly* into the water; then add the foil packets later.)

The environment in which you work also affects your culinary success. The more efficient your kitchen, the more capable—and relaxed—you're likely to feel. For your best efforts, make the following habits an integral part of your kitchen routine.

Always keep your kitchen well stocked. This automatically makes any meal preparation smoother. Develop a routine of taking frequent inventory, replenishing as needed. Attach lists of the staples you use to the pantry door and the side of the refrigerator or freezer for an easy, ongoing inventory (and a head start on your weekly shopping list). Make a note of any item that seems to be running low. Remember that staples should include "emergency items"—such as the components for quick meals when guests arrive unexpectedly.

Make weekly shopping lists. Base your shopping lists on these inventories plus your weekly menu plan (a "must" for successful weight control). Take advantage of sales by stocking up on frequently used canned foods and products that can be stored in the freezer. (For supermarket strategies, see the introduction to *Treat Yourself Like Company*.)

Organize for easy clean-up.

• Wipe up spills *immediately*, before they spread. Always have paper towels or extra sponges on hand.

• Wipe down the sink, range, and counters as you work. It's more efficient, more sanitary, and more morale-boosting than letting the work pile up.

• Wash cooking utensils as you use them, or soak pans in water (cool water for eggs, milk, or starchy foods; hot water for other foods). When soaking pans, always fill the pan *above* the cooking line.

• Let plates and glasses dry by themselves in the dish drainer, if you're not using the dishwasher.

• Cover infrequently used china, glasses, and serving pieces with clear plastic. This eliminates the need to wash them before using.

• When talking on the phone, use your free hand to do some nearby tidying up. This will make the chore more pleasant, and the job is done before you realize you've been working.

(See "Organizing Your Kitchen" for additional tips.)

We also suggest you make use of some very helpful material—the book you are holding. Take the time to leaf through *all* the introductions. You'll find helpful suggestions to make your culinary efforts easy, organized, swift, creative—and enjoyable, so that you will appear as fabulous as the dishes you are preparing.

ORGANIZING YOUR KITCHEN

As any good craftsperson can tell you, the proper tools and a well-organized work space are prerequisites for doing your best work. Craftsmanship in the kitchen is no different. It's essential to have the proper tools of the culinary trade in order to achieve the best results. This means an adequate supply of equipment in good condition and efficiently organized. It's equally important to have your work space arranged for maximum results with minimal difficulties.

According to experts, the ideal kitchen should be divided into separate work centers for the major activities: preparation, cooking, serving, clean-up, and storage. A work center may be arranged in a "U," an "L," a corridor, along one wall, or as an island. Each area should include the equipment, supplies, and utensils needed for the tasks performed there, storage space for these items, and an adequate work surface. Of course, this perfect arrangement isn't always possible, but an awareness of the ideal can help you to organize the space you have for the best results possible.

The placement of major appliances and the storage space for equipment and foods influence the flow of work and the energy expended in preparing meals, serving, and cleaning up. Items that are frequently used should be kept near the equipment they are used with first. Supplies used infrequently can be kept in less accessible areas. Here's a Grade-A arrangement:

WHAT	WHERE
Range and sink	Close together
Equipment such as dishes, cutting board, wastebasket	Near the sink
Cleaning supplies	Under the sink (If there are young children in the house, *put safety locks* on the cabinet doors or store poisonous items elsewhere, well out of the youngsters' reach.)
Utensils initially used with water (e.g., tea kettle, coffee maker, double boiler, etc.)	Near the sink
Cooking utensils that are used without water	Near the range
Foods that require boiling water	Near the range (Never store foods near household chemicals, over heat sources, or in cabinets through which water or drain pipes pass.)
Containers for leftovers	Near the refrigerator
Container of baking soda and/or fire extinguisher	Near the range (Although baking soda is useful for putting out small grease fires, the fire department recommends having a fire extinguisher in case of a larger blaze.)
Basic first-aid kit (including burn ointment, disinfectant, adhesive bandages, etc.)	Within easy reach

Creating Additional Space

You can often create additional storage space simply by reorganizing your cabinets and drawers. Check cabinets to make sure that valuable space isn't being taken up by infrequently used equipment, serving accessories, or foods. Any item that hasn't been used within the past year should be stored elsewhere, given to someone who can use it, or discarded. Try to arrange cabinets so that you can easily identify and reach all the items stored there. (See *Magic in Minutes* for additional tips about efficiently arranged food cupboards.)

New space can be created, or existing space put to greater use, by utilizing inexpensive, easy-to-install accessories.

• Shallow metal or plastic stacking shelves or turntables add extra storage levels wherever additional space is needed.

• Dividers, racks, or other holders placed in drawers make utensils and gadgets easier to find. (This arrangement also helps prevent bending, denting, and breakage.)

• Slide-out drawers and large turntables give extra storage space in floor-level cabinets.

• Special racks attached to the back of cabinet or closet doors can hold spices, cleaning supplies, paper bags, etc.

• If space is available between counter tops and overhanging cabinets, attach drawers or baskets under the cabinets to hold paper towels, kitchen wrap, utensils, etc. (This space can also be utilized to display attractive but infrequently used platters, trays, or casseroles.)

• Hooks on the inside of under-the-sink cabinet doors can be used to hold dish towels (after they have dried).

• A fold-down shelf can provide extra work space if a permanent shelf isn't practical.

• Walls and even the ceiling can be utilized, too. For example, pegboards or grids can be hung on walls to hold tools, gadgets, and cookware. Ceiling-mounted pot racks can hold larger pans and utensils.

• Out-of-the-kitchen areas (e.g., linen closets, the basement, etc.) can be converted into additional storage space for infrequently used equipment or extra canned goods. (Make certain that all such foods are stored at temperatures between 32° and 70°F.)

Check housewares departments and restaurant supply stores for other ideas.

The Tools You Need

Having the proper tools makes any task easier, so take inventory of what you have before you decide what additional equipment you may need.

Sometimes, just a few small purchases can enable you to handle difficult chores with a snap of the fingers. In deciding what supplies to purchase, be realistic about the available space, the type of cooking you do, and your personal preferences. Some gadgets and cookware may be cleverly designed and fascinating but not practical for your purposes. Choose only those items that you will actually use.

Cookware

SUGGESTED BASIC EQUIPMENT

- double boiler
- saucepans with covers—1-, 2-, and 4-quart
- saucepot or Dutch oven with cover—6-quart
- skillets with covers—8-, 9-, or 10-inch and 12-inch

Efficient cookware has the following characteristics: straight sides, flat bottom, tight-fitting cover, heat-resistant or ovenproof handle firmly anchored to the pot, well-balanced design, smooth surface (no dirt-collecting crevices). Pots and pans should conduct heat evenly, be dent-resistant, and fit the burners on your range.

Cookware comes in various materials; each has its own advantages and disadvantages.

Aluminum and copper conduct heat the most evenly. Both materials are best for top-of-the-stove cookware—skillets, saucepans, or pots. Aluminum is moderately priced and lightweight. The heavier the gauge (thickness), the more durable. Copper looks attractive, but good-quality copper is very expensive. It should be heavy gauge and, for easier cleaning, lined with another metal (e.g., tin).

Cast iron is very durable and comparatively inexpensive. Since it heats slowly and retains heat well, it's good for long, slow cooking and may be used either on top of the range or in the oven. However, cast iron is heavy to handle and must be seasoned to prevent rust.

Ovenproof glass and glass-ceramic have the advantage of versatility. Since they take quick changes of temperature without warping, cracking, or crazing and retain heat well, they can go from freezer to oven to table, where they double as serving pieces. However, they are not generally recommended for top-of-the-range cooking because they are relatively poor conductors of heat and produce uneven results unless foods are cooked in liquid.

Stainless steel is exceptionally durable and easy to clean, but somewhat more expensive than other materials (except copper). Used alone, stainless steel is not a good heat conductor and has a tendency to warp and develop hot spots. Therefore, it is usually combined with other metals (e.g., copper or aluminum) to ensure more even heat distribution.

Nonstick finishes permit cooking without fat, or with only small amounts. They also make cleaning up easier since foods usually don't stick. However, nonstick surfaces require special care (follow the manufacturer's directions). Because nonstick finishes tend to become scratched, use only wooden or plastic utensils with them, never metal.

Bakeware

SUGGESTED BASIC EQUIPMENT

- cake pans—8-inch round, 8 x 8 x 2-inch square, and 9 x 13 x 2-inch rectangular
- casseroles—1-, 2-, and 3-quart, and individuals
- custard cups—6- and 10-ounce sets
- jelly-roll pan—13 x 10½ x 1-inch (can double as baking sheet)
- loaf pans—7⅜ x 3⅝ x 2¼-inch and individual-serving size (preferably one for each family member)
- muffin pan—12-cup with 2½-inch-diameter cups
- pie pans and plates—7- and 8-inch
- quiche dish—8-inch
- roasting pans with racks—one small, one large

Some casseroles are both ovenproof and flameproof. Although slightly more costly, they are well worth the money, for they are much more useful. Weigh the options in making your purchase.

Cutting Tools

Slicing, paring, boning, chopping, and carving are essential cookery steps. Having appropriate, good-quality tools speeds each task and makes it easier. Your kitchen should be equipped with:

- bread knife with serrated edge
- carving knife and 2-tined fork with finger guard
- chef's knife—all-purpose knife
- grapefruit knife with curved, serratted edge—for scooping flesh from fruits and vegetables
- paring knife—for paring and slicing fruits, vegetables, etc.

Blades come in carbon steel, stainless steel, and high-carbon stainless steel. Plain carbon steel takes and holds the keenest edge but rusts and darkens easily. It also discolors some foods. Stainless steel won't rust but doesn't hold an edge as well as carbon. Blades made of high-carbon stainless steel combine the best features of both.

Basic Kitchen Tools

blender
can/bottle/jar openers (hand or electric)
colander
cooking fork, long-handled
cooling racks (wire)
corkscrew
cutting board (those made of polyethylene are better than wood)
flour sifter
funnel
garlic press
grater, flat or 4-sided
ladle
measuring cups (graduated nest of dry measures and a liquid measure with pouring lip)
measuring spoons
meat mallet
mixer (electric)

mixing bowls (small and large)
pancake turner
pastry brush
pepper mill
pot holders
rolling pin
rubber scraper
scale for weighing foods
sieve
spoons (large, slotted and solid)
spoons, wooden
steamer basket or insert
storage containers for freezer and refrigerator (various sizes)
tea strainer
thermometers (meat, oven, freezer-refrigerator)
trivets
vegetable brush (stiff)
whisks, large and small (for different size bowls)

We have listed the basic equipment that makes work in the kitchen flow quickly, smoothly, and easily. Of course, many additional items are available (such as the food processor), as a trip through your local housewares department will demonstrate. However, in making purchases, buy only those items that will really be useful and be sure that they are sturdy and well-made.

ORGANIZING
YOUR FOOD PREPARATION

Now that your kitchen is set up, you're ready to cook. The recipes in this book are all quick and easy. None takes more than an hour to prepare, and many can be made in 30 minutes or less.

Before you begin, it's important to keep a few things in mind. A well-written recipe is not just a listing of ingredients and instructions. It more closely resembles a clear message sent from someone who knows how to prepare a specific dish to someone who wants to make it. There are reason and logic to the way in which a good recipe is written, and for optimum results, it should be followed *exactly*. Always read the entire recipe through before starting. Read it more than once, if necessary; don't just scan it. Make sure you have all the items you need on hand. Form a clear picture in your mind as to how you will proceed and what the finished dish will look like.

"Mise en Place"

Advance preparation is an essential time-saving step in cooking. French chefs have a name for this; they call it *"mise en place"*—everything in its proper place. All precooking procedures, such as dicing, chopping, and chilling of ingredients and the weighing and measuring of amounts, should be carried out so that everything is set to go *before* you begin to combine and cook.

Position everything you need within convenient reach before you actually start cooking. Make sure that all ingredients are at the proper temperatures. ("Room temperature" usually means 68° to 72°F.) Try to plan the preparation so you can reuse some utensils without interrupting your work to wash them (e.g., when using measuring spoons, measure dry ingredients before liquid ones). The best way of assuring consistent results is to measure accurately, using standard measuring utensils. Measurements of dry ingredients should always be *level* unless otherwise specified. Always combine *in the order specified in the recipe*. If the recipe is new to you, don't substitute. Once you have tried the dish, you can blend in your own creativity by making minor adjustments.

Recipes usually specify cooking times as well as observable checkpoints (e.g., "until browned, about 15 minutes"). Since many variables can affect timing, the visual checkpoints are generally more accurate and realistic. Some recipes include instructions to preheat the oven. If you don't preheat, add approximately 5 to 10 minutes to the cooking time.

Last, but far from least, make certain that any recipe you attempt gives exact measurements, includes all essential ingredients, and explains each step clearly. Bear in mind that your best bet for a successful recipe is a reliable source.

Some Basics About Our Recipes

It's the feeling of our chefs and home economists that fresh is usually better than processed. Therefore, all the recipes in this book use fresh vegetables unless otherwise specified. Frozen or canned can usually be substituted, but cooking times may have to be adjusted, and the finished product may differ a little in taste and/or texture. To help you in purchasing, we have included charts of vegetable yields for fresh and frozen produce (see pages 311–314).

The expert use of seasonings can make the difference between a successful cook and one who is only so-so. The herbs we use are *dried* unless otherwise indicated. If you are substituting fresh herbs, use approximately four times the amount of dried (e.g., 1 teaspoon chopped fresh basil, instead of ¼ teaspoon dried basil leaves). In substituting ground (powdered) herbs, use about ⅛ the amount of fresh (e.g., ⅛ teaspoon ground thyme, instead of 1 teaspoon chopped fresh thyme); in substituting ground for dried herbs, use about ½ the amount of dried (e.g., ½ teaspoon ground thyme, instead of 1 teaspoon dried thyme leaves).

Spices also liven up a dish. Most of our recipes suggest the *ground* form, which is a very concentrated source of flavor. Therefore, in substituting fresh for ground, use approximately eight times as much (e.g., 1 teaspoon minced ginger root, instead of ⅛ teaspoon ground ginger).

Some recipes use freshly ground pepper and/or fresh garlic. If peppercorns and pepper mill are not available, substitute regular ground black pepper in the same amount as the freshly ground. Garlic powder may be substituted for fresh garlic; however, this will give the dish a slightly different taste. If powder is preferred, use half the amount of fresh. Generally, 1 garlic clove will yield about ½ teaspoon minced; therefore substitute ¼ teaspoon powder for 1 garlic clove, minced.

Dried herbs and spices should usually not be kept for more than a year. As a rule of thumb, if the seasoning is aromatic, it is still potent. If the aroma has diminished, you may have to use a larger amount of seasoning than the recipe calls for.

Vegetable oils come in many forms and are used for several different purposes. Oils such as corn, cottonseed, peanut, safflower, sesame (*light*),

soybean, and sunflower—or any combination of these—may be used whenever vegetable oil is called for in a recipe. Since olive oil and Chinese (*dark*)
sesame oil have distinctive flavors, their use has been specifically indicated.

Reduced-calorie margarine is available in two forms, tub and stick. When
this product is called for in a recipe, use the tub form.

The standard that we have used for broiling is four inches from the
heat source. If it is necessary to broil closer or farther away, the appropriate distance has been indicated.

You should be able to prepare just about every recipe in this book using
basic-size pots and pans. It's always best to use the pan size recommended
in the recipe. However, chances are a substitution will work just as well.
(A chart of some common pan substitutions can be found in the Appendix, page 315.) The size called for is determined by the volume of food
the pan holds; when substituting, use one as close to the recommended
size as possible. If the pan is too small, the food may boil over; if it is too
large, the food may dry out or burn. To determine the dimensions of a
baking pan, measure across the top, between the inside edges. To determine
the volume, measure the amount of water the pan holds when it is completely filled. When you use a different size pan than the one recommended, it may be necessary to adjust the suggested cooking time by 5 to
10 minutes (or rely on the observable checkpoints). *If you substitute glass
or glass-ceramic for metal, reduce the oven temperature by 25°F.*

A NOTE ON RECIPE EXPANSIONS

To make this book adaptable to various serving needs, we have provided expansions for most of the recipes. To increase the recipe yield,
some of the ingredients can merely be multiplied by the additional number
of servings; however this does not hold true for everything and frequently
special care must be taken when increasing herbs, spices, and liquid. There
is no one formula that can be applied to all ingredients; therefore, when
increasing a recipe, it is important that the expansion chart be followed
closely. The following abbreviations have been used: t = teaspoon/s;
T = tablespoon/s; c = cup/s; qt = quart/s; oz = ounce/s; lb = pound/s;
pkg = package/s; pkt = packet/s; min = minute/s.

When increasing a recipe, it will be necessary to increase the pan size
accordingly. We have supplied a chart (Appendix, page 315) for saucepans
and casseroles. However, when increasing the size of a skillet to accommo-

date an expanded recipe, there is no one rule that can be followed; we have, therefore, included skillet sizes with the recipes to which they apply.

A NOTE ON RECIPE SYMBOLS

 The clock face on recipes indicates that they can be prepared in 30 minutes or less.

 The penny appears on budget recipes.

Now your dish is done to perfection and you're ready to serve it. To enhance perfection, serve cold foods on chilled plates and hot foods on warmed plates. To chill plates and glassware, refrigerate them for approximately 5 minutes before serving. Plates and platters can be heated by placing them in a warm oven (no more than 200°F.) for 5 to 10 minutes before serving, or by putting them in a warmer or on a warming tray.

For portion control, remember to divide the dish evenly when serving so that each portion will be the same size. For the benefit of those following the Weight Watchers Food Plan, we have included per-serving Exchange Information for all of the recipes in this book and, since most people are concerned about nutrition, we have also included per-serving nutrition analyses for calories, protein, fat, carbohydrate, sodium, and cholesterol (see Appendix, pages 317–348).

Magic in Minutes

◆◆◆

Appetizer
Pizza Pie

Soups
Bacon-Flavored Corn Chowder
Cheddar-Chicken Soup
Quick Minestrone

Sandwiches
Broiled Ham 'n' Cheese with Mustard Dressing
Hot Open-Face Turkey Sandwich
Hot Open-Face Roast Beef Sandwich

Entrées
Chicken Tacos
Puffy Fruit Omelet
Spicy Garbanzos
Broiled Mustard-Scrod with Wine Sauce
Sole (or Flounder) Véronique
Oven-Fried Chicken with Orange-Teriyaki Sauce
Oriental Beef and Vegetable Stir-Fry
Orange-Ginger-Glazed Pork Chops
Spaghetti Carbonara
Oriental Chicken Livers en Brochette

Side Dishes
Hot Potato Salad
Macaroni-Cheddar Salad
Puffy Pancake
Potato-Vegetable Casserole

Desserts
Hot Fruit Compote with Coconut Topping
Glazed "Danish"
Orange Loaf Bars

Are you searching for a way to be a kitchen magician on practically a moment's notice? One of the answers can be found right in your cupboard.

By always having on hand an adequate supply of the basic staples used in day-to-day cooking, you'll be assured of being able to put together a dinner for unexpected guests or a swiftly prepared meal on a rush-hour day. You'll also cut down on time-consuming trips to the supermarket. Being able to always have foods on hand requires a knowledge of proper storage techniques. Here are a few suggestions for efficient use of your food cupboard.

• Store cans, bottles, and boxes in a cool, dry place to retard changes in color in canned fruits and vegetables and to prevent oils from turning rancid. The ideal temperature for a food cupboard is 50°F.; it should not rise above 70°F., nor fall below freezing.

• Don't keep canned foods for more than a year, since they may lose flavor and nutrients. Mark the date of purchase on stored foods and rotate them on your shelves so that the oldest items are used first.

• Watch out for danger signals: cans with bulges or leaks; spurting liquid when the container is opened; mold or an "off" odor; bulging lids on jars; cloudiness and/or film inside jars; the appearance of gas bubbles. *Never taste any food that you suspect may have spoiled.* Discard it or return it to the store where it was purchased.

• Don't buy dented or rusted cans, and keep stored containers dust-free.

• Once a can has been opened, store the leftovers in covered glass jars or plastic containers in the refrigerator. After boxed items, such as crackers, rice, or pasta, have been opened, store them in *airtight containers.*

A well-arranged cupboard works best. Attach self-stick labels to the shelves, describing what should be stored there, so that family members can always store groceries in the proper places. Space permitting, reserve one shelf (or part of a shelf) for "emergency" supplies—items that can be prepared quickly when you're given short notice. Recipes and menus for last-minute meals can also be kept there.

Don't discount the value of eye appeal, either. To liven up dark areas, put colorful paper on the shelves. Use paper towels to line drawers; they can easily be discarded and replaced when they get soiled.

15

SEASONINGS AND WINES

With a wave of your culinary wand, the seasoning shelves and the wine cellar can turn simple food into spectacular fare. Herbs, spices, and wines enhance flavors and make foods more exciting. However, a little goes a long way, so use them judiciously.

Herbs are the leaves, roots, flowers, and seeds of plants that generally grow in temperate climates. *Spices* are the nuts, fruits, seeds, and bark of tropical plants. When buying dried herbs, select whole leaves rather than the ground or powdered forms. The leaf will hold its flavor longer and can always be ground or crushed. Herbs and spices should be stored in a dark, cool, dry area away from heat and sunlight (never near the stove). Always label the containers with the date of purchase and check periodically for freshness: a good test of seasonings is to rub some in the palm of your hand and sniff to see how aromatic it is. (See "Organizing Your Food Preparation," page 9, for ways to estimate amounts when substituting fresh herbs for dried, or fresh spices for ground ones.)

Wines should be stored in a cool area. Unopened bottles should be placed on their sides, not standing up. The cork can be removed more easily when it is moist.

The following chart lists some of the staples you might want to keep on hand. Your personal preferences and cooking needs should be the deciding factors.

HERBS AND SPICES

Allspice, ground
Basil leaves
Bay leaves
Chili powder
Chives
Cinnamon (ground and stick)
Cloves (ground and whole)
Curry powder
Garlic powder
Ginger, ground

Mustard, powdered
Nutmeg, ground
Oregano leaves
Paprika
Pepper: white, black (ground and whole), red (ground and crushed)
Rosemary leaves
Tarragon leaves
Thyme leaves

——— CONDIMENTS AND MISCELLANEOUS STAPLES ———

Aromatic bitters
Bacon bits, imitation
Baking powder and soda
Barbecue sauce
Bread crumbs
Browning sauce
Canned tomato sauce, puree, and paste*
Canned vegetables, fruits, juices, and legumes*
Capers*
Cereal
Chili sauce
Cocoa (unsweetened)
Coconut (shredded)*
Cream of tartar
Dry legumes
Extracts and flavorings
Flour
Garlic cloves
Gelatin (flavored and unflavored)
Honey

Horseradish*
Hot sauce
Instant broth and seasoning mixes
Ketchup
Lemon and lime juices*
Mayonnaise and salad dressings*
Mustard
Olive oil
Olives*
Onions
Peanut butter*
Pickle relish*
Pickles*
Reduced-calorie flavored spreads (e.g., apricot, grape, strawberry)
Seeds (caraway, poppy, sesame)
Soy and teriyaki sauces
Sugar
Syrups
Vegetable oil
Vinegar
Worcestershire sauce

——————————— WINES ———————————

Red
White

Marsala
Dry sherry

* Refrigerate once opened.

Pizza Pie

MAKES 2 SERVINGS, ½ PIE EACH *or* 4 SERVINGS, ¼ PIE EACH

4 ready-to-bake refrigerated butter-milk flaky biscuits (1 ounce each)
2 teaspoons olive or vegetable oil
½ cup each diced onion and green bell pepper
½ cup tomato sauce
½ teaspoon each oregano leaves and basil leaves

Dash pepper
2 ounces mozzarella cheese, shredded
1 tablespoon plus 1 teaspoon grated Parmesan cheese

Preheat oven to 400°F. On sheet of wax paper place biscuits next to each other; cover with another sheet of wax paper and roll dough to form one circle about 8 inches in diameter and ⅛ inch thick. Remove paper and fit dough into 7-inch pie pan; using fork, prick bottom and sides of dough. Bake until lightly browned, 8 to 10 minutes.

While crust is baking, in small nonstick skillet heat oil; add vegetables and sauté until soft. Add tomato sauce and seasonings and cook, stirring constantly, until mixture thickens. Pour sauce over baked crust; sprinkle with mozzarella cheese, then Parmesan cheese, and bake until cheese is melted and lightly browned, 10 to 15 minutes. Cut pie in half or into quarters.

Bacon-Flavored Corn Chowder

MAKES 2 SERVINGS, ABOUT 1½ CUPS EACH

For a thicker, sweeter chowder, use canned cream-style corn instead of whole-kernel corn.

2 teaspoons margarine
½ cup each diced onion and celery
1 tablespoon plus 1½ teaspoons all-purpose flour
1½ cups skim milk
1 cup drained canned whole-kernel corn

1 teaspoon imitation bacon bits, crushed
⅛ teaspoon each salt and powdered mustard
Dash white pepper
Garnish: ground nutmeg

In 1-quart saucepan heat margarine over medium-high heat until bubbly and hot; stir in onion and celery. Cover pan and cook until vegetables are soft, 2 to 3 minutes. Add flour and cook, stirring constantly with wire whisk, for 1 minute longer; continuing to stir, gradually add milk and bring to a boil. Reduce heat and cook, stirring constantly, until mixture is smooth and thickened, 2 to 3 minutes. Add remaining ingredients except nutmeg and continue stirring and cooking until ingredients are thoroughly combined and mixture is hot. Pour into soup bowls and garnish each portion with dash nutmeg.

For Additional Servings Use

	3 servings	4 servings	6 servings
margarine	1 T	1 T + 1 t	2 T
onions and celery	¾ c each	1 c each	1½ c each
flour	2 T + ¾ t	3 T	¼ c + 1½ t
milk	2¼ c	3 c	1 qt + ½ c
corn	1½ c	2 c	3 c
bacon bits	1½ t	2 t	1 T
salt and mustard	⅛ t each	¼ t each	¼ t each, or to taste
pepper	dash	⅛ t	⅛ t, or to taste

Cheddar-Chicken Soup

 MAKES 2 SERVINGS, ABOUT 2 CUPS EACH

Here's a way to combine some items from the refrigerator and the pantry for a hearty and inexpensive meal.

2 teaspoons margarine
½ cup each chopped onion, celery, and carrot
2 teaspoons all-purpose flour
1 cup water
1 packet instant chicken broth and seasoning mix
½ cup frozen asparagus cuts and tips

½ cup skim milk
2 ounces Cheddar cheese, shredded
4 ounces skinned and boned cooked chicken, diced
1 cup cooked small macaroni (e.g., small shells, tubetti, ditalini, small elbows, etc.)
1 teaspoon Worcestershire sauce
Dash each salt and white pepper

In 1½- or 2-quart saucepan heat margarine over medium heat until bubbly and hot; add onion, celery, and carrot and sauté until vegetables are tender. Sprinkle vegetables with flour and stir quickly to combine; gradually stir in water. Add broth mix and, stirring constantly, bring to a boil. Add asparagus and cook, stirring, for about 3 minutes; add milk and cheese and continue stirring and cooking until cheese melts. Reduce heat to low, add remaining ingredients, and cook until thoroughly heated.

For Additional Servings Use

	3 servings	4 servings	6 servings
margarine	1 T	1 T + 1 t	2 T
onions, celery, and carrots	¾ c each	1 c each	1½ c each
flour	1 T	1 T + 1 t	2 T
water	1½ c	2 c	3 c
broth mix	1½ pkt	2 pkt	3 pkt
asparagus and milk	¾ c each	1 c each	1½ c each
cheese	3 oz	4 oz	6 oz
chicken	6 oz	8 oz	12 oz
macaroni	1½ c	2 c	3 c
Worcestershire sauce	1½ t	2 t	1 T
salt and pepper	dash each	⅛ t each	⅛ to ¼ t each

Quick Minestrone

MAKES 2 SERVINGS, ABOUT 2 CUPS EACH

A lot of ingredients right from your pantry and very little effort will produce this hearty meal-in-a-bowl.

2 teaspoons olive oil
3 ounces diced Canadian-style bacon
2 garlic cloves, minced
½ cup each chopped onion, celery, carrot, and zucchini
1¼ cups water
1 cup tomato juice
6 ounces drained canned pink beans or red kidney beans

2 tablespoons chopped fresh basil or 1 teaspoon dried
1 packet instant beef broth and seasoning mix
⅛ teaspoon each oregano leaves and pepper
½ cup cooked ditalini (small tube macaroni)
2 tablespoons chopped fresh parsley

In 2-quart saucepan heat oil over medium heat; add bacon and garlic and sauté briefly (*do not brown garlic*). Add onion, celery, carrot, and zucchini and cook, stirring occasionally, until vegetables are tender, about 5 minutes; add remaining ingredients except ditalini and parsley and bring to a boil. Reduce heat and let simmer, stirring occasionally, for about 15 minutes; add ditalini and parsley and let simmer until heated.

For Additional Servings Use

	3 servings	4 servings	6 servings
oil	1 T	1 T + 1 t	2 T
bacon	4½ oz	6 oz	9 oz
garlic	3 cloves	4 cloves	6 cloves
onions, celery, carrots, and zucchini	¾ c each	1 c each	1½ c each
water	1¾ c	2½ c	3¾ c
tomato juice	1½ c	2 c	3 c
beans	9 oz	12 oz	1 lb 2 oz
basil	2 T fresh or 1 t dried	3 T fresh or 1½ t dried	¼ c fresh or 1¾ to 2 t dried
broth mix	1½ pkt	2 pkt	3 pkt
oregano leaves and pepper	⅛ t each	⅛ to ¼ t each	¼ t each
ditalini	¾ c	1 c	1½ c
parsley	3 T	¼ c	⅓ c

Broiled Ham 'n' Cheese with Mustard Dressing

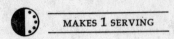 MAKES 1 SERVING

1 slice rye bread, lightly toasted
2 ounces sliced boiled ham
1 ounce Swiss cheese, sliced
½ medium tomato, thinly sliced

2 teaspoons part-skim ricotta cheese
1½ teaspoons plain lowfat yogurt
1 teaspoon Dijon-style mustard
½ teaspoon chopped chives

Preheat broiler. Place toast on a broiling pan; top toast with ham, then cheese, then tomato slices. In small bowl stir together remaining ingredients; spoon dressing over tomato slices and broil until dressing bubbles and cheese is melted.

Hot Open-Face Turkey Sandwich

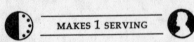 MAKES 1 SERVING

1 teaspoon margarine
2 tablespoons sliced mushrooms
1 teaspoon all-purpose flour
⅓ cup water
½ packet (about ½ teaspoon) instant chicken broth and seasoning mix

4 ounces sliced skinned cooked turkey
1 slice pumpernickel or rye bread, toasted
2 each tomato slices and romaine, iceberg, or loose-leafed lettuce leaves

In small saucepan heat margarine over medium-high heat until hot and bubbly; add mushrooms and sauté until browned. Sprinkle flour over mixture and stir to combine; gradually stir in water. Add broth mix and cook, stirring constantly, until mixture thickens. Reduce heat to low, add turkey, and let simmer until turkey is heated. On plate arrange turkey slices on toast and pour gravy over turkey; garnish with tomato and lettuce.

Hot Open-Face
Roast Beef Sandwich

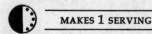 MAKES 1 SERVING

1 teaspoon margarine
2 tablespoons diced onion
1 teaspoon all-purpose flour
⅓ cup water
½ packet (about ½ teaspoon) instant beef broth and seasoning mix

4 ounces sliced roast beef
1 slice rye bread, toasted
2 each tomato slices and romaine, iceberg, or loose-leafed lettuce leaves
1 teaspoon prepared horseradish

In small saucepan heat margarine over medium-high heat until bubbly and hot; add onion and sauté until translucent. Sprinkle flour over mixture and stir to combine; gradually stir in water. Add broth mix and cook, stirring constantly, until mixture thickens. Reduce heat to low, add roast beef, and let simmer until meat is heated. On plate arrange meat slices on toast and pour gravy over meat; garnish with tomato and lettuce and serve with horseradish.

Chicken Tacos

MAKES 2 SERVINGS, 1 TACO EACH

This is a delicious way to use up leftover chicken. If desired, taco shells can be heated, prior to filling, in toaster-oven at 300°F. for about 5 minutes.

2 teaspoons vegetable oil
½ cup sliced onion
2 garlic cloves, minced
1 medium tomato, chopped
½ cup tomato sauce
Dash each hot sauce, oregano
   leaves, salt, and pepper

4 ounces skinned and boned
   cooked chicken, diced
2 taco shells
1 ounce Cheddar cheese, shredded
½ cup shredded lettuce

In 9- or 10-inch skillet heat oil; add onion and garlic and sauté until onion is translucent, about 5 minutes. Add tomato, tomato sauce, and seasonings and cook, stirring occasionally, for 5 minutes; add chicken and cook until heated through. Divide chicken mixture into taco shells; top each portion with ½ ounce cheese and ¼ cup lettuce.

For Additional Servings Use

	3 servings	4 servings	6 servings
oil	1 T	1 T + 1 t	2 T
onions	¾ c	1 c	1½ c
garlic	2 cloves	3 cloves	3 cloves
tomatoes	1½ medium	2 medium	3 medium
tomato sauce	¾ c	1 c	1½ c
hot sauce, oregano leaves, salt, and pepper	dash each	⅛ t each	⅛ t each
chicken	6 oz	8 oz	12 oz
taco shells	3	4	6
cheese	1½ oz	2 oz	3 oz.
lettuce	¾ c	1 c	1½ c
skillet	10-inch	10- or 12-inch	12-inch

Puffy Fruit Omelet

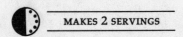

MAKES 2 SERVINGS

2 medium kiwi fruit, peeled (at
  room temperature)
½ cup strawberries
2 large eggs, separated
2 teaspoons confectioners' sugar,
  divided

½ teaspoon vanilla extract
Dash salt
2 teaspoons margarine

Slice 1 kiwi fruit and cut remaining kiwi fruit into wedges; set aside. Slice half of the strawberries, leaving remaining berries whole; set aside.

Preheat oven to 325°F. In small mixing bowl, using electric mixer on high speed, beat egg whites until foamy; add 1 teaspoon sugar and the vanilla and salt and beat until stiff peaks form. In separate bowl beat yolks until thick and lemon colored; gently fold whites into yolks until well combined.

In 10-inch nonstick omelet pan (or skillet) that has an oven-safe or removable handle heat margarine over low heat until bubbly and hot; pour in egg mixture and, using back of spoon, lightly press center down so that edges of omelet are higher than center. Cook until bottom of omelet is golden, about 5 minutes; transfer pan to oven and bake for 5 to 6 minutes (a knife inserted in center should come out dry).

Using spatula, loosen edges of omelet. Arrange fruit slices over half of omelet; fold other half over fruit and carefully slide omelet onto warm platter. Sprinkle with remaining teaspoon sugar and serve with reserved kiwi fruit wedges and whole berries.

Spicy Garbanzos

1 teaspoon vegetable oil	¾ cup canned crushed tomatoes
¼ cup diced onion	½ cup water
1 garlic clove, minced	Dash hot sauce
½ cup chopped green bell pepper	12 ounces drained canned chick-peas
½ teaspoon chili powder	(garbanzo beans)
⅛ teaspoon ground cumin	⅛ teaspoon each salt and pepper

In 1½-quart saucepan heat oil; add onion and garlic and sauté until onion is softened. Add green pepper and sauté for 5 minutes longer; stir in chili powder and cumin. Add tomatoes, water, and hot sauce; cover and let simmer for 10 minutes. Stir in chick-peas, salt, and pepper and let simmer, uncovered, until beans are heated through and sauce is slightly thickened, about 10 minutes longer.

For Additional Servings Use

	3 servings	4 servings	6 servings
oil	1½ t	2 t	1 T
onions	⅓ c + 2 t	½ c	¾ c
garlic	1½ cloves	2 cloves	3 cloves
green peppers	¾ c	1 c	1½ c
chili powder	¾ t	1 t	1½ t
cumin	⅛ t	¼ t	¼ t, or to taste
tomatoes	1 c + 2 T	1½ c	2¼ c
water	¾ c	1 c	1½ c
hot sauce	dash	dash	dash to ⅛ t
chick-peas	1 lb 2 oz	1½ lb	2¼ lb
salt and pepper	⅛ t each	¼ t each	¼ t each, or to taste

Broiled Mustard-Scrod with Wine Sauce

MAKES 2 SERVINGS

1 teaspoon margarine	1 tablespoon mayonnaise
1 tablespoon minced shallots or onion	½ teaspoon prepared mustard
10 ounces scrod fillets*	2 tablespoons lemon juice
Dash each salt and white pepper	¼ cup dry white wine
	1 tablespoon chopped fresh parsley

In small skillet heat margarine until bubbly and hot; add shallots (or onion) and sauté briefly (*do not brown*). Spread shallot mixture over bottom of shallow baking pan that is large enough to hold fish in single layer; sprinkle scrod with salt and pepper and place in single layer over vegetable mixture. In small bowl combine mayonnaise and mustard; spread mixture evenly over fillets, then drizzle with lemon juice. Broil 3 inches from heat source until fish flakes easily at the touch of a fork, 8 to 10 minutes depending on thickness of fillets.

Transfer fish to serving platter and keep warm. Transfer pan juices and vegetables remaining in pan to small skillet; add wine and cook over high heat until liquid is reduced, about 3 minutes. Pour sauce over fillets; sprinkle with parsley.

* Cod, flounder, or haddock fillets may be substituted for the scrod.

For Additional Servings Use

	3 servings	4 servings	6 servings
margarine	1½ t	2 t	1 T
shallots or onions	1 T + 1½ t	2 T	3 T
scrod	15 oz	1¼ lb	1 lb 14 oz
salt and white pepper	dash each	⅛ t each	⅛ t each, or to taste
mayonnaise	1 T + 1½ t	2 T	3 T
mustard	¾ t	1 t	1½ t
lemon juice	3 T	¼ c	⅓ c
wine	⅓ c + 2 t	½ c	¾ c
parsley	1 T	2 T	3 T

Sole (or Flounder) Véronique

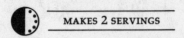

MAKES 2 SERVINGS

Fish with a flair and a surprise touch, all in less than 30 minutes.

2 thick sole or flounder fillets, 5
   ounces each
¼ teaspoon salt
Dash pepper
¼ cup dry white wine
1 tablespoon minced shallots or
   onion
2 teaspoons lemon juice

1 tablespoon margarine
1 teaspoon all-purpose flour
¼ cup skim milk (at room
   temperature)
40 small seedless green grapes (or
   24 large, cut into halves)
3 tablespoons thawed frozen dairy
   whipped topping

Season fish with salt and pepper and transfer to 9- or 10-inch nonstick skillet; add wine, shallots (or onion), and lemon juice and bring to a boil. Reduce heat, cover pan, and let simmer until fish flakes easily at the touch of a fork, 2 to 3 minutes. Remove pan from heat and, using a slotted pancake turner, carefully transfer fillets to a warmed serving platter; set aside and keep warm. Pour pan juices into small heatproof cup and reserve.

    In same skillet heat margarine over medium-high heat until bubbly and hot; add flour and stir until blended. Gradually stir in milk and cook, stirring constantly, until mixture comes to a boil. Reduce heat, add grapes, whipped topping, and reserved pan juices and stir to combine; cook until heated through. Drain any liquid that has accumulated on serving platter into sauce and stir to combine; pour sauce over fish.

For Additional Servings Use

	3 servings	4 servings	6 servings
sole or flounder	3 fillets (5 oz each)	4 fillets (5 oz each)	6 fillets (5 oz each)
salt	¼ t	½ t	¾ t
pepper	dash	⅛ t	⅛ to ¼ t
wine	⅓ c + 2 t	½ c	¾ c
shallots or onions	1 T + 1½ t	2 T	3 T
lemon juice	1 T	1 T + 1 t	2 T
margarine	1 T + 1½ t	2 T	3 T
flour	1½ t	2 t	1 T
milk	⅓ c + 2 t	½ c	¾ c
grapes	60 small or 36 large	80 small or 48 large	120 small or 72 large
whipped topping	¼ c + 1½ t	⅓ c + 2 t	½ c + 1 T
skillet	10-inch	10- or 12-inch	12-inch

Oven-Fried Chicken with Orange-Teriyaki Sauce

 MAKES 2 SERVINGS

To enhance the Oriental effect, garnish with scallion brushes (see introduction to Good Lookin' Cookin', page 287).

Chicken	Sauce
10 ounces skinned and boned chicken breasts, cut into 4 pieces	**2 teaspoons margarine**
1½ ounces (½ cup plus 2 tablespoons) cornflake crumbs	**2 tablespoons thinly sliced scallion (green onion)**
2 tablespoons grated orange peel	**½ garlic clove, minced**
2 tablespoons thawed frozen concentrated orange juice (no sugar added)	**2 tablespoons teriyaki sauce**
	1 tablespoon plus 1 teaspoon reduced-calorie orange marmalade (16 calories per 2 teaspoons)
	1 tablespoon water

To Prepare Chicken: Preheat oven to 350°F. Using paper towels pat chicken dry; set aside. On sheet of wax paper, or on paper plate, combine cornflake crumbs and orange peel. Pour juice into small bowl; dip chicken pieces into juice, then into crumb mixture, coating thoroughly and pressing any remaining crumbs firmly onto chicken. Arrange coated chicken on baking sheet and bake for 10 to 15 minutes; turn pieces over and bake until chicken is tender and coating is crisp, about 5 minutes longer.

To Prepare Sauce: While chicken is baking, in small saucepan heat margarine over medium heat until bubbly and hot; add scallion and garlic and sauté until scallion slices are soft. Reduce heat to low, add remaining ingredients, and cook until sauce is hot and slightly thickened; serve with chicken.

For Additional Servings Use

	3 servings	4 servings	6 servings
chicken	15 oz (cut into 6 pieces)	1¼ lb (cut into 8 pieces)	1 lb 14 oz (cut into 12 pieces)
cornflake crumbs	2¼ oz (1 c less 1 T)	3 oz (1¼ c)	4½ oz (2 c less 2 T)
orange peel	3 T	¼ c	⅓ c
orange juice	3 T	¼ c	⅓ c + 2 t
margarine	1 T	1 T + 1 t	2 T
scallions	3 T	¼ c	⅓ c + 2 t
garlic	½ clove	1 clove	1½ cloves
teriyaki sauce	3 T	¼ c	⅓ c
marmalade	2 T	2 T + 2 t	¼ c
water	1 T + 1½ t	2 T	3 T

Oriental Beef
and Vegetable Stir-Fry

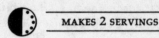 MAKES 2 SERVINGS

10 ounces ground beef
1 tablespoon teriyaki sauce
½ teaspoon each minced pared
ginger root and minced fresh
garlic
½ cup frozen tiny peas
¼ cup dry sherry
¾ cup water

1 packet instant beef broth and
seasoning mix
2 teaspoons each soy sauce and
cornstarch
1½ cups cooked vermicelli (very
thin spaghetti), hot
½ cup chopped scallions (green
onions)

In bowl combine beef, teriyaki sauce, ginger, and garlic; form into large patty and broil on rack in broiling pan, turning once, until browned on both sides, about 5 minutes. Let cool slightly, then crumble.

In 12-inch nonstick skillet combine beef, peas, and sherry; cook, stirring constantly, for about 2 minutes. Stir in water and broth mix. In small cup combine soy sauce and cornstarch, stirring to dissolve cornstarch; add to beef mixture and cook, stirring constantly, until thickened. Add cooked vermicelli and toss to combine; serve sprinkled with scallions.

For Additional Servings Use

	3 servings	*4 servings*	*6 servings*
ground beef	15 oz	1¼ lb	1 lb 14 oz
teriyaki sauce	1 T + 1½ t	2 T	3 T
ginger root	½ t	¾ t	1 t
garlic	¾ t	1 t	1½ t
peas	¾ c	1 c	1½ c
sherry	⅓ c + 2 t	½ c	¾ c
water	1 c + 2 T	1½ c	2¼ c
broth mix	1½ pkt	2 pkt	3 pkt
soy sauce and cornstarch	1 T each	1 T + 1 t each	2 T each
vermicelli	2¼ c	3 c	4½ c
scallions	¾ c	1 c	1½ c
skillet	12-inch	wok	wok

Orange-Ginger-Glazed Pork Chops

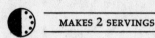 MAKES 2 SERVINGS

Delicious served with Far East Broccoli (see page 75).

12 ounces pork loin chops (½ inch thick)
2 teaspoons vegetable oil
1 tablespoon minced shallots or onion
½ cup orange juice (no sugar added)
1 tablespoon plus 1 teaspoon reduced-calorie orange marmalade (16 calories per 2 teaspoons)

1 teaspoon each firmly packed brown sugar, prepared mustard, and teriyaki sauce
¼ teaspoon ground ginger
1 small orange, sliced

On rack in broiling pan broil chops for about 3 minutes on each side.

While chops are broiling, in small nonstick saucepan heat oil; add shallots (or onion) and sauté briefly, being careful not to burn. Add remaining ingredients, except chops, and bring to a boil. Cook over high heat, stirring occasionally, until mixture is reduced and thickened, about 5 minutes.

Arrange chops in shallow flameproof casserole that is large enough to hold them in 1 layer; using some of the glaze, spread both sides of each chop evenly and broil, turning once, until glaze is browned, about 3 minutes on each side. Serve with orange slices and remaining glaze.

For Additional Servings Use

	3 servings	4 servings	6 servings
pork chops	1 lb 2 oz	1½ lb	2¼ lb
oil	1 T	1 T + 1 t	2 T
shallots or onions	1 T + 1½ t	2 T	3 T
orange juice	¾ c	1 c	1½ c
marmalade	2 T	2 T + 2 t	¼ c
sugar, mustard, and teriyaki sauce	1½ t each	2 t each	1 T each
ginger	¼ t	¼ t	½ t
oranges	1½ small	2 small	3 small

Spaghetti Carbonara

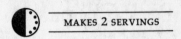 MAKES 2 SERVINGS

2 teaspoons margarine
½ cup diced onion
1 garlic clove, minced
4 ounces Canadian-style bacon, diced
½ cup skim milk

2 eggs
¼ teaspoon freshly ground pepper
1½ cups cooked thin spaghetti (hot)
1 tablespoon plus 1 teaspoon grated Parmesan cheese

In 2-quart saucepan heat margarine over medium heat until bubbly and hot; add onion and garlic and sauté until onion is translucent. Add bacon and cook, stirring constantly, for about 3 minutes. Reduce heat to low.

In small bowl beat together milk and eggs; *very slowly* pour egg mixture into saucepan, stirring constantly. Continue stirring and cook over low heat until mixture is thickened; stir in pepper. Add hot spaghetti and toss to combine; sprinkle with Parmesan cheese.

For Additional Servings Use

	3 servings	4 servings	6 servings
margarine	1 T	1 T + 1 t	2 T
onions	¾ c	1 c	1½ c
garlic	1½ cloves	2 cloves	3 cloves
bacon	6 oz	8 oz	12 oz
skim milk	¾ c	1 c	1½ c
eggs	3	4	6
pepper	¼ t	½ t	¾ t
spaghetti	2¼ c	3 c	4½ c
cheese	2 T	2 T + 2 t	¼ c

Oriental Chicken Livers en Brochette

MAKES 2 SERVINGS, 2 SKEWERS EACH

Elaborate-looking but easy and economical. Prepare the marinade early in the day, since livers should marinate for at least 4 hours.

2 tablespoons each rice vinegar and teriyaki sauce
1½ teaspoons firmly packed brown sugar
1 teaspoon each minced pared ginger root and minced fresh garlic

10 ounces chicken livers
1 medium green bell pepper, seeded and cut into 1-inch squares
12 cherry tomatoes
8 medium mushroom caps (about 1½-inch diameter each)

In bowl combine vinegar, teriyaki sauce, sugar, ginger, and garlic; add livers and toss to coat. Cover and refrigerate for at least 4 hours, tossing once (if preferred, livers may be marinated overnight).

Preheat broiler. Onto each of four 12-inch skewers, thread an equal amount of livers, ¼ of the pepper squares, 3 cherry tomatoes, and 2 mushroom caps, alternating ingredients; reserve marinade. Place skewers on rack in broiling pan and broil, turning once and brushing frequently with reserved marinade, until livers are browned and firm, 4 to 5 minutes on each side. Arrange skewers on serving platter.

For Additional Servings Use

	3 servings	4 servings	6 servings
vinegar and teriyaki sauce	3 T each	¼ c each	⅓ c each
sugar	2¼ t	1 T	1 T + 1½ t
ginger and garlic	1 t each	2 t each	2½ t each
livers	15 oz	1¼ lb	1 lb 14 oz
green peppers	1½ medium	2 medium	3 medium
cherry tomatoes	18	24	36
mushroom caps	12	16	24
skewers	6	8	12

Hot Potato Salad

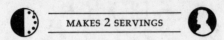

MAKES 2 SERVINGS

For uniform cooking, use small all-purpose potatoes and, for ease of handling, let cool slightly before peeling.

2 teaspoons vegetable oil
½ cup each diced onion and green
  bell pepper
1 teaspoon all-purpose flour
¾ cup water
1 packet instant chicken broth and
  seasoning mix

2 teaspoons cider vinegar
½ teaspoon superfine sugar
Dash pepper
9 ounces peeled cooked potatoes,
  thinly sliced

In 9- or 10-inch nonstick skillet heat oil; add onion and green pepper and cook, stirring occasionally, until vegetables are tender. Sprinkle flour over mixture and cook, stirring constantly, for 1 minute; gradually stir in water. Add broth mix and bring to a boil. Reduce heat and let simmer until mixture thickens; stir in vinegar, sugar, and pepper. Add potato slices and cook until thoroughly heated, 2 to 3 minutes longer.

For Additional Servings Use

	3 servings	4 servings	6 servings
oil	1 T	1 T + 1 t	2 T
onions and green peppers	¾ c each	1 c each	1½ c each
flour	1½ t	2 t	1 T
water	1 c + 2 T	1½ c	2¼ c
broth mix	1½ pkt	2 pkt	3 pkt
vinegar	1 T	1 T + 1 t	2 T
sugar	¾ t	1 t	1½ t
pepper	dash	⅛ t	⅛ t, or to taste
potatoes	13½ oz	1 lb 2 oz	1 lb 11 oz
skillet	10-inch	10- or 12-inch	12-inch

Macaroni-Cheddar Salad

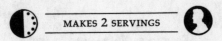

MAKES 2 SERVINGS

1½ cups cooked elbow macaroni, chilled

½ cup diagonally sliced celery (¼-inch slices)

2 ounces Cheddar cheese, shredded

2 tablespoons diced onion

¼ teaspoon salt

4 pimiento-stuffed green olives, sliced

1 tablespoon each mayonnaise and plain lowfat yogurt

Dash pepper

4 iceberg, romaine, or loose-leafed lettuce leaves, chilled

½ medium tomato, chilled

Dash paprika

In bowl combine all ingredients except lettuce, tomato, and paprika, tossing to mix well; cover and refrigerate until ready to serve.

To serve, arrange lettuce on serving plate and top with macaroni mixture; cut tomato into wedges and arrange around salad. Sprinkle macaroni mixture with paprika.

For Additional Servings Use

	3 servings	4 servings	6 servings
macaroni	2¼ c	3 c	4½ c
celery	1 c	1 c	1½ c
cheese	3 oz	4 oz	6 oz
onions	3 T	¼ c	⅓ c + 2 t
salt	¼ t	½ t	¾ t
olives	6	8	12
mayonnaise and yogurt	1 T + 1½ t each	2 T each	3 T each
pepper	dash	⅛ t	⅛ to ¼ t
lettuce	6 leaves	8 leaves	12 leaves
tomatoes	½ medium	1 medium	1½ medium
paprika	dash	⅛ t	⅛ to ¼ t

Puffy Pancake

 MAKES 2 SERVINGS, ½ PANCAKE EACH *or*
4 SERVINGS, ¼ PANCAKE EACH

This is a good breakfast entrée as well as a side dish.

2 large eggs
½ cup less 1½ teaspoons
  all-purpose flour
½ cup skim milk
Dash ground nutmeg

1 tablespoon plus 1 teaspoon
  margarine
2 teaspoons confectioners' sugar
1 tablespoon plus 1½ teaspoons
  lemon juice

Preheat oven to 425°F. In medium bowl beat eggs until fluffy; alternately beat in flour and milk, then add nutmeg (do not overbeat; mixture should be lumpy).

Heat 12-inch nonstick skillet that has a metal or removable handle; add margarine and tilt skillet until margarine is melted and coats pan. Pour batter into pan and immediately transfer to upper-third portion of oven; bake for 15 to 20 minutes (pancake should be puffy and browned). Sprinkle pancake with sugar and bake for 1 minute longer. Sprinkle with lemon juice.

Potato-Vegetable Casserole

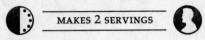

MAKES 2 SERVINGS

Hearty enough to serve as an entrée.

4 ounces Muenster cheese, shredded
¾ cup plain lowfat yogurt
1 teaspoon Dijon-style mustard
Dash freshly ground pepper
6 ounces peeled boiled potatoes,
    thinly sliced

1 cup each cooked cauliflower florets
    and thinly sliced carrots
¼ cup chopped scallions (green
    onions)

In small bowl combine first 4 ingredients. In shallow 2-quart flameproof casserole arrange potatoes, cauliflower, and carrots; sprinkle with scallions and top with yogurt mixture. Broil until cheese is melted and begins to brown, about 7 minutes.

For Additional Servings Use

	3 servings	4 servings	6 servings
cheese	6 oz	8 oz	12 oz
yogurt	1 c + 2 T	1½ c	2¼ c
mustard	1½ t	2 t	1 T
pepper	dash	⅛ t	⅛ to ¼ t
potatoes	9 oz	12 oz	1 lb 2 oz
cauliflower and carrots	1½ c each	2 c each	3 c each
scallions	⅓ c + 2 t	½ c	¾ c

Hot Fruit Compote with Coconut Topping

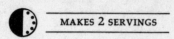

MAKES 2 SERVINGS

Fruit Mixture

4 dried apricot halves
1 large pitted prune, cut in half
1 tablespoon each raisins and
  lemon juice
1 teaspoon firmly packed brown
  sugar
Dash ground allspice

½ small Golden Delicious apple,
  cored, pared, and chopped
1½ to 2 teaspoons water (optional)

Topping

4 graham crackers (2½-inch
  squares), made into fine crumbs
2 teaspoons margarine, softened
1 teaspoon shredded coconut

To Prepare Fruit Mixture: In small nonstick saucepan combine first 5 ingredients; cook over low heat until sugar melts and fruit is plumped. Add apple and, if mixture is dry, water; cover and let simmer until apple is tender.

Spray two 6-ounce custard cups with nonstick cooking spray; spoon an equal amount of fruit mixture into each cup.

To Prepare Topping and Bake: Preheat oven to 425°F. In bowl combine all ingredients for topping, stirring to mix well. Sprinkle an equal amount of crumb mixture over each portion of fruit mixture and bake until topping is browned, about 5 minutes.

For Additional Servings Use

	4 servings	6 servings	8 servings
apricots	8 halves	12 halves	16 halves
prunes	3 medium or 2 large	3 large	6 medium or 4 large
raisins and lemon juice	2 T each	3 T each	¼ c each
sugar	2 t	1 T	1 T + 1 t
allspice	⅛ t	⅛ t	¼ t
apples	1 small	1½ small	2 small
water (optional)	1 T	1 to 2 T	2 T
graham crackers	8	12	16
margarine	1 T + 1 t	2 T	2 T + 2 t
coconut	2 t	1 T	1 T + 1 t

Glazed "Danish"

 MAKES 2 SERVINGS, 1 "DANISH" EACH

2 ready-to-bake refrigerated buttermilk flaky biscuits (1 ounce each)

2 teaspoons reduced-calorie red raspberry spread (16 calories per 2 teaspoons)

1 teaspoon shredded coconut

1 teaspoon confectioners' sugar, dissolved in about ⅛ teaspoon water

Preheat oven to 400°F. On nonstick baking sheet bake biscuits for 3 minutes. Remove biscuits from oven and, using metal 1-teaspoon measure, make an indentation in center of each; fill each indentation with 1 teaspoon raspberry spread. Return biscuits to oven and bake until golden brown, 3 to 4 minutes.

Sprinkle raspberry portion of each "Danish" with ½ teaspoon coconut; let cool, then drizzle biscuit portion of each with an equal amount of the dissolved sugar, avoiding coconut-topped center. Serve warm.

For Additional Servings Use

	3 servings	*4 servings*	*6 servings*
biscuits	3 (1 oz each)	4 (1 oz each)	6 (1 oz each)
raspberry spread	1 T	1 T + 1 t	2 T
coconut	1½ t	2 t	1 T
sugar	1½ t, dissolved in ⅛ to ¼ t water	2 t, dissolved in ¼ t water	1 T, dissolved in ¼ to ½ t water

Orange Loaf Bars

MAKES 2 SERVINGS, 2 BARS EACH

⅓ cup plus 2 teaspoons self-rising flour

1 egg

2 tablespoons thawed frozen concentrated orange juice (no sugar added)

1 tablespoon plus 1 teaspoon reduced-calorie orange marmalade (16 calories per 2 teaspoons)

2 teaspoons each granulated sugar and margarine

½ teaspoon vanilla extract

Preheat oven to 350°F. Spray a 7⅜ x 3⅝ x 2¼-inch loaf pan with nonstick cooking spray; set aside.

In small mixing bowl combine all ingredients and, using an electric mixer on low speed, beat 30 seconds just to combine; pour into sprayed pan and bake for about 25 minutes (until cake tester inserted in center comes out clean). Remove loaf from pan and cool on wire rack. Cut cooled loaf into 4 equal bars.

For Additional Servings Use

	4 servings	6 servings	8 servings
flour	¾ c	1 c + 2 T	1½ c
eggs	2	3	4
orange juice	¼ c	⅓ c + 2 t	½ c
marmalade	2 T + 2 t	¼ c	⅓ c
sugar and margarine	1 T + 1 t each	2 T each	2 T + 2 t each
vanilla	1 t	1½ t	2 t
baking pan	8 x 8 x 2-inch	8 x 8 x 2-inch	two 8 x 8 x 2-inch
Method: bake for	about 35 min.	about 40 min.	about 35 min.

Simple Skillet Specialties

✦

Entrées

Shrimp Fandango

Chicken Marsala

Chicken Velouté

Kasha-Chicken Combo

Mexican Stir-Fry

Parmesan Chicken

Skillet Chicken and Garbanzos

Deviled Lamb

Frankfurter-Vegetable Stir-Fry

Sweet 'n' Sour Cabbage and Bacon Sauté

Bacon-Liver Burgers

Quick Liver, Tomato, 'n' Onion Sauté

Side Dishes

Bacon-Corn Fritters

Chili-Cheese Corn Fritters

Potato-Carrot Fritters

Carrot-Asparagus Toss

Glazed Fruited Carrots

Grapes, Seeds, 'n' Sprouts

Oriental Vegetable Stir-Fry

"Pan-Fried" Spaghetti Squash

Potatoes O'Brien

Skillet Yams and Apples

Thanks to that invaluable time-honored utensil, the skillet, it is possible to easily prepare one-dish specialties that are real palate-pleasers with a minimum of fuss and a maximum of tastiness. This chapter serves up simple skillet recipes that will tempt even the most fastidious appetite.

In addition to many entrée possibilities, vegetables are particularly suitable for skillet cookery because they can be quickly sautéed or stir-fried—ideal methods for preparing vegetables so that they stay colorful, crisp, and nutritious.

Combining vegetables with herbs or spices and a little margarine or vegetable oil—and using quick-cooking techniques—can lend that special touch that makes the ordinary *extra*ordinary. The chart on page 44 lists seasonings that go well with various vegetables, although you can always let your taste buds be your guide.

For additional skillet vegetable recipes, see *Meal Mates* and *Good Lookin' Cookin'*.

In selecting skillets, bear in mind that the material from which the skillet is made affects its efficiency as well as its cost. (See "Organizing Your Kitchen", page 3, for the comparative merits of aluminum, copper, cast iron, and stainless steel, as well as nonstick cookware.) Although ovenproof glass and glass-ceramic are fine for use in the oven, they are *not* generally recommended for top-of-the-stove cookery since they are relatively poor conductors of heat and produce uneven results unless foods are cooked in liquid. Be sure to use wooden or plastic utensils—never metal—with nonstick cookware, to avoid scratching the finish.

To ensure even cooking and proper balance on the stove, a skillet should have a perfectly flat bottom. For safety's sake, as well as for even cooking and energy conservation, try to use the burner that best fits the size of your skillet.

Choose plain cookware with sturdy, heat-resistant or flameproof handles. Although skillets with intricate designs or crevices may look attractive, they can be difficult to clean, which also makes them less efficient in the long run, since shiny, clean cookware works better than dull, dark, or dirty pans.

VEGETABLES	COMPLEMENTARY SEASONINGS
artichokes	bay leaf, savory
asparagus	tarragon
beets	bay leaf, caraway seed, dill, fennel, mustard seed, savory, tarragon, thyme
broccoli	oregano, tarragon
brussels sprouts	sage
cabbage	caraway seed, dill, mint, mustard seed, savory, tarragon
carrots	bay leaf, dill, marjoram, mint, oregano, sage, thyme
cauliflower	caraway seed, dill
corn	chili powder
eggplant	basil, garlic, marjoram, oregano, sage
green beans	basil, dill, marjoram, mint, oregano, savory, tarragon, thyme
mushrooms	garlic, oregano, paprika, rosemary, thyme
peas	dill, marjoram, mint, oregano, rosemary, sage, savory
potatoes	bay leaf, caraway seed, chives, mint, oregano, paprika, rosemary, thyme
rutabaga	basil
spinach	marjoram, nutmeg, rosemary
summer squash	basil, rosemary
tomatoes	basil, bay leaf, dill, garlic, oregano, sage
turnips	caraway seed

Here are some tips to help keep your skillets in tip-top shape.

• Never place a hot skillet in water; the sudden change in temperature can warp the pan. Allow it to cool first.

• If food is stuck to the pan, soak the pan in warm sudsy water to loosen particles, then scour, if necessary.

• Wash greasy skillets in hot, sudsy water until all traces of grease are gone. Rinse and dry.

• After cleaning a cast-iron skillet, dry it immediately to prevent rusting.

• To prevent skillets as well as other types of cookware from acquiring a musty odor, store them *uncovered*.

Skillets come in a variety of sizes; choose the ones most appropriate to your needs. The size is determined by the diameter. Just make sure that the skillet you use will accommodate the amount of food that is to be prepared in it. For single portions, or when preparing a small quantity, a

6-inch skillet (2-cup capacity) is usually suitable. A 7- or 8-inch skillet has approximately a 3-cup capacity and a 10-inch skillet about twice that much. If you are feeding a large family, preparing for guests, or making extra portions to freeze, you will probably want to use a larger skillet— one with a 12-inch diameter (2½-quart capacity). These sizes are available in most housewares or department stores. If you find that an even larger size would better meet your needs, your best bet is to try a restaurant supply store or a specialty housewares shop. Woks, which generally have a 5-quart capacity, are suitable substitutes for very large skillets.

With the help of the recipes in this chapter, don't be surprised if your skillet becomes your favorite piece of kitchen equipment.

Shrimp Fandango

MAKES 2 SERVINGS

Peanut oil is excellent for recipes requiring high degrees of direct heat since it has a very high smoke point (the temperature at which it will begin to smoke). If peanut oil is not available, another vegetable oil can be substituted.

1 tablespoon peanut oil
¼ cup each diced yellow and red bell peppers (large dice)
1 garlic clove, minced
10 ounces shelled and deveined large shrimp
¼ cup dry vermouth
½ cup Chinese snow peas (stem ends and strings removed),* steamed until tender-crisp

½ cup julienne-cut carrots (matchstick pieces),* steamed until tender-crisp
½ cup sliced scallions (green onions)
Dash each salt and hot sauce
1 cup cooked long-grain rice, hot (optional)

In 10-inch skillet heat oil over medium heat; add peppers and garlic and sauté until peppers are tender, about 2 minutes. Increase heat to high; add shrimp and cook, stirring constantly, until shrimp begin to turn pink, about 2 minutes. Add vermouth; continue to stir and cook until liquid is reduced, about 2 minutes. Add remaining ingredients except rice; cook, stirring constantly, until heated through. If desired, serve over hot rice.

* Frozen snow peas may be substituted for the fresh and broccoli florets may be substituted for the carrots.

For Additional Servings Use

	3 servings	4 servings	6 servings
oil	1 T + 1½ t	2 T	3 T
peppers	¾ c	1 c	1½ c
garlic	1½ cloves	2 cloves	3 cloves
shrimp	15 oz	1¼ lb	1 lb 14 oz
vermouth	⅓ c + 2 t	½ c	¾ c
snow peas, carrots, and scallions	¾ c each	1 c each	1½ c each
salt and hot sauce	dash each	dash each	dash each
rice (optional)	1½ c	2 c	3 c
skillet	10-inch	12-inch	12-inch or wok

Chicken Marsala

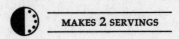 MAKES 2 SERVINGS

1 tablespoon plus 1 teaspoon
  margarine
10 ounces skinned and boned
  chicken breasts
1 tablespoon minced shallots or
  onion
⅓ cup dry Marsala wine
¼ cup prepared instant chicken
  broth and seasoning mix
  (prepared according to packet
  directions), at room temperature

1 teaspoon all-purpose flour
20 small seedless green grapes,
  cut into halves
¼ teaspoon salt
Dash freshly ground pepper

In 9- or 10-inch nonstick skillet heat margarine over medium heat until bubbly and hot; add chicken and cook, turning once, until browned on both sides. Add shallots (or onion) and cook until softened; add wine and cook, stirring occasionally, until liquid becomes slightly syrupy, about 4 minutes.

In measuring cup or small bowl combine broth and flour, stirring to dissolve flour; pour over chicken mixture and cook, stirring constantly, until sauce thickens. Add grapes and stir to combine; sprinkle with salt and pepper and serve.

For Additional Servings Use

	3 servings	4 servings	6 servings
margarine	2 T	2 T + 2 t	¼ c
chicken	15 oz	1¼ lb	1 lb 14 oz
shallots or onions	1 T + 1½ t	2 T	3 T
wine	½ c	⅔ c	1 c
broth	⅓ c + 2 t	½ c	¾ c
flour	1½ t	2 t	1 T
grapes	30 small	40 small	60 small
salt	¼ t	½ t	¾ t
pepper	dash	⅛ t	⅛ t, or to taste
skillet	10-inch	12-inch	12-inch

Chicken Velouté

In the world of haute cuisine, velouté is one of the basic sauces. It is a white sauce in which a light stock replaces the milk.

1 tablespoon margarine, divided
10 ounces skinned and boned
   chicken breasts
2 tablespoons minced shallots or
   onion
2 teaspoons all-purpose flour
¾ cup water

1 packet instant chicken broth and
   seasoning mix
¼ cup canned plum tomatoes,
   chopped
¼ teaspoon salt
1 cup cooked long-grain rice (hot)
1 tablespoon chopped fresh parsley

In 10-inch skillet heat 2 teaspoons margarine until bubbly and hot; add chicken and cook, turning once, until browned on both sides and, when pierced with fork, juices run clear. Remove from skillet and keep warm.

In same skillet heat remaining margarine until bubbly and hot; add shallots (or onion) and sauté lightly (*do not brown*). Sprinkle with flour and stir quickly to combine; gradually stir in water. Add broth mix and cook over medium heat, stirring constantly, until thickened. Reduce heat to low, add tomatoes and salt, and cook for 5 minutes longer; add browned chicken, turning to coat with sauce. Cook for 5 minutes, stirring occasionally. Serve chicken and sauce over rice and sprinkle with parsley.

For Additional Servings Use

	3 servings	4 servings	6 servings
margarine	1 T + 1½ t	2 T	3 T
chicken	15 oz	1¼ lb	1 lb 14 oz
shallots or onions	3 T	¼ c	⅓ c + 2 t
flour	1 T	1 T + 1 t	2 T
water	1 c + 2 T	1½ c	2¼ c
broth mix	1½ pkt	2 pkt	3 pkt
tomatoes	⅓ c + 2 t	½ c	¾ c
salt	¼ t	½ t	¾ t
rice	1½ c	2 c	3 c
parsley	1 T	2 T	3 T
skillet	10-inch	12-inch	12-inch to brown chicken, then use 2-quart saucepan for remainder of recipe
Method: brown chicken in	1 T margarine	1 T + 1 t margarine	2 T margarine

Kasha-Chicken Combo

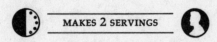

MAKES 2 SERVINGS

This is a marvelous recipe for using up leftovers; we've used chicken, but any cooked meat can be substituted. If cooked meat is not available, it's also delicious with drained canned tuna.

2 ounces uncooked buckwheat
   groats (kasha)
1 egg, lightly beaten
¼ cup each diced onion and red
   bell pepper
1 teaspoon margarine

1 packet instant chicken broth and
   seasoning mix
¾ cup hot water
6 ounces skinned and boned cooked
   chicken, diced
½ medium tomato, diced

In small bowl combine kasha and egg. Heat 9-inch nonstick skillet over high heat; add kasha mixture and cook, stirring constantly, until kasha is dry and grains are separated (*be careful not to burn*). Reduce heat to low and add onion, red pepper, and margarine, stirring to combine; sprinkle mixture with broth mix, then add water. Cover skillet and let mixture simmer until all liquid has been absorbed, 8 to 10 minutes. Add chicken and tomato and continue cooking over low heat, stirring occasionally, until chicken is heated.

For Additional Servings Use

	4 servings	*6 servings*	*8 servings*
groats	4 oz	6 oz	8 oz
eggs	2	3	4
onions and red peppers	½ c each	¾ c each	1 c each
margarine	2 t	1 T	1 T + 1 t
broth mix	2 pkt	3 pkt	4 pkt
water	1½ c	2¼ c	3 c
chicken	12 oz	1 lb 2 oz	1½ lb
tomatoes	1 medium	1½ medium	2 medium
skillet	10-inch	12-inch	wok or 3-qt saucepan

Mexican Stir-Fry

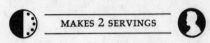

MAKES 2 SERVINGS

Staples from the pantry and leftover chicken join to make up this spicy 15-minute dish.

1 tablespoon vegetable oil
½ cup chopped onion
2 garlic cloves, minced
½ cup each diced red and green bell peppers
2 tablespoons chopped drained canned chili peppers
½ cup each tomato puree and water
1 packet instant chicken broth and seasoning mix

½ teaspoon chili powder
⅛ teaspoon ground red pepper
4 ounces drained canned pinto or red kidney beans
4 ounces skinned and boned cooked chicken, diced
1 cup cooked long-grain rice
1 tablespoon plus 1 teaspoon shredded Cheddar cheese

In 10-inch nonstick skillet heat oil over medium heat; add onion and garlic and sauté for 3 minutes. Add bell and chili peppers and sauté until vegetables are tender-crisp, about 2 minutes longer; stir in puree, water, broth mix, chili powder, and ground red pepper and bring to a boil. Reduce heat to low and cook for about 5 minutes to blend flavors; add beans, chicken, and rice and cook until thoroughly heated. Serve sprinkled with cheese.

For Additional Servings Use

	3 servings	4 servings	6 servings
vegetable oil	1 T + 1½ t	2 T	3 T
onions	¾ c	1 c	1½ c
garlic	3 cloves	4 cloves	6 cloves
bell peppers	¾ c each	1 c each	1½ c each
chili peppers	3 T	¼ c	⅓ c + 2 t
puree and water	¾ c each	1 c each	1½ c each
broth mix	1½ pkt	2 pkt	3 pkt
chili powder	¾ t	1 t	1½ t
ground red pepper	⅛ t	¼ t	¼ t, or to taste
beans	6 oz	8 oz	12 oz
chicken	6 oz	8 oz	12 oz
rice	1½ c	2 c	3 c
cheese	2 T	2 T + 2 t	¼ c
skillet	12-inch	12-inch	wok or 4-qt saucepan

Parmesan Chicken

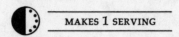

MAKES 1 SERVING

2 tablespoons buttermilk (made
   from skim milk)
½ ounce grated Parmesan cheese
4 ounces skinned and boned chicken
   breast, pounded to about ¼-inch
   thickness
1 teaspoon all-purpose flour

⅛ teaspoon salt
Dash each garlic powder, onion
   powder, and pepper
3 tablespoons plain dried bread
   crumbs
2 teaspoons vegetable oil

In small bowl combine milk and cheese. Sprinkle chicken with flour and
seasonings, then dip into buttermilk mixture, coating both sides and using
entire mixture; on sheet of wax paper, or on paper plate, dip chicken into
bread crumbs, turning to coat both sides with crumbs.

   In small nonstick skillet heat oil; add chicken and cook, turning once,
until browned on both sides.

For Additional Servings Use

	2 servings	*3 servings*	*4 servings*
buttermilk	¼ c	⅓ c + 2 t	½ c
cheese	1 oz	1½ oz	2 oz
chicken	8 oz	12 oz	15 oz
flour	2 t	1 T	1 T + 1 t
salt	¼ t	¼ t	½ t
garlic powder, onion powder, and pepper	dash each	dash each	⅛ t each
bread crumbs	⅓ c + 2 t	½ c + 1 T	¾ c
oil	1 T + 1 t	2 T	2 T + 2 t
skillet	9- or 10-inch	10-inch	12-inch

Skillet Chicken and Garbanzos

MAKES 2 SERVINGS
---

2 teaspoons all-purpose flour
Dash each salt and pepper
5 ounces skinned and boned chicken
  breasts, cut into 3 x 1-inch pieces
1 teaspoon each margarine and olive
  or vegetable oil
½ cup diced green bell pepper

¼ cup diced onion
2 medium tomatoes, blanched,
  peeled, and chopped
8 ounces drained canned chick-peas
  (garbanzo beans)
1 packet instant chicken broth and
  seasoning mix

In large plastic bag combine flour, salt, and pepper; add chicken and shake until pieces are slightly coated. In 9- or 10-inch nonstick skillet combine margarine and oil and heat over high heat until margarine is bubbly and hot; add chicken and sauté until lightly browned on all sides. Remove chicken from skillet and set aside.

Reduce heat to medium; add green pepper and onion to skillet and cook, stirring occasionally, until vegetables are tender, 1 to 2 minutes. Add tomatoes, chick-peas, and broth mix and stir to combine; return chicken to skillet. Reduce heat to low, cover skillet, and let simmer until tomatoes are reduced to a puree, 10 to 15 minutes.

For Additional Servings Use

	3 servings	4 servings	6 servings
flour	1 T	1 T + 1 t	2 T
salt and pepper	dash each	⅛ t each	⅛ to ¼ t each
chicken	8 oz	10 oz	15 oz
margarine and oil	1½ t each	2 t each	1 T each
green peppers	¾ c	1 c	1½ c
onions	⅓ c + 2 t	½ c	¾ c
tomatoes	3 medium	4 medium	6 medium
chick-peas	12 oz	1 lb	1½ lb
broth mix	1½ pkt	2 pkt	3 pkt
skillet	12-inch	12-inch	wok or 3-qt saucepan

Deviled Lamb

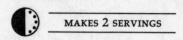

MAKES 2 SERVINGS

When a dish is referred to as "deviled," the tang you taste is frequently mustard.

8 ounces boned cooked lamb, cut
  into ¼-inch-thick slices
1 tablespoon plus 1 teaspoon
  Dijon-style mustard

¼ teaspoon ground thyme
1 tablespoon plus 1½ teaspoons
  plain dried bread crumbs
1 tablespoon vegetable oil

Spread both sides of each lamb slice with thin coating of mustard; sprinkle with thyme, then coat each slice lightly with an equal amount of crumbs, being sure to use all of crumbs.

In 10-inch nonstick skillet heat oil over medium heat; add lamb and cook, turning once, until browned on both sides, about 2 minutes on each side.

For Additional Servings Use

	3 servings	4 servings	6 servings
lamb	12 oz	1 lb	1½ lb
mustard	2 T	2 T + 2 t	¼ c
thyme	¼ t	½ t	¾ t
bread crumbs	2 T + ¾ t	3 T	¼ c + 1½ t
oil	1 T + 1½ t	2 T	3 T
skillet	10-inch	12-inch	12-inch

Frankfurter-Vegetable Stir-Fry

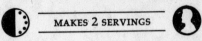

MAKES 2 SERVINGS

2 teaspoons vegetable oil
½ cup each sliced onion and thinly
   sliced carrot and green bell pepper
1 small garlic clove, minced, or ½
   teaspoon garlic powder
1 cup shredded green cabbage
6 ounces frankfurters, sliced

¼ cup prepared instant chicken
   broth and seasoning mix
   (prepared according to packet
   directions), at room temperature
1 teaspoon each cornstarch and
   soy sauce

In 9- or 10-inch nonstick skillet heat oil over medium heat; add onion,
carrot, pepper, and garlic and sauté until onion is translucent, about 5
minutes. Reduce heat to low and add cabbage; cover skillet and cook,
stirring occasionally, until cabbage becomes wilted, about 10 minutes. Add
frankfurters and cook until heated through. In measuring cup or small
bowl combine broth, cornstarch, and soy sauce, stirring to dissolve cornstarch; pour over frankfurter mixture and cook, stirring constantly, until
slightly thickened.

For Additional Servings Use

	3 servings	4 servings	6 servings
oil	1 T	1 T + 1 t	2 T
onions, carrots, and peppers	¾ c each	1 c each	1½ c each
garlic	1 small clove or ½ t powder	2 small cloves or 1 t powder	1 large clove or 1½ t powder
cabbage	1½ c	2 c	3 c
frankfurters	9 oz	12 oz	1 lb 2 oz
broth	⅓ c + 2 t	½ c	¾ c
cornstarch and soy sauce	1½ t each	2 t each	1 T each
skillet	12-inch	12-inch	wok or 3-qt saucepan

Sweet 'n' Sour Cabbage and Bacon Sauté

 MAKES 2 SERVINGS

2 teaspoons vegetable oil
6 ounces Canadian-style bacon, cut into cubes
1 cup sliced onions
4 cups shredded green cabbage (about half of a 1½-pound head)

1 tablespoon plus 1½ teaspoons white vinegar
1½ teaspoons firmly packed brown sugar
Dash pepper

In 10-inch nonstick skillet heat oil; add bacon and onions and sauté until browned. Add cabbage and stir until thoroughly combined; add remaining ingredients and cook, stirring occasionally, until cabbage is tender and liquid has evaporated.

For Additional Servings Use

	3 servings	*4 servings*	*6 servings*
oil	1 T	1 T + 1 t	2 T
bacon	9 oz	12 oz	1 lb 2 oz
onions	1½ c	2 c	3 c
cabbage	6 c	8 c	12 c
vinegar	2 T	3 T	¼ c
sugar	2¼ t	1 T	1 T + 1½ t
pepper	dash	⅛ t	⅛ t, or to taste
skillet	12-inch	12-inch	wok or 4-qt saucepan

Bacon-Liver Burgers

MAKES 1 SERVING, 2 BURGERS

Frequently, potatoes are riced rather than mashed. A ricer is a utensil designed for pressing soft foods through a perforated container so that the food emerges in the form of strands that are about the diameter of a grain of rice.

5 ounces chicken livers
¼ cup each minced onion and celery
3 ounces peeled cooked potato, mashed or riced
1½ teaspoons imitation bacon bits, crushed

Dash each salt and pepper
2¼ teaspoons seasoned dried bread crumbs
1½ teaspoons margarine
2 teaspoons ketchup

1. In 8-inch nonstick skillet cook livers over high heat just until they lose red color, 2 to 3 minutes; transfer to bowl and, using a fork, mash.

2. In same skillet combine onion and celery; cover and cook over low heat until vegetables are soft.

3. Add cooked vegetables, potato, bacon bits, salt, and pepper to mashed livers and mix until thoroughly combined; shape mixture into 2 equal patties.

4. On sheet of wax paper, or on paper plate, press patties into crumbs, turning to coat both sides.

5. In clean skillet heat margarine over medium-high heat until bubbly and hot; add patties and cook until browned on all sides, 2 to 4 minutes. Serve with ketchup.

For Additional Servings Use

	2 servings	3 servings	4 servings
livers	10 oz	15 oz	1¼ lb
onions and celery	½ c each	¾ c each	1 c each
potatoes	6 oz	9 oz	12 oz
bacon bits	1 T	1 T + ½ t	2 T
salt	⅛ t	⅛ t	¼ t
pepper	dash	dash	⅛ t
bread crumbs	1 T + 1½ t	2 T + ¾ t	3 T
margarine	1 T	1 T + 1½ t	2 T
ketchup	1 T + 1 t	2 T	2 T + 2 t
skillet	9-inch	10-inch	12-inch
Method: step 3	form 4 equal patties	form 6 equal patties	form 8 equal patties

Quick Liver, Tomato, 'n' Onion Sauté

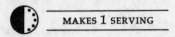 MAKES 1 SERVING

2 teaspoons margarine, divided
½ cup sliced onion (separated into rings)
1 medium tomato, cut into 5 slices
¼ teaspoon marjoram leaves

1 tablespoon plus 1½ teaspoons all-purpose flour
¼ teaspoon salt
Dash freshly ground pepper
5 ounces calf liver, thinly sliced
Garnish: parsley sprigs

1. In 8-inch skillet heat half of the margarine; add onion rings in a single layer and sauté just until lightly browned and tender (*not soft*). Remove from skillet and keep warm.

2. In same skillet arrange tomato slices in a single layer and cook each side briefly; gently remove from skillet and set aside with onions. Sprinkle vegetables with marjoram and keep warm.

3. On sheet of wax paper, or on paper plate, combine flour, salt, and pepper; dredge liver in seasoned flour, turning slices to coat all sides.

4. In same skillet heat remaining margarine until bubbly and hot; add liver and sauté, turning once, until done to taste (*do not overcook*); remove to serving plate and top with onion rings and tomato slices. Serve garnished with parsley sprigs.

For Additional Servings Use

	2 servings	3 servings	4 servings
margarine	1 T + 1 t	2 T	2 T + 2 t
onions	1 c	1½ c	2 c
tomatoes	2 medium	3 medium	4 medium
marjoram leaves	½ t	¾ t	1 t
flour	3 T	¼ c + 1½ t	⅓ c + 2 t
salt	½ t	¾ t	1 t
pepper	dash	dash	⅛ t
liver	10 oz	15 oz	1¼ lb
skillet	10-inch	10- or 12-inch	12-inch

Bacon-Corn Fritters

 MAKES 2 SERVINGS, 2 FRITTERS EACH

½ cup drained canned whole-kernel corn
3 tablespoons all-purpose flour
1 egg
1 tablespoon imitation bacon bits

½ teaspoon double-acting baking powder
Dash pepper
2 teaspoons vegetable oil

In small bowl combine first 6 ingredients, stirring well. In 10-inch nonstick skillet heat oil over medium heat until hot but not smoking. Spoon batter into skillet, forming 4 equal fritters (about ¼ cup batter for each fritter); cook until edges bubble and fritters are browned on bottom. Turn fritters over and cook until browned on other side.

For Additional Servings Use

	4 servings	*6 servings*
corn	1 c	1½ c
flour	⅓ c + 2 t	½ c + 1 T
eggs	2	3
bacon bits	2 T	3 T
baking powder	1 t	1½ t
pepper	dash	dash to ⅛ t
oil	1 T + 1 t	2 T
Method: use 2 t oil for each 4 fritters and prepare in	2 batches	3 batches

Chili-Cheese Corn Fritters

 MAKES 2 SERVINGS, 3 FRITTERS EACH

This can also be used as an entrée.

3 ounces Cheddar cheese, shredded
½ cup drained canned whole-kernel corn
1 egg
3 tablespoons plain dried bread crumbs

⅛ teaspoon each garlic powder, onion powder, chili powder, and double-acting baking powder
Dash each salt and ground red pepper
1 tablespoon vegetable oil

In 1-quart mixing bowl combine all ingredients except oil; let stand a few minutes for flavors to blend.

In 10-inch nonstick skillet heat oil over medium heat until hot but not smoking; spoon corn mixture into skillet, forming 6 equal fritters. Using the back of a spoon, press top of each fritter to flatten slightly; cook until browned on bottom. Turn fritters over and cook until browned on other side.

For Additional Servings Use

	4 servings	6 servings
cheese	6 oz	9 oz
corn	1 c	1½ c
eggs	2	3
bread crumbs	⅓ c + 2 t	½ c + 1 T
garlic powder, onion powder, chili powder, and baking powder	¼ t each	¼ t each
salt and red pepper	⅛ t each	⅛ t each
oil	2 T	3 T
Method: use 1 T oil for each 6 fritters and prepare in	2 batches	3 batches

Potato-Carrot Fritters

 MAKES 2 SERVINGS, 2 FRITTERS EACH

4½ ounces pared potato, grated
½ cup grated carrot
1 egg, lightly beaten
3 tablespoons all-purpose flour
2 tablespoons buttermilk (made from skim milk)

1 tablespoon plus 1½ teaspoons chopped scallion (green onion)
¼ teaspoon salt
⅛ teaspoon garlic powder
Dash each baking soda and pepper
2 teaspoons vegetable oil

In bowl combine all ingredients except oil. In 9-inch nonstick skillet heat oil over high heat until hot but not smoking. Drop potato mixture by heaping tablespoonsful into skillet, forming 4 equal fritters; using the back of spoon, press top of each fritter to flatten slightly. Reduce heat to medium and cook until fritters are browned on bottom; turn fritters over and cook until browned on other side.

For Additional Servings Use

	4 servings	6 servings
potatoes	9 oz	13½ oz
carrots	1 c	1½ c
eggs	2	3
flour	⅓ c + 2 t	½ c + 1 T
buttermilk	¼ c	⅓ c + 2 t
scallions	3 T	¼ c + 1½ t
salt	½ t	¾ t
garlic powder	¼ t	¼ t
baking soda	⅛ t	⅛ t
pepper	dash	dash to ⅛ t
oil	1 T + 1 t	2 T
Method: use 2 t oil for each 4 fritters and prepare in	2 batches	3 batches

Carrot-Asparagus Toss

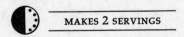 MAKES 2 SERVINGS

2 teaspoons each peanut oil and minced shallots
1 cup diagonally sliced carrots, blanched
12 asparagus spears, sliced diagonally and blanched

2 tablespoons water
1 teaspoon soy sauce
⅛ teaspoon each salt and pepper

In 9-inch skillet heat oil; add shallots and sauté until softened. Add carrots and asparagus and sauté for 3 minutes; stir in water and continue sautéing until liquid has evaporated. Stir in soy sauce, salt, and pepper and serve hot.

For Additional Servings Use

	3 servings	*4 servings*	*6 servings*
oil and shallots	1 T each	1 T + 1 t each	2 T each
carrots	1½ c	2 c	3 c
asparagus	18 spears	24 spears	36 spears
water	3 T	¼ c	⅓ c
soy sauce	1½ t	2 t	1 T
salt and pepper	⅛ t each	¼ t each	¼ t each, or to taste
skillet	9-inch	10-inch	12-inch

Glazed Fruited Carrots

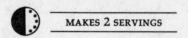

MAKES 2 SERVINGS

2 teaspoons margarine
2 tablespoons dry vermouth
1 teaspoon firmly packed brown
  sugar
½ teaspoon cornstarch, dissolved in
  1½ teaspoons water
1 package (10 ounces) frozen sliced
  carrots (about 2 cups), cooked
  according to package directions

10 small seedless green grapes, cut
  into halves
1 tablespoon raisins
Dash salt (optional)

In small nonstick skillet melt margarine over low heat; add vermouth and sugar and stir until sugar is melted. Add dissolved cornstarch and cook, stirring constantly, until mixture thickens; stir in carrots, grapes, raisins, and if desired, salt. Continue cooking and stirring until carrots and fruits are coated with sauce and thoroughly heated.

For Additional Servings Use

	3 servings	*4 servings*	*6 servings*
margarine	1 T	1 T + 1 t	2 T
vermouth	3 T	¼ c	⅓ c + 2 t
sugar	1½ t	2 t	1 T
cornstarch	¾ t, dissolved in 2 t water	1 t, dissolved in 1 T water	1½ t, dissolved in 1 T water
carrots	1½ pkg (about 3 c)	2 pkg (about 4 c)	3 pkg (about 6 c)
grapes	15 small	20 small	30 small
raisins	1 T + 1½ t	2 T	3 T
salt (optional)	dash	dash	dash to ⅛ t
skillet	8-inch	10-inch	12-inch

Grapes, Seeds, 'n' Sprouts

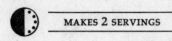 MAKES 2 SERVINGS

2 teaspoons each margarine and
   sunflower seed
10 small seedless red or green grapes

2 tablespoons dry white wine
1 cup cooked brussels sprouts
Dash salt

In small nonstick skillet heat margarine over medium-high heat until bubbly and hot; add seeds and stir until golden brown. Add grapes and wine; bring to a boil. Reduce heat to medium, add sprouts and salt, and cook, stirring constantly, until thoroughly heated.

For Additional Servings Use

	3 servings	*4 servings*	*6 servings*
margarine and sunflower seed	1 T each	1 T + 1 t each	2 T each
grapes	15 small	20 small	30 small
wine	3 T	¼ c	⅓ c + 2 t
brussels sprouts	1½ c	2 c	3 c
salt	dash	⅛ t	⅛ t, or to taste
skillet	8-inch	10-inch	12-inch

Oriental Vegetable Stir-Fry

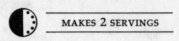 MAKES 2 SERVINGS

1½ teaspoons peanut oil
¼ cup diagonally sliced scallions
(green onions)
½ garlic clove, minced
1 cup diagonally sliced celery
(thin slices)
¾ cup Chinese snow peas (stem
ends and strings removed)*

½ cup diced red bell pepper
⅓ cup water
2 teaspoons soy sauce
1 teaspoon cornstarch
⅛ teaspoon ground ginger
Dash each salt and pepper

In 9-inch skillet or wok heat oil over high heat; add scallions and garlic and stir-fry for 1 minute. Add remaining vegetables and cook, stirring quickly and frequently, for 2 minutes. In measuring cup or small bowl combine water, soy sauce, and cornstarch, stirring to dissolve cornstarch; pour mixture over vegetables. Add seasonings and cook, stirring constantly, until snow peas are tender-crisp and sauce thickens.

* Frozen snow peas may be substituted for the fresh.

For Additional Servings Use

	3 servings	4 servings	6 servings
oil	2¼ t	1 T	1 T + 1½ t
scallions	⅓ c + 2 t	½ c	¾ c
garlic	½ clove	1 clove	1½ cloves
celery	1½ c	2 c	3 c
snow peas	1 c + 2 T	1½ c	2¼ c
red peppers	¾ c	1 c	1½ c
water	½ c	⅔ c	1 c
soy sauce	1 T	1 T + 1 t	2 T
cornstarch	1½ t	2 t	1 T
ginger	⅛ t	⅛ t	¼ t
salt and pepper	dash each	⅛ t each	⅛ t each, or to taste
skillet	10-inch or wok	12-inch or wok	12-inch or wok

"Pan-Fried" Spaghetti Squash

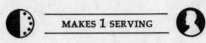

MAKES 1 SERVING

An excellent way to use up that leftover squash.

1½ teaspoons margarine
¼ cup diced onion
1½ cups cooked spaghetti squash

⅛ teaspoon salt
Dash pepper

In small nonstick skillet heat margarine until bubbly and hot; add onion and sauté until golden brown. Add squash, spreading over surface of pan; sprinkle with salt and pepper and cook, turning with a spatula, until browned on both sides.

For Additional Servings Use

	2 servings	3 servings	4 servings
margarine	1 T	1 T + 1½ t	2 T
onions	½ c	¾ c	1 c
squash	3 c	4½ c	6 c
salt	¼ t	¼ t	½ t
pepper	dash	dash	⅛ t
skillet	9- or 10-inch	10-inch	12-inch

Potatoes O'Brien

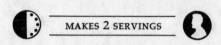

MAKES 2 SERVINGS

In the culinary world, the term "O'Brien" refers to cubed potatoes that are prepared with onions, green bell peppers, and red bell peppers or pimientos.

1 teaspoon each vegetable oil and
  margarine
½ cup diced green bell pepper
2 tablespoons diced onion
9 ounces peeled cooked potatoes,
  cut into cubes

¼ cup diced pimientos
¼ teaspoon salt
Dash each pepper and paprika

In 9-inch nonstick skillet combine oil and margarine and heat until margarine is bubbly and hot; add green pepper and onion and sauté over medium-high heat, stirring occasionally, until onion is translucent, about 3 minutes. Reduce heat and add remaining ingredients; cook, stirring occasionally, until potatoes are thoroughly heated, about 5 minutes.

For Additional Servings Use

	3 servings	4 servings	6 servings
oil and margarine	1½ t each	2 t each	1 T each
green peppers	¾ c	1 c	1½ c
onions	3 T	¼ c	⅓ c + 2 t
potatoes	13½ oz	1 lb 2 oz	1 lb 11 oz
pimientos	⅓ c + 2 t	½ c	¾ c
salt	¼ t	½ t	¾ t
pepper and paprika	dash each	⅛ t each	⅛ to ¼ t each
skillet	10-inch	12-inch	12-inch

Skillet Yams and Apples

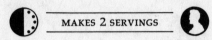

MAKES 2 SERVINGS

1 tablespoon margarine
2 small Golden Delicious apples,
   cored, pared, and cut into cubes
2 tablespoons minced onion
2 teaspoons firmly packed brown
   sugar

1 teaspoon lemon juice
¼ teaspoon salt
⅛ teaspoon ground cinnamon
Dash ground nutmeg (optional)
6 ounces peeled cooked yams,
   chilled and cut into 1-inch cubes*

In 10-inch skillet heat margarine over medium heat until bubbly and hot; add apples and onion and sauté, stirring occasionally, until apples are soft, 4 to 5 minutes. Sprinkle evenly with sugar, lemon juice, and seasonings and cook, stirring constantly, until sugar is melted; add yam cubes and cook, stirring occasionally, until yams are thoroughly heated.

* Sweet potatoes may be substituted for the yams.

For Additional Servings Use

	3 servings	4 servings	6 servings
margarine	1 T + 1½ t	2 T	3 T
apples	3 small	4 small	6 small
onions	3 T	¼ c	⅓ c + 2 t
sugar	1 T	1 T + 1 t	2 T
lemon juice	1½ t	2 t	1 T
salt	¼ t	½ t	¾ t
cinnamon	⅛ t, or to taste	¼ t	¼ to ½ t
nutmeg (optional)	dash	⅛ t	⅛ to ¼ t
yams	9 oz	12 oz	1 lb 2 oz
skillet	10-inch	12-inch	12-inch

Cocktail Quickies

Appetizers and Snacks
Spinach-Stuffed Mushrooms
Marinated Roasted Peppers
Far East Broccoli
Spinach Turnovers
Crostini Appetizer
Cheddar-Beer Crackers
Scallion-Cheese Rounds
Herbed Romano Sticks
Sesame Breadsticks
Caramel Corn
Glazed Popcorn Treat
Peanut-Corn Crunch
Spicy Popcorn Snack
"Orange-Crème" Stuffed Prunes

Dips
Cucumber-Yogurt Dip
Spicy Blue Cheese Dip or Dressing
Zippy Parsley Dip

Beverages
Apple Tonic
Orange Tonic
Cran-Orange Tonic
"Mai Tai"
"Martini"
Mimosa
Champagne Cocktail
Crème de Champagne Cocktail
Mocha-Almond Delight
Golden "Eggnog"
Apple-Ale Punch
Tropical Wine Punch

Have you ever missed your own party? Not because you weren't there, but because you had to be *every*where—with frantic last-minute preparations?

Entertain the welcome thought that you can be a guest at your own party. The not-so-secret ingredients are coordination and advance planning—of everything from casseroles to coasters, from drinks to decor.

Here's a chapter of recipes that will make it easier for you to host America's favorite type of bash: the cocktail party. You'll find easy-to-prepare recipes ranging from popular popcorn to champagne cocktails. What they have in common is ease of preparation.

Having a party is like concocting the perfect dish: you need to know how to mix the right ingredients. Here are some tips for a successful party.

Plan every detail. The very first step is to draw up written lists of whom you want to invite, what you'll serve, how you'll decorate, what supplies you'll need, as well as a time schedule for accomplishing each task. Get as many chores as possible out of the way ahead of time. (For instance, paper goods and nonperishables can be purchased way in advance.)

Here's another hint: keep a *post*-party record of guests, foods, and decorations, plus your comments about what went well and what didn't, to make planning the next one easier.

Blend a varied mixture of guests. Whether the party is intimate or huge, a mixture of personalities creates a more lively atmosphere. Include some guests who know each other to assure easy conversation, but add the surprise element of new people, too. Draw guests from various groups so that conversation doesn't disintegrate into an evening of shoptalk. Don't be afraid to mix ages, either. Compatibility isn't a matter of decades, but of mutual interests.

Set a festive stage. Going to the effort of decorating tells your guests you think they are "special" and puts them in a party mood the minute they walk through the door. Background music adds a nice touch, but avoid mood music; instead, tune in to lively toe-tapping songs. (Just keep it low enough so guests don't have to compete with the stereo.)

Create an eye-catching table. Place platters and dishes in an attractive arrangement on a bright cloth, using a centerpiece as the focal point. The centerpiece can be a simple floral arrangement, or for more variety, a group of bud vases, each containing a different color or type of flower. For a foliage effect, mass some low plants together. Or combine fresh fruits and vegetables to make a centerpiece that's really good enough to eat—for example, dark eggplant, bright oranges, purple grapes, and vivid strawberries in a wicker basket.

Light the scene. Lighting has a powerful effect on mood, as any stage or film technician can verify. How bright or dim depends on the mood you want to create. A soft diffused glow is both inviting and flattering. To create a supper club atmosphere, try changing your light bulbs to pink or amber for the evening. Of course, nothing is more effective than candlelight.

Serve appropriate foods. Cocktail party fare means finger foods—things that people can help themselves to easily and that don't need to be cut. Stay away from "runny" items—people don't want to have to worry about their clothes.

Hint: As an aid to the weight-conscious, when you set out bottles of wine, add some bottles of mineral water and diet soft drinks; then your guests can unobtrusively pour soda into a wine glass.

Be savvy about glassware. Festive beverages are what cocktail parties are all about, and it's sophisticated to know the kind of glassware to serve them in. The all-purpose wine glass is acceptable everywhere, but you may want to have some other members of the glass family on hand. These include brandy inhalers, claret glasses, goblets, sherry glasses, and rock glasses (sometimes called Old-Fashioned glasses), as well as the *coup* (or "champagne cocktail" or "saucer" glass) and the *"trumpet,"* appropriate for sparkling wines (these lovely glasses can also double as servers for sherbets and other light desserts).

Hints: Storing glassware upside down prevents dust from collecting in the bowls and keeps them ready for swift serving. Never put fine glassware into a dishwasher unless you want nicks and cracks in them. Crystal wine glasses should always be washed in clear water without detergents.

The major ingredient is you! Whether a party takes wing or not depends in large part on the mood of the host or hostess. A frantic host makes guests feel uncomfortable. But if you are relaxed and obviously enjoying the party, your guests will enjoy it, too. You should be available to your company, not out in the kitchen. Then your focus can be where it should be: putting your friends at ease.

Spinach-Stuffed Mushrooms

MAKES 2 SERVINGS, 4 STUFFED MUSHROOMS EACH

8 large mushrooms (about 2-inch
diameter each)
1 tablespoon margarine
2 tablespoons minced shallots or
onion
1 cup well-drained cooked chopped
spinach (fresh or frozen)
½ cup cooked long-grain rice

2 ounces shredded Fontina cheese*
Dash each salt and freshly ground
pepper
¼ cup prepared instant chicken
broth and seasoning mix
(prepared according to packet
instructions)

Rinse mushrooms and, using paper towels, gently dry. Remove and chop stems, reserving caps. In small nonstick skillet heat margarine until bubbly and hot; add chopped mushroom stems and shallots (or onion) and sauté until all liquid has evaporated. Add spinach, rice, cheese, salt, and pepper and stir to combine.

Preheat oven to 400°F. Fill each reserved mushroom cap with an equal amount of spinach mixture; transfer stuffed mushrooms to an 8 x 8 x 2-inch baking pan. Add broth to pan and bake until mushrooms are tender when pierced with a fork, 20 to 25 minutes; serve hot.

* Mozzarella cheese may be substituted for the Fontina cheese.

For Additional Servings Use

	4 servings	*6 servings*	*12 servings*
mushrooms	16 large	24 large	48 large
margarine	2 T	3 T	⅓ c + 2 t
shallots or onions	¼ c	⅓ c + 2 t	¾ c
spinach	2 c	3 c	6 c
rice	1 c	1½ c	3 c
cheese	4 oz	6 oz	12 oz
salt and pepper	dash each	⅛ t each	¼ t each
broth	½ c	½ c	¾ c
skillet	10-inch	12-inch	wok or 4-qt saucepan

Marinated Roasted Peppers

MAKES 2 SERVINGS

This recipe can be prepared early in the day, or even the day before; remember, at least 30 minutes must be allowed for marinating.

2 medium red bell peppers
2 medium green bell peppers
1 tablespoon freshly squeezed
   lemon juice

1 teaspoon mashed drained canned
   anchovies
Dash pepper

Preheat broiler. On baking sheet broil red and green peppers 3 inches from heat source, turning frequently until charred on all sides; transfer peppers to brown paper bag and let stand until cool enough to handle.

Fit strainer into small bowl and peel peppers over bowl; remove and discard stem ends and seeds, allowing juice from peppers to drip into bowl. Cut each pepper into strips and add to bowl; add remaining ingredients and stir to combine. Cover and let marinate for at least 30 minutes.

For Additional Servings Use

	4 servings	6 servings	12 servings
red and green peppers	4 medium each	6 medium each	12 medium each
lemon juice	2 T	3 T	⅓ c
anchovies	2 t	1 T	2 T
pepper	dash	⅛ t	¼ t

Far East Broccoli

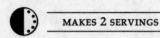 MAKES 2 SERVINGS

Chilled, this is good as an hors d'oeuvre; hot it's delicious as a side dish.

1 tablespoon each rice vinegar and Chinese sesame oil

1 teaspoon each soy sauce and prepared mustard

1 package (10-ounce) frozen broccoli spears, steamed until tender-crisp and drained (chill if desired)*

In salad bowl combine vinegar, oil, soy sauce, and mustard; add broccoli and toss to coat.

* 2 cups fresh broccoli florets may be substituted for the broccoli spears.

For Additional Servings Use	4 servings	6 servings	12 servings
vinegar and oil	2 T each	3 T each	⅓ c + 2 t each
soy sauce and mustard	2 t each	1 T each	2 T each
broccoli	2 pkg frozen or 4 c fresh	3 pkg frozen or 6 c fresh	6 pkg frozen or 12 c fresh

Spinach Turnovers

 MAKES 2 SERVINGS, 2 TURNOVERS EACH

1 teaspoon margarine
2 tablespoons minced onion
¼ cup thawed frozen chopped
  spinach
2 teaspoons part-skim ricotta cheese

1 teaspoon grated Parmesan cheese
2 ready-to-bake refrigerated
  buttermilk flaky biscuits (1
  ounce each)

In small nonstick skillet heat margarine over medium heat until bubbly and hot; add onion and sauté until translucent, about 2 minutes. Add spinach to skillet and cook, stirring occasionally, until moisture has evaporated. Remove from heat and stir in cheeses, stirring until combined; set aside.

Preheat oven to 400°F. Spray cookie sheet with nonstick cooking spray and set aside. Between 2 sheets of wax paper roll each biscuit into a circle, about 6 inches in diameter; cut each circle in half. Mound an equal amount of spinach mixture onto center of each biscuit half; moisten edges of dough with water and fold each half, turnover fashion, to enclose filling. Seal edges by pressing with tines of a fork. Transfer turnovers to sprayed cookie sheet and bake until browned, 8 to 10 minutes; serve hot.

For Additional Servings Use

	4 servings	6 servings	12 servings
margarine	2 t	1 T	2 T
onions	¼ c	⅓ c + 2 t	¾ c
spinach	½ c	¾ c	1½ c
ricotta cheese	1 T + 1 t	2 T	¼ c
Parmesan cheese	2 t	1 T	2 T
biscuits	4 (1 oz each)	6 (1 oz each)	12 (1 oz each)

Crostini Appetizer

 MAKES 2 SERVINGS, 1 CROSTINI EACH

Bake in conventional oven or in a toaster-oven.

1 teaspoon olive oil
1 tablespoon minced onion
½ garlic clove
¼ cup blanched, peeled, seeded, and chopped tomato
1 teaspoon mashed drained canned anchovies

Dash each oregano leaves and freshly ground pepper
2 slices French bread (1 ounce each), toasted
1 teaspoon grated Parmesan cheese

Preheat oven to 400°F. In small nonstick skillet heat oil; add onion and garlic and sauté over medium heat until onion is translucent. Remove and discard garlic. Add tomato, anchovies, oregano, and pepper to onion and cook, stirring occasionally, for about 3 minutes.

Place bread slices on sheet of foil and place on baking sheet; spread an equal amount of anchovy mixture over each slice. Sprinkle each with ½ teaspoon cheese and bake until top is browned, 10 to 15 minutes; serve hot.

For Additional Servings Use

	4 servings	6 servings	12 servings
oil	2 t	1 T	2 T
onions	2 T	3 T	⅓ c + 2 t
garlic	½ clove	1 clove, cut	2 cloves, cut
tomatoes	½ c	¾ c	1½ c
anchovies	2 t	1 T	2 T
oregano leaves and pepper	dash each	⅛ t each	¼ t each
French bread	4 slices (1 oz each)	6 slices (1 oz each)	12 slices (1 oz each)
cheese	2 t	1 T	2 T

Cheddar-Beer Crackers

 MAKES 2 SERVINGS, 8 CRACKERS EACH

⅓ cup plus 2 teaspoons all-purpose flour
¼ teaspoon double-acting baking powder
Dash salt

2 teaspoons margarine
¼ cup beer
1 ounce sharp Cheddar cheese, shredded
½ teaspoon poppy seed

Preheat oven to 450°F. In bowl combine first 3 ingredients; with pastry blender, or 2 knives used scissors-fashion, cut in margarine until mixture resembles coarse meal. Add beer and cheese and stir to combine.

Onto nonstick baking sheet drop batter by heaping teaspoonsful, forming 16 mounds and leaving a space of about 1 inch between each. Sprinkle each mound with an equal amount of poppy seed and bake until lightly browned, 8 to 10 minutes. Remove crackers to wire rack to cool.

For Additional Servings Use

	4 servings	6 servings	12 servings
flour	¾ c	1 c + 2 T	2¼ c
baking powder	½ t	¾ t	1½ t
salt	⅛ t	⅛ t, or to taste	¼ t
margarine	1 T + 1 t	2 T	¼ c
beer	½ c	¾ c	1½ c
cheese	2 oz	3 oz	6 oz
poppy seed	1 t	1½ t	1 T
Method: form	32 mounds	48 mounds	96 mounds

Scallion-Cheese Rounds

 MAKES 2 SERVINGS, 6 ROUNDS EACH

12 sesame melba rounds
⅓ cup cottage cheese
2 tablespoons diced scallion (green
  onion)

2 teaspoons each grated Parmesan
  cheese and mayonnaise
Dash garlic powder
¼ teaspoon paprika

Preheat broiler. Arrange sesame rounds on nonstick cookie sheet and set aside. In small bowl combine remaining ingredients except paprika and mix well; spoon an equal amount of mixture (about 1 heaping teaspoonful) onto each round. Sprinkle each with paprika and broil until cheese is bubbly, about 1 minute; serve hot.

For Additional Servings Use

	4 servings	6 servings	12 servings
melba rounds	24	36	72
cottage cheese	⅔ c	1 c	2 c
scallions	¼ c	⅓ c + 2 t	¾ c
Parmesan cheese and mayonnaise	1 T + 1 t each	2 T each	¼ c each
garlic powder	dash to ⅛ t	⅛ t	¼ t
paprika	½ t	¾ t	1½ t

Herbed Romano Sticks

MAKES 2 SERVINGS

These sticks can be baked in a conventional oven or in a toaster-oven.

⅓ cup plus 2 teaspoons all-purpose flour

Dash each oregano leaves, garlic powder, ground red pepper, and salt

1 tablespoon plus 1 teaspoon margarine

2 tablespoons plain lowfat yogurt

2 teaspoons grated Romano cheese*

1. In mixing bowl combine flour and seasonings; with pastry blender, or 2 knives used scissors-fashion, cut in margarine until mixture resembles coarse meal. Add yogurt and mix thoroughly to form dough.

2. Form dough into a ball, wrap in plastic wrap, and refrigerate until chilled, about 1 hour.

3. Preheat oven to 400°F. Between 2 sheets of wax paper roll dough to about ⅛-inch thickness; remove paper and cut dough into strips, each about 4 inches long and ½ inch wide. Fold each strip in half, forming 2-inch-long strips, and twist each slightly.

4. Place strips on nonstick baking sheet (or toaster-oven tray that has been sprayed with nonstick cooking spray) and sprinkle each with an equal amount of cheese; bake until golden brown, about 15 minutes. Serve warm.

* Grated Parmesan cheese may be substituted for the Romano cheese.

For Additional Servings Use

	4 servings	6 servings	12 servings
flour	¾ c	1 c + 2 T	2¼ c
seasonings	dash each	⅛ t each	⅛ t each
margarine	2 T + 2 t	¼ c	½ c
yogurt	¼ c	⅓ c + 2 t	¾ c
cheese	1 T + 1 t	2 T	¼ c

Sesame Breadsticks

 MAKES 10 SERVINGS, 2 STICKS EACH

Any leftovers may be refrigerated for use at another time. To reheat in oven or toaster-oven, wrap in foil; to reheat in microwave oven, wrap in plastic wrap.

Preheat oven to 400°F. Spray cookie sheet with nonstick cooking spray and set aside.

Using a *10-ounce package refrigerated buttermilk flaky biscuits (10 biscuits)*, separate biscuits and cut each in half; roll each half between palms of hands into a 6-inch-long strip. Place strips on sprayed cookie sheet. In metal measuring cup, or other small flameproof container, melt *1 tablespoon plus 2 teaspoons margarine;* brush each biscuit strip with an equal amount of melted margarine and sprinkle each with ¼ *teaspoon sesame seed.* Bake until golden brown, 5 to 8 minutes.

Caramel Corn

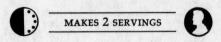

MAKES 2 SERVINGS

2 cups prepared plain popcorn
1½ teaspoons granulated sugar

1 teaspoon light corn syrup
2 teaspoons margarine

Place popcorn in large bowl and set aside. In metal ¼-cup measure, or other small flameproof container, combine sugar and syrup; cook over low heat, stirring constantly, until sugar is melted. Add margarine and stir until melted; pour over popcorn and toss quickly to thoroughly coat. Let stand until popcorn is dry and coating hardened.

For Additional Servings Use

	4 servings	*6 servings*	*12 servings*
popcorn	4 c	6 c	12 c
sugar	1 T	1 T + 1½ t	3 T
syrup	2 t	1 T	2 T
margarine	1 T + 1 t	2 T	¼ c

Glazed Popcorn Treat

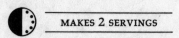 MAKES 2 SERVINGS

2 cups prepared plain popcorn, hot
2 tablespoons raisins, chopped
2 dried apricot halves, chopped
1 date, pitted and chopped

1 teaspoon sunflower seed
2 teaspoons each margarine and
  firmly packed light brown sugar

In serving bowl combine first 5 ingredients; set aside. In small skillet melt margarine over low heat; add sugar and stir until sugar is melted. Pour over popcorn mixture and toss until popcorn is coated.

For Additional Servings Use

	4 servings	*6 servings*	*12 servings*
popcorn	4 c	6 c	12 c
raisins	¼ c	⅓ c + 2 t	¾ c
apricots	4 halves	6 halves	12 halves
dates	2	3	6
sunflower seed	2 t	1 T	2 T
margarine and sugar	1 T + 1 t each	2 T each	¼ c each

Peanut-Corn Crunch

MAKES 2 SERVINGS

---

1 cup prepared plain popcorn
2 tablespoons raisins
1½ teaspoons sunflower seed

3 tablespoons chunky-style peanut
butter

In small bowl combine first 3 ingredients and set aside. In small nonstick saucepan heat peanut butter over low heat, stirring constantly, until softened; pour over popcorn mixture and stir until entire mixture is thoroughly coated.

Line each of four 2½-inch-diameter muffin pan cups with a paper baking cup; spoon an equal amount of mixture into each and, using the back of a spoon, press mixture firmly into cup. Remove filled paper cups from muffin pan and refrigerate until mixture is firm, about 30 minutes.

For Additional Servings Use

	4 servings	*6 servings*	*12 servings*
popcorn	2 c	3 c	6 c
raisins	¼ c	⅓ c + 2 t	¾ c
sunflower seed	1 T	1 T + 1½ t	3 T
peanut butter	⅓ c + 2 t	½ c + 1 T	1 c + 2 T
paper baking cups	8	12	24

Spicy Popcorn Snack

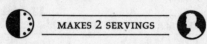

MAKES 2 SERVINGS

4 cups prepared plain popcorn
2 teaspoons each tomato paste and
   water

¼ teaspoon each salt, garlic
   powder, chili powder, and
   vegetable oil

Place popcorn in large bowl and set aside. Preheat oven to 250°F.

In metal ¼-cup measure, or other small flameproof container, combine remaining ingredients; cook over low heat until mixture bubbles. Pour oil mixture over popcorn and toss quickly to thoroughly coat. Spread coated popcorn on jelly-roll pan and bake until dry, 3 to 5 minutes.

For Additional Servings Use

	4 servings	6 servings	12 servings
popcorn	8 c	12 c	24 c
tomato paste and water	1 T + 1 t each	2 T each	¼ c each
salt, garlic powder, chili powder, and oil	½ t each	¾ t each	1½ t each

"Orange-Crème" Stuffed Prunes

 MAKES 2 SERVINGS, 3 STUFFED PRUNES EACH

6 large pitted prunes
1 cup hot water
1 tablespoon plus 1 teaspoon
  part-skim ricotta cheese

½ teaspoon granulated sugar
¼ teaspoon grated orange peel
Ground cinnamon

In small bowl combine prunes and hot water; let stand until prunes are softened, about 10 minutes.

In separate bowl combine cheese, sugar, and orange peel, mixing well. Drain prunes, discarding liquid. Stuff each prune with an equal amount of cheese mixture and sprinkle each with dash cinnamon.

For Additional Servings Use

	4 servings	*6 servings*	*12 servings*
prunes	12 large	18 large	36 large
hot water	1½ c	1½ c	2 c
cheese	2 T + 2 t	¼ c	½ c
sugar	1 t	1½ t	1 T
orange peel	½ t	¾ t	1½ t
cinnamon	dash each prune	dash each prune	dash each prune

Cucumber-Yogurt Dip

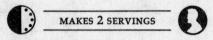

MAKES 2 SERVINGS

Use with crudités or as a salad dressing.

1 medium cucumber, pared, seeded, and coarsely grated
1 teaspoon minced scallion (green onion)
½ garlic clove, mashed with ¼ teaspoon salt
⅛ teaspoon ground cumin
Dash white pepper
½ cup plain lowfat yogurt

Squeeze and discard liquid from cucumber. In bowl combine cucumber, scallion, and seasonings; add yogurt and stir to combine. Serve at room temperature or chilled.

For Additional Servings Use

	4 servings	6 servings	12 servings
cucumbers	2 medium	3 medium	6 medium
scallions	2 t	1 T	2 T
garlic	½ clove, with ¼ t salt	1 clove, with ½ t salt	2 cloves, with 1 t salt
cumin	⅛ t	¼ t	½ t
white pepper	dash	⅛ t	¼ t
yogurt	1 c	1½ c	3 c

Spicy Blue Cheese Dip or Dressing

 MAKES 2 SERVINGS, ABOUT ¼ CUP EACH

Delicious with crudités or a tossed salad.

⅓ cup cottage cheese
1 ounce Danish blue cheese
2 tablespoons plain lowfat yogurt
1½ teaspoons each minced scallion
 (green onion) and chopped fresh
 parsley

¼ teaspoon each prepared
 horseradish and Worcestershire
 sauce*
⅛ teaspoon Dijon-style mustard
Dash white pepper

Combine cottage and blue cheeses and push through a sieve into a bowl; add remaining ingredients and stir until thoroughly combined.

* For more tang, use ½ teaspoon each horseradish and Worcestershire sauce.

For Additional Servings Use

	4 servings	*6 servings*	*12 servings*
cottage cheese	⅔ c	1 c	2 c
blue cheese	2 oz	3 oz	6 oz
yogurt	¼ c	⅓ c + 2 t	¾ c
scallions and parsley	1 T each	1 T + 1½ t each	3 T each
horseradish and Worcestershire sauce	¾ t each	1⅛ t each	2¼ t each
mustard	¼ t	¼ to ½ t	¾ t
white pepper	dash	dash	⅛ t

Zippy Parsley Dip

 MAKES 2 SERVINGS, ABOUT ⅓ CUP EACH

Serve with crudités or as a salad dressing.

½ cup parsley sprigs, rinsed and thoroughly dried with paper towels

2 tablespoons chopped onion

2 teaspoons mayonnaise

½ teaspoon mashed drained canned anchovies

½ garlic clove

Dash pepper

⅓ cup cottage cheese

In blender container combine all ingredients except cheese and process until pureed, scraping down sides of container as necessary; add cheese and process just until smooth (do not puree or mixture will be too thin). Refrigerate, covered, until chilled (chilling will thicken mixture slightly).

For Additional Servings Use

	4 servings	*6 servings*	*12 servings*
parsley sprigs	1 c	1½ c	3 c
onions	¼ c	⅓ c + 2 t	¾ c
mayonnaise	1 T + 1 t	2 T	¼ c
anchovies	1 t	1½ t	1 T
garlic	1 clove	1½ cloves	3 cloves
pepper	dash	dash to ⅛ t	⅛ to ¼ t
cottage cheese	⅔ c	1 c	2 c

Apple Tonic

 MAKES 1 SERVING, ABOUT 1 CUP

Chill 10-ounce highball glass. In blender container combine ¾ *cup chilled diet tonic water (4 calories per 8 fluid ounces)* and 1 tablespoon plus 1 tea-spoon *thawed frozen concentrated apple juice (no sugar added)*; process until frothy. Pour into chilled glass and, if desired, add ice cubes; serve immediately.

Variation: Substitute club soda for the tonic water.

For Additional Servings Use	2 servings	3 servings	4 servings
tonic water	1½ c	2¼ c	3 c
apple juice	2 T + 2 t	¼ c	⅓ c

Orange Tonic

 MAKES 1 SERVING, ABOUT 1 CUP

Chill 10-ounce highball glass. In blender container combine ¾ *cup chilled diet tonic water (4 calories per 8 fluid ounces)* and 2 tablespoons *thawed frozen concentrated orange juice (no sugar added)*; process until frothy. Pour into chilled glass and, if desired, add ice cubes; serve immediately.

For Additional Servings Use	2 servings	3 servings	4 servings
tonic water	1½ c	2¼ c	3 c
orange juice	¼ c	⅓ c + 2 t	½ c

Cran-Orange Tonic

 ———— MAKES 1 SERVING, ABOUT 1 CUP ————

⅓ cup plus 2 teaspoons chilled low-calorie cranberry juice cocktail (35 calories per 6 fluid ounces)

2 tablespoons thawed frozen concentrated orange juice (no sugar added)

½ cup diet tonic water (4 calories per 8 fluid ounces)

2 ice cubes

Chill 10-ounce highball glass. In blender container combine juices and process just until mixed; add tonic water and process at low speed until foamy, about 15 seconds. Place ice cubes in chilled glass, pour in tonic mixture, and serve immediately.

For Additional Servings Use —————

	2 servings	*3 servings*	*4 servings*
cranberry juice	¾ c	1 c + 2 T	1½ c
orange juice	¼ c	⅓ c + 2 t	½ c
tonic water	1 c	1½ c	2 c

"Mai Tai"

 MAKES 2 SERVINGS, ABOUT ⅔ CUP EACH

2 tablespoons thawed frozen concentrated orange juice (no sugar added)

1 tablespoon plus 1 teaspoon thawed frozen concentrated pineapple-orange juice (no sugar added)

1 teaspoon each freshly squeezed lemon juice and lime juice

½ teaspoon granulated sugar

⅛ teaspoon rum extract

½ cup chilled club soda

Garnish: 2 lemon or lime slices

Chill two 5½-ounce rock glasses. In blender container combine all ingredients except soda and garnish; process until frothy. Turn off motor and add soda; process at low speed just until combined. Divide mixture into chilled glasses and garnish each portion with a lemon or lime slice; serve immediately.

For Additional Servings Use

	4 servings	6 servings	8 servings
orange juice	¼ c	⅓ c + 2 t	½ c
pineapple-orange juice	2 T + 2 t	¼ c	⅓ c
lemon and lime juices	2 t each	1 T each	1 T + 1 t each
sugar	1 t	1½ t	2 t
extract	¼ t	¼ t, or to taste	½ t
club soda	1 c	1½ c	2 c

"Martini"

MAKES 2 SERVINGS

¼ cup each dry sherry and dry
  vermouth
½ teaspoon freshly squeezed lemon
  juice

4 ice cubes
2 green olives

Chill two stemmed cocktail glasses and a cocktail shaker; add sherry, vermouth, and lemon juice to shaker and shake to combine. Add ice cubes and shake until mixture is thoroughly chilled. Strain "martini" mixture into chilled glasses, add 1 olive to each, and serve immediately.

For Additional Servings Use

	4 servings	6 servings	8 servings
sherry and vermouth	½ c each	¾ c each	1 c each
lemon juice	1 t	1½ t	2 t
ice cubes	4	4	4
olives	4	6	8

Mimosa

 MAKES 2 SERVINGS, ABOUT ½ CUP EACH

½ cup each chilled dry champagne
  and club soda
1 tablespoon thawed frozen
  concentrated orange juice (no
  sugar added)

Garnish: 2 mint sprigs

Chill two trumpet champagne glasses. In blender container, combine all ingredients except garnish and process at high speed until smooth and frothy, about 30 seconds. Divide mixture into chilled glasses and garnish each with a mint sprig; serve immediately.

For Additional Servings Use

	4 servings	6 servings	8 servings
champagne and club soda	1 c each	1½ c each	2 c each
orange juice	2 T	3 T	¼ c

Champagne Cocktail

 MAKES 2 SERVINGS, ABOUT ½ CUP EACH

½ cup chilled orange juice (no sugar added)
1 tablespoon freshly squeezed lemon juice

1 teaspoon grenadine syrup
⅛ teaspoon brandy extract
2 ice cubes
½ cup chilled pink champagne

Chill two champagne cocktail glasses. In blender container combine juices, syrup, and extract and process for about 1 second; with motor running add ice cubes, 1 at a time, processing after each addition until all ice is dissolved. Turn motor off and add champagne; process at low speed until combined, about 1 second. Divide cocktail into chilled glasses and serve immediately.

For Additional Servings Use

	4 servings	*6 servings*	*8 servings*
orange juice	1 c	1½ c	2 c
lemon juice	2 T	3 T	¼ c
syrup	2 t	1 T	1 T + 1 t
extract	¼ t	¼ t, or to taste	½ t
ice cubes	3	4	5
champagne	1 c	1½ c	2 c

Crème de Champagne Cocktail

 MAKES 2 SERVINGS, ABOUT ½ CUP EACH

1 egg white
½ cup chilled dry champagne
2 tablespoons thawed frozen dairy
  whipped topping

1 teaspoon lime juice (no sugar
  added)
½ teaspoon superfine sugar
Dash brandy extract

Chill two champagne cocktail glasses. In blender container process egg white at high speed until thick and foamy; add remaining ingredients and process until combined. Divide cocktail into chilled glasses and serve immediately.

For Additional Servings Use

	4 servings	*6 servings*	*8 servings*
egg whites	2	3	4
champagne	1 c	1½ c	2 c
whipped topping	¼ c	⅓ c + 2 t	½ c
lime juice	2 t	1 T	1 T + 1 t
sugar	1 t	1½ t	2 t
brandy extract	⅛ t	⅛ to ¼ t	¼ t

Mocha-Almond Delight

 MAKES 4 SERVINGS, ABOUT ½ CUP EACH

6 ounces chocolate dietary frozen
  dessert
1 cup coffee, chilled
⅓ cup thawed frozen dairy whipped
  topping

¼ teaspoon almond extract
Ground nutmeg (optional)

Chill a serving bowl. In blender container combine frozen dessert and coffee and process until smooth; add whipped topping and extract and process until combined. Place blender container in freezer and let chill for 10 minutes;* process for about 30 seconds. Pour into chilled bowl and use a 4-ounce ladle to serve; serve in punch glasses. If desired, sprinkle each portion with dash nutmeg.

* If prepared a few hours before serving, place blender container in refrigerator; transfer to freezer about 10 minutes before serving and proceed as directed.

Golden "Eggnog"

 MAKES 1 SERVING, ABOUT ¾ CUP

½ cup skim milk
1½ ounces vanilla dietary frozen
  dessert
1 tablespoon thawed frozen dairy
  whipped topping

½ teaspoon granulated sugar
⅛ teaspoon each rum extract and
  brandy extract
Dash ground nutmeg

In blender container combine all ingredients except nutmeg and process until smooth; pour into champagne cocktail glass and sprinkle with nutmeg.

For Additional Servings Use

	2 servings	*3 servings*	*4 servings*
skim milk	1 c	1½ c	2 c
frozen dessert	3 oz	4½ oz	6 oz
whipped topping	2 T	3 T	¼ c
sugar	1 t	1½ t	2 t
extracts	¼ t each	¼ to ½ t each	½ t each
nutmeg	dash each portion	dash each portion	dash each portion

Apple-Ale Punch

 MAKES 4 SERVINGS, ABOUT 1 CUP EACH *or* 8 SERVINGS,
ABOUT ½ CUP EACH

*Place punch (or serving) bowl into a larger bowl that has been lined
with ice—punch will be chilled but not diluted.*

2½ cups chilled diet ginger ale (2
calories per 8 fluid ounces)

1⅓ cups chilled apple juice (no
sugar added)

3 tablespoons freshly squeezed
lemon juice

2 teaspoons grenadine syrup

2 lemons, thinly sliced

In punch (or serving) bowl combine all ingredients except lemon slices
and stir to mix; float lemon slices in punch and serve chilled.

For Additional Servings Use

	6 servings, about 1 cup each or 12 servings, about ½ cup each	8 servings, about 1 cup each or 16 servings, about ½ cup each
ginger ale	3¾ c	1 qt + 1 c
apple juice	2 c	2⅔ c
lemon juice	¼ c	⅓ c
syrup	1 T	1 T + 1 t

Tropical Wine Punch

 MAKES 4 SERVINGS, ABOUT 1 CUP EACH *or* 8 SERVINGS,
ABOUT ½ CUP EACH

1¾ cups chilled diet ginger ale (2
calories per 8 fluid ounces)
1⅓ cups chilled pineapple juice (no
sugar added)

1 cup chilled dry white wine
1 lemon, thinly sliced
1 lime, thinly sliced

In punch (or serving) bowl combine first 3 ingredients, stirring to mix;
float lemon and lime slices in punch and place bowl in larger bowl lined
with ice. Serve chilled.

For Additional Servings Use

	6 servings, about 1 cup each or 12 servings, about ½ cup each	8 servings, about 1 cup each or 16 servings, about ½ cup each
ginger ale	2½ c + 2 T	3½ c
pineapple juice	2 c	2⅔ c
wine	1½ c	2 c

Guests Are Coming

◆◆◆

Appetizers
Asparagus Vinaigrette
Yogurt-Caraway Quiche

Entrées
Lamb and Bean Salad with Vinaigrette Dressing
Salad Niçoise
Chicken-Mushroom Crêpes
Ham 'n' Cabbage Crêpes
Seafood Crêpes
Haddock Provençale
Rolled Stuffed Flounder Fillets
Sautéed Chili-Shrimp
Shrimp and Linguini with Basil-Caper Sauce
Chicken Diane
Crispy Cinnamon-Chicken Bake
Fiesta Chicken

Side Dishes
Potato-Cheese Pie
Creamy Pasta with Broccoli

Sauce
Orange Sauce

Desserts and Snacks
Apple Dumplings
Apple-Raisin Turnovers
Quick Shortcakes
Sticky Raisin Buns
Strawberry Chiffon
Wine-Poached Pears
Peanut Butter Brittle

The announcement that "Company is coming" need not be the cue for a flurry of frantic last-minute preparations. A little advance planning can help you entertain with flair and without fuss, even on those occasions when someone drops by "for a minute" and remains for dinner.

PLANNING THE RIGHT MENU

On those occasions when you do expect company, plan your menu with care. Choose tried-and-true recipes (never treat guests like guinea pigs), but do take into account food preferences, your budget, and the seasonal availability of foods. Since guests may be late, it's wise to choose dishes that can wait if dinner must be delayed, or that cook so quickly that you don't have to finish them until your company has arrived.

Decide on the main dish first. Then choose vegetables that will complement it by providing contrasting colors and textures. You can always count on a tossed salad as a perfect accompaniment. The taste-contrast theory applies even to the salad dressing. For example, a bland salad dressing provides an appetizing contrast to a highly spiced entrée, and a spicy dressing will add zing to a bland meal. With a light main course, such as fish, a heavy or creamy dressing is right, while a hearty entrée can be balanced by a light vinaigrette dressing.

Dessert should also complement the main dish. A hearty entrée is best followed by a light dessert (like sherbet); a light entrée, such as salad, calls for a hearty dessert (like a cobbler).

Finally, review the overall menu to make sure that flavors are harmonious and that the colors, textures, and shapes offer agreeable variety. Then prepare a written work schedule that includes both shopping and preparation times. (For suggestions about coping successfully in the supermarket, see the introduction to *Treat Yourself Like Company*.) Always begin your preparations with the dish that takes longest to cook.

BUFFETS

Space limitations often present a hurdle to entertaining. That's one reason (aside from convenience) that buffet service is growing in popularity. It's a sensible way to serve when dining space is at a premium, and it's very much in keeping with the informal "do-it-yourself" attitude of the '80s. However, buffet serving still requires attention to detail. Again—consult your budget and draw up a written menu, work schedule, and shopping list. Keep the menu simple by selecting foods that can be combined on one plate, so guests won't have to do a juggling act with too many dishes. Choose foods that look attractive, do not require a knife, and won't splatter or drip during serving and eating. And remember to make it easy for yourself by avoiding recipes that call for too many pots and pans.

Take a realistic look at how much actual table space you have, and invite only as many guests as you can serve comfortably. Then select the type of buffet service that will be most appropriate: plate, table, or tray.

With *plate service*, the plates, forks, napkins, etc., are set up on a buffet or accessory table. Guests help themselves and carry their dishes, napkins, and flatware to wherever they wish to sit.

With *table service*, the buffet is arranged on a serving table, chest, or any other suitable piece of furniture. Guests may be seated at card tables, folding snack tables, etc., which have regular place settings.

If *tray service* is your choice, each guest should be provided with a tray (about 12 x 18 inches) that serves as a miniature table from which to dine. On each one, arrange a mat (to prevent slippage), napkin, plate, flatware, and any other necessary items.

Whichever service you prefer, be sure to place the buffet table so that guests can move around it easily. If space permits, leave enough room between serving dishes so that people can put plates down as they serve themselves.

Whether you are planning an intimate sit-down dinner or catering a large buffet, investing some advance effort allows you to be cool and collected when your guests arrive, instead of frazzled from being cooped up in the kitchen for hours. Being able to enjoy the occasion as much as your guests gives you a party mood as well as a party look.

Asparagus Vinaigrette

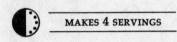 MAKES 4 SERVINGS

This can also be used as a salad.

2 tablespoons rice vinegar
1 tablespoon each lemon juice, olive oil, and water
¼ teaspoon each powdered mustard and grated lemon peel

Dash each salt and white pepper
24 asparagus spears, cooked and chilled
2 tablespoons chopped pimiento

In jar that has tight-fitting cover combine all ingredients except vegetables; cover and shake well.

In shallow dish arrange asparagus spears; add dressing and gently turn spears in dressing to coat. Sprinkle with pimiento.

For Additional Servings Use

	6 servings	8 servings
vinegar	3 T	¼ c
lemon juice, oil, and water	1 T + 1½ t each	2 T each
mustard and lemon peel	¼ t each, or to taste	½ t each
salt and pepper	dash each, or to taste	⅛ t each
asparagus	36 spears	48 spears
pimientos	3 T	¼ c

Yogurt-Caraway Quiche

MAKES 4 SERVINGS

An appetizer that can substitute as an entrée.

For 8 servings, double all ingredients and divide filling mixture into 2 pastry shells.

Crust

1 frozen Basic Pastry Shell (in quiche dish), see page 180

Filling

2 teaspoons margarine
¾ cup chopped onions
1 ounce Canadian-style bacon, chopped

4 eggs, beaten
¼ cup plain lowfat yogurt
3 ounces Swiss cheese, shredded
½ teaspoon caraway seed
Dash pepper
Dash salt (optional)

To Prepare Crust: Preheat oven to 450°F. Using tines of fork, prick pastry shell in several places; line shell with foil and bake for 5 minutes. Remove foil and bake until golden brown, 10 to 15 minutes longer (if shell has not been frozen, bake for 5 to 8 minutes); remove crust from oven and reduce oven temperature to 350°F.

To Prepare Quiche: In small nonstick skillet heat margarine until bubbly and hot; add onions and bacon and sauté until onions are translucent.

In medium bowl combine eggs and yogurt; stir in onion mixture and remaining ingredients for filling. Pour into baked crust; bake until set, about 20 minutes. Serve warm.

Lamb and Bean Salad with Vinaigrette Dressing

MAKES 4 SERVINGS

For that perfect summer luncheon.

8 ounces boned cooked lamb, cut into matchstick pieces

8 ounces drained canned small white beans

½ cup chopped scallions (green onions)

½ cup red wine vinegar

2 tablespoons water

1 tablespoon olive or vegetable oil

½ teaspoon pepper

¼ teaspoon each oregano leaves and salt

2 tablespoons chopped fresh parsley

In 2-quart bowl combine lamb, beans, and scallions. In jar that has a tight-fitting cover combine remaining ingredients except parsley; cover, shake well, and pour over bean mixture. Toss well, then cover and refrigerate for 2 hours; toss again after about 1 hour. Just before serving sprinkle with parsley.

For Additional Servings Use

	6 servings	8 servings
lamb	12 oz	1 lb
beans	12 oz	1 lb
scallions and vinegar	¾ c each	1 c each
water	3 T	¼ c
oil	1 T + 1½ t	2 T
pepper	¾ t	1 t
oregano leaves	½ t	½ t
salt	¼ t, or to taste	½ t

Salad Niçoise

MAKES 4 SERVINGS

This refreshing, colorful salad comes to us from the beautiful city of Nice, on the French Riviera. Niçoise usually refers to a dish that includes tomatoes, anchovies, tuna, garlic, and black olives, but combinations vary with each cook.

Salad

8 ounces drained canned chunk white tuna, flaked

16 chilled iceberg lettuce leaves, torn into bite-size pieces

2 chilled medium tomatoes, each cut into 8 wedges

8 pitted black olives, sliced

4 large eggs, hard-cooked and cut into 8 wedges each

Dressing

2 tablespoons olive oil

1 tablespoon plus 1 teaspoon white wine vinegar

2 teaspoons each chopped fresh basil, mashed drained canned anchovies, and lemon juice

1 teaspoon Dijon-style mustard

To Prepare Salad: In large salad bowl combine first 4 ingredients and toss; arrange egg wedges over tuna mixture and set aside.

To Prepare Dressing and Serve: In blender container combine remaining ingredients and process at low speed until smooth, scraping mixture down from sides of container as necessary. Pour dressing over salad and serve immediately.

For Additional Servings Use

	6 servings	*8 servings*
tuna	12 oz	1 lb
lettuce	24 leaves	32 leaves
tomatoes	3 medium	4 medium
olives	12 pitted	16 pitted
eggs	6 large	8 large
oil	3 T	¼ c
vinegar	2 T	2 T + 2 t
basil, anchovies, and lemon juice	1 T each	1 T + 1 t each
mustard	1½ t	2 t

Chicken-Mushroom Crêpes

MAKES 4 SERVINGS, 2 CRÊPES EACH

Thaw filling overnight in the refrigerator; let crêpes thaw at room temperature for 10 to 15 minutes before using.

4 servings frozen Chicken-Mushroom Crêpe Filling (see page 184), thawed

8 frozen crêpes (see Basic Crêpes, page 182), thawed

2 tablespoons chopped fresh parsley

Preheat oven to 400°F. Spoon half serving of thawed filling onto center of each crêpe and fold sides of crêpe over to enclose filling. Spray casserole that is large enough to hold crêpes in 1 layer with nonstick cooking spray; transfer crêpes to casserole, seam-side down, and bake until heated through and lightly browned, 15 to 20 minutes. Serve sprinkled with parsley.

For 6 or 8 servings, use 6 or 8 servings of filling and 12 or 16 crêpes.

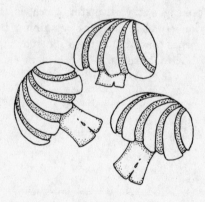

Ham 'n' Cabbage Crêpes

 MAKES 4 SERVINGS, 2 CRÊPES EACH

Let filling thaw overnight in the refrigerator; let Béchamel thaw for several hours in the refrigerator, and let crêpes thaw at room temperature for 10 to 15 minutes before using.

4 servings frozen Béchamel (see
  page 192), thawed
2 tablespoons plus 2 teaspoons dry
  sherry
Dash each salt and ground nutmeg

4 servings frozen Ham 'n' Cabbage
  Crêpe Filling (see page 183),
  thawed
8 frozen crêpes (see Basic Crêpes,
  page 182), thawed
Garnish: ground nutmeg

Preheat oven to 400°F. In 1-quart saucepan combine thawed Béchamel, sherry, salt, and nutmeg and heat (*do not boil*). In bowl combine thawed filling with ⅔ cup of the Béchamel mixture.

Spoon an equal amount of filling mixture onto center of each crêpe and fold sides of crêpe over filling to enclose. Spray 4 shallow individual casseroles with nonstick cooking spray; transfer 2 crêpes to each casserole, seam-side down. Spoon an equal amount of remaining Béchamel mixture over each portion of crêpes and bake until heated through, about 10 minutes. Serve sprinkled with nutmeg.

For Additional Servings Use

	6 servings	8 servings
Béchamel	6 servings	8 servings
sherry	¼ c	⅓ c
salt and nutmeg	dash each	⅛ t each
filling	6 servings	8 servings
crêpes	12	16
Method: combine filling with	1 c Béchamel mixture	1⅓ c Béchamel mixture

Seafood Crêpes

MAKES 4 SERVINGS, 2 CRÊPES EACH

Let filling thaw overnight in the refrigerator; let Béchamel thaw for several hours in the refrigerator and let crêpes thaw at room temperature for 10 to 15 minutes before using.

4 servings frozen Seafood Crêpe
  Filling (see page 185), thawed
4 servings frozen Béchamel (see
  page 192), thawed

8 frozen crêpes (see Basic Crêpes,
  page 182), thawed
Garnish: ground nutmeg

Preheat oven to 400°F. In bowl combine thawed filling with ½ cup thawed Béchamel, stirring to mix well. Spoon an equal amount of filling mixture onto center of each crêpe and fold sides of crêpe over filling to enclose. Spray 4 shallow individual casseroles with nonstick cooking spray; transfer 2 crêpes to each casserole, seam-side down. Spoon an equal amount of remaining Béchamel over each portion of crêpes and bake until heated through, about 10 minutes. Serve sprinkled with nutmeg.

For 6 or 8 servings, use 6 or 8 servings each of the filling and the Béchamel and 12 or 16 crêpes.

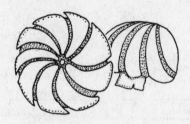

Haddock Provençale

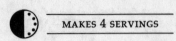 MAKES 4 SERVINGS

The term "Provençale" means "as prepared in Provence, France." Originally, this referred to dishes redolent with garlic; today, in American cuisine, Provençale generally indicates that tomatoes and garlic have been used.

For an extra-special treat, substitute scallops for the haddock.

1¼ pounds boned haddock, cut into 1-inch pieces
3 tablespoons all-purpose flour
¼ teaspoon each salt and pepper
1 tablespoon plus 1 teaspoon vegetable oil
2 teaspoons olive oil

1 garlic clove, minced
2 medium tomatoes, cut into wedges
1 tablespoon plus 1 teaspoon dry vermouth
2 teaspoons chopped fresh basil or ½ teaspoon dried

Rinse fish in cold water; pat dry with paper towels. On sheet of wax paper, or on paper plate, combine flour, salt, and pepper; dredge fish in flour mixture, coating all sides and using up all of mixture.

In 12-inch nonstick skillet combine oils and heat over medium-high heat; add fish and garlic and sauté until lightly browned. Reduce heat, add remaining ingredients, and cook until thoroughly heated.

For Additional Servings Use

	6 servings	8 servings
haddock	1 lb 14 oz	2½ lb
flour	¼ c + 1½ t	⅓ c + 2 t
salt and pepper	¼ t each	½ t each
vegetable oil	2 T	2 T + 2 t
olive oil	1 T	1 T + 1 t
garlic	2 cloves	3 cloves
tomatoes	3 medium	4 medium
vermouth	2 T	2 T + 2 t
basil	1 T fresh or ¾ t dried	1 T + 1 t fresh or 1 t dried
skillet	12-inch	wok

Rolled Stuffed Flounder Fillets

MAKES 4 SERVINGS

2 teaspoons margarine
½ cup finely diced onion
1 garlic clove, minced
¼ cup each finely diced celery and carrot
¼ cup minced red bell pepper
1 cup thinly sliced mushrooms
Dash each salt, white pepper, and ground thyme

2 tablespoons chopped fresh parsley, divided
4 flounder fillets, 5 ounces each
1 tablespoon plus 1 teaspoon each grated Parmesan cheese and mayonnaise
½ teaspoon Dijon-style mustard
1 tablespoon lemon juice
Garnish: lemon slices and parsley

In small nonstick skillet heat margarine until bubbly and hot; add onion and garlic and sauté briefly. Add celery, carrot, and red pepper; cover and cook over medium-low heat, stirring occasionally, until vegetables are tender, about 5 minutes. Add mushrooms and seasonings, stirring to combine. Increase heat to medium-high and cook, uncovered, until all moisture has evaporated; stir in half of parsley. Spoon an equal amount of mixture onto center of each fillet and roll fish to enclose; place stuffed fish rolls in a layer, seam-side down, in shallow casserole.

Preheat oven to 400°F. In small bowl combine cheese, mayonnaise, and mustard; spread mixture evenly over fillets and sprinkle with lemon juice. Bake until fish is lightly browned and flakes easily when tested with a fork, about 20 minutes; sprinkle with remaining parsley. Serve garnished.

For Additional Servings Use

	6 servings	8 servings
margarine	1 T	1 T + 1 t
onions	¾ c	1 c
garlic	1½ cloves	2 cloves
celery, carrots, and red peppers	⅓ c + 2 t each	½ c each
mushrooms	1½ c	2 c
salt, white pepper, and thyme	dash each, or to taste	⅛ t each
parsley	3 T	¼ c
fillets	6 (5 oz each)	8 (5 oz each)
cheese and mayonnaise	2 T each	2 T + 2 t each
mustard	¾ t	1 t
lemon juice	1 T	2 T
skillet	9- or 10-inch	10-inch

Sautéed Chili-Shrimp

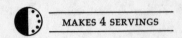

MAKES 4 SERVINGS

2 tablespoons olive oil
4 cups broccoli florets*
1 cup each diced onions and red or
  green bell peppers
1¼ pounds shelled and deveined
  shrimp

1 garlic clove, minced, or ⅛
  teaspoon garlic powder
¼ cup chili sauce
¼ teaspoon each salt and thyme
  leaves
Garnish: lemon wedges

1. In wok or 4-quart saucepan heat oil over medium-high heat; add broccoli florets and sauté until tender-crisp, about 3 minutes (broccoli will turn bright green).

2. Add onions and peppers to broccoli and sauté until onions are translucent, about 2 minutes.

3. Push vegetables to side of pan and add shrimp and garlic; sauté, stirring occasionally, until shrimp begin to turn pink, 2 to 3 minutes.

4. Add remaining ingredients except garnish and stir all ingredients in pan together to combine; cook until shrimp turn bright pink and mixture is hot. Serve garnished with lemon wedges.

* Two 10-ounce packages of frozen chopped broccoli may be substituted. Thaw broccoli and add to hot oil with onions and peppers; proceed with Steps 2, 3, and 4 as directed.

For Additional Servings Use

	6 servings	8 servings
oil	3 T	¼ c
broccoli	6 c fresh or three 10-oz pkg frozen	8 c fresh or four 10-oz pkg frozen
onions and peppers	1½ c each	2 c each
shrimp	1 lb 14 oz	2½ lb
garlic	2 cloves or ¼ t powder	2 cloves or ¼ t powder
chili sauce	⅓ c + 2 t	½ c
salt and thyme leaves	½ t each	½ t each
pan	wok or 4-qt saucepan	wok

Shrimp and Linguini with Basil-Caper Sauce

MAKES 4 SERVINGS

---

2 tablespoons olive oil, divided
½ cup chopped onion, divided
4 garlic cloves, minced, divided
2 teaspoons mashed drained canned anchovies
1¼ pounds shelled and deveined shrimp
3½ cups canned plum tomatoes, chopped

1½ cups thinly sliced mushrooms
¼ cup drained capers, rinsed
2 tablespoons chopped fresh basil or 2 teaspoons dried
½ teaspoon crushed red pepper
3 cups cooked linguini (flat spaghetti), hot
Garnish: chopped and whole fresh basil

In 12-inch nonstick skillet heat half of the oil; add half each of the onion and garlic and sauté briefly, about 2 minutes. Add anchovies and stir to combine; add shrimp and cook over high heat, stirring constantly, just until shrimp turn pink. Immediately transfer mixture to bowl; set aside.

In same skillet heat remaining oil; add remaining onion and garlic and sauté briefly, about 2 minutes. Add tomatoes and bring to a boil; add mushrooms, capers, basil, and pepper and cook over medium heat, stirring occasionally, for 15 to 20 minutes. Add shrimp mixture and cook just until heated through; serve over hot linguini and garnish with basil.

For Additional Servings Use

	6 servings	8 servings
oil	3 T	¼ c
onions	¾ c	1 c
garlic	6 cloves	8 cloves
anchovies	1 T	1 T + 1 t
shrimp	1 lb 14 oz	2½ lb
tomatoes	5¼ c	7 c
mushrooms	2¼ c	3 c
capers	⅓ c + 2 t	½ c
basil	3 T fresh or 1 T dried	¼ c fresh or 1 T + 1 t dried
pepper	¾ t	1 t
linguini	4½ c	6 c
pan	3-qt saucepan	4-qt saucepan

Chicken Diane

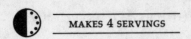

MAKES 4 SERVINGS

Serve with hot rice or noodles and a tossed green salad.

2 tablespoons plus 2 teaspoons
  margarine, divided
1¼ pounds skinned and boned
  chicken breasts
½ cup minced onion

¼ cup chopped fresh parsley
2 tablespoons plus 2 teaspoons each
  steak sauce and dry sherry
2 teaspoons each Worcestershire
  sauce and Dijon-style mustard

In 12-inch nonstick skillet heat half of the margarine over medium heat until bubbly and hot; add chicken and cook, turning frequently, until lightly browned on all sides and, when pierced with a fork, juices run clear. Remove chicken to a plate and keep warm.

In same skillet heat remaining margarine until bubbly and hot; add onion and sauté until translucent, 1 to 1½ minutes. Reduce heat and add remaining ingredients except chicken; cook, stirring occasionally, until heated through. Return chicken to skillet and turn to coat with sauce.

For Additional Servings Use

	6 servings	8 servings
margarine	¼ c	⅓ c
chicken	1 lb 14 oz	2½ lb
onions	¾ c	1 c
parsley	⅓ c	½ c
steak sauce and sherry	¼ c each	⅓ c each
Worcestershire sauce and Dijon-style mustard	1 T each	1 T + 1 t each
skillet	12-inch	wok

Crispy Cinnamon-Chicken Bake

| MAKES 4 SERVINGS | |

1½ ounces cornflake crumbs (½ cup plus 2 tablespoons)
1 tablespoon plus 1 teaspoon granulated brown sugar
2 teaspoons each ground cinnamon and grated orange peel

½ teaspoon salt
½ cup buttermilk (made from skim milk)
3 pounds chicken parts, skinned*
1 tablespoon plus 1 teaspoon vegetable oil

Preheat oven to 400°F. In blender container combine cornflake crumbs, sugar, cinnamon, orange peel, and salt and process until well blended; pour mixture onto sheet of wax paper or paper plate.

Pour buttermilk into bowl; dip chicken parts into buttermilk, then coat with crumb mixture, pressing crumbs into chicken and being sure to use all of buttermilk and crumb mixture. Using oil, grease nonstick baking pan that is large enough to hold chicken in 1 layer; add coated chicken parts and bake until tender, about 30 minutes.

* 3 pounds chicken parts will yield about 1 pound cooked meat.

For Additional Servings Use

	6 servings	8 servings
cornflake crumbs	2¼ oz (1 c less 1 T)	3 oz (1¼ c)
sugar	2 T	2 T + 2 t
cinnamon and orange peel	1 T each	1 T + 1 t each
salt	¾ t	1 t
buttermilk	¾ c	1 c
chicken	4½ lb	6 lb
oil	2 T	2 T + 2 t

Fiesta Chicken

MAKES 4 SERVINGS

An appetizing and attractive one-dish meal in about 45 minutes.

1 tablespoon plus 1 teaspoon margarine

1 cup each diced onions and green bell peppers

1¼ pounds skinned and boned chicken breasts, cut into cubes

2 cups canned crushed tomatoes

4 ounces uncooked converted rice

8 large pimiento-stuffed green olives, thinly sliced

1 teaspoon salt

¼ teaspoon garlic powder

¼ teaspoon crushed saffron (optional)

⅛ teaspoon pepper

Preheat oven to 400°F. In 4-quart flameproof casserole heat margarine over medium heat until bubbly and hot; add onions and green peppers and sauté until vegetables are tender, 2 to 3 minutes.

Remove casserole from heat and add remaining ingredients; stir until thoroughly combined. Cover casserole and bake until rice has absorbed liquid, 30 to 35 minutes.

For Additional Servings Use

	6 servings	8 servings
margarine	2 T	2 T + 2 t
onions and green peppers	1½ c each	2 c each
chicken	1 lb 14 oz	2½ lb
tomatoes	3 c	4 c
rice	6 oz	8 oz
olives	12 large	16 large
salt	1½ t	2 t
garlic powder	½ t	½ t
saffron (optional)	¼ t	½ t
pepper	⅛ t, or to taste	¼ t

Tutti-"Fruiti"
Milk Shake

Strawberry Fizz

Chicken Tacos

Curried Papaya
Chicken

Grapes, Seeds,
'n' Sprouts

Cauliflower Polonaise

Monte Cristo Sandwich

Tabouli

Quick Liver
Tomato 'n' Onion Sauté

Oriental Chicken Livers
en Brochette

Kidney Bean 'n' Ham
Soup with
Herbed Romano Sticks

Creamy Cauliflower
Soup

Vanilla Fudge Swirl

Orange Spanish
"Cream"

Turkey Pot Pie

Orange-Ginger-
Glazed Pork Chops

Far East Broccoli

Ham 'n' Cabbage Crêpes
(top)

Seafood Crêpes

Buttermilk-Herb
Dressing

Tuna-Macaroni Salad

"Martini" / Mimosa

Cheese-Filled Pears

Potato-Cheese Pie

MAKES 4 SERVINGS, 1 PIE EACH

Perfect accompanied by a large tossed salad.

4 large eggs

12 ounces pared potatoes, grated

1⅓ cups cottage cheese

¼ cup diced green bell pepper

2 tablespoons diced onion

2 teaspoons salt

⅛ teaspoon pepper

Preheat oven to 375°F. In large bowl beat eggs well; add remaining ingredients and stir to combine.

Spray four 5¼ x 1½-inch foil tart pans with nonstick cooking spray; divide potato mixture into pans and bake until top of each pie is golden brown and mixture is set, about 45 minutes. To serve, invert pies onto serving platter.

For Additional Servings Use

	6 servings	*8 servings*
eggs	6 large	8 large
potatoes	1 lb 2 oz	1½ lb
cheese	2 c	2⅔ c
green peppers	⅓ c + 2 t	½ c
onions	3 T	¼ c
salt	1 T	1 T + 1 t
pepper	⅛ t, or to taste	¼ t

Creamy Pasta with Broccoli

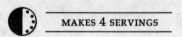

MAKES 4 SERVINGS

4½ ounces uncooked fettuccine
1 tablespoon plus 1 teaspoon olive
  oil
1 garlic clove, minced
1⅓ cups part-skim ricotta cheese
2 cups cooked broccoli florets,*
  reserve ½ cup cooking liquid

½ teaspoon salt
¼ teaspoon freshly ground pepper
1 tablespoon plus 1 teaspoon grated
  Parmesan cheese

In 4-quart saucepan cook fettuccine in boiling water to cover, according to package directions.

While pasta is cooking, in 9- or 10-inch skillet heat oil; add garlic and sauté until golden. Add ricotta cheese and cook, stirring occasionally, until cheese begins to melt and bubbles appear; add reserved cooking liquid, salt, and pepper and stir to combine.

Drain fettuccine well and return to saucepan; add cheese mixture and broccoli and toss lightly to combine. Serve each portion sprinkled with 1 teaspoon Parmesan cheese.

* Chopped fresh or frozen broccoli may be substituted.

For Additional Servings Use

	6 servings	8 servings
fettuccine	6¾ oz	9 oz
oil	2 T	2 T + 2 t
garlic	2 cloves	2 cloves
ricotta cheese	2 c	2⅔ c
broccoli	3 c with ¾ c liquid	4 c with 1 c liquid
salt	1 t	1 t
pepper	¼ t, or to taste	½ t
Parmesan cheese	2 T	2 T + 2 t
skillet	10- or 12-inch	12-inch

Orange Sauce

 MAKES 4 SERVINGS, ABOUT ¼ CUP EACH

Perfect over broiled chicken.

1 tablespoon plus 1 teaspoon
  margarine
2 teaspoons all-purpose flour
1 cup orange juice (no sugar added)

¼ cup lemon juice
1 teaspoon aromatic bitters, or to
  taste

In small saucepan heat margarine over medium-low heat until bubbly and hot; add flour and cook, stirring constantly, until thoroughly combined, about 1 minute. Gradually stir in orange juice and cook, stirring constantly, until mixture thickens, 2 to 3 minutes; stir in remaining ingredients and cook until thoroughly heated.

For Additional Servings Use

	6 servings	*8 servings*
margarine	2 T	2 T + 2 t
flour	1 T	1 T + 1 t
orange juice	1½ c	2 c
lemon juice	⅓ c	½ c
bitters	1 t, or to taste	1 to 1½ t, or to taste

Apple Dumplings

MAKES 5 SERVINGS, 1 DUMPLING EACH

---

1 package (5 ounces) refrigerated buttermilk flaky biscuits (5 biscuits)

1 tablespoon plus 2 teaspoons margarine, softened

2½ teaspoons superfine sugar

2 teaspoons ground cinnamon

5 small baking apples, cored and pared

¼ cup plus 1 tablespoon thawed frozen dairy whipped topping

Separate biscuits and roll each between 2 sheets of wax paper into 4-inch circle; set aside.

Preheat oven to 375°F. In small bowl cream together margarine, sugar, and cinnamon to a smooth paste. Set 1 apple on each biscuit circle and spoon an equal amount of margarine mixture onto top of each apple; gently fold 4 corners of each biscuit over each apple and pinch dough to seal. Carefully set each dumpling into a 6-ounce custard cup; bake until biscuits are golden brown and apples are soft, about 30 minutes. To serve, top each dumpling with 1 tablespoon whipped topping.

For Additional Servings Use

	8 servings	*10 servings*
biscuits	8 (1 oz each)	one 10-oz pkg (10 biscuits)
margarine	2 T + 2 t	3 T + 1 t
sugar	1 T + 1 t	1 T + 2 t
cinnamon	1 T + ¼ t	1 T + 1 t
apples	8 small	10 small
topping	½ c	½ c + 2 T

Apple-Raisin Turnovers

MAKES 4 SERVINGS, 1 TURNOVER EACH

2 teaspoons margarine
2 small apples, cored, pared, and
thinly sliced
Dash apple pie spice
¼ cup raisins

4 ready-to-bake refrigerated
buttermilk flaky biscuits (1
ounce each)
1 teaspoon confectioners' sugar

1. In small nonstick skillet heat margarine over medium-high heat until bubbly and hot; add apples and spice and cook, stirring constantly, until apple slices are coated with margarine. Reduce heat to low and stir in raisins; cover and let simmer until apple slices are soft, 3 to 5 minutes. Remove from heat.

2. Roll each biscuit between 2 sheets of wax paper, forming 4 circles, each about 4 inches in diameter; spoon an equal amount of fruit mixture onto half of each circle. Moisten edges of dough with water, then fold dough over to enclose filling; using finger or tines of a fork, press edges together to seal.

3. Preheat oven to 400°F. Spray baking sheet with nonstick cooking spray; arrange turnovers on sheet, cover lightly, and refrigerate for about 5 minutes.

4. Transfer baking sheet to middle of center oven rack and bake until turnovers are lightly browned, about 10 minutes; transfer turnovers to serving plate and sprinkle each with ¼ teaspoon sugar.

For Additional Servings Use

	6 servings	8 servings	12 servings
margarine	1 T	1 T + 1 t	2 T
apples	3 small	4 small	6 small
apple pie spice	⅛ t	⅛ t	¼ t
raisins	⅓ c + 2 t	½ c	¾ c
biscuits	6 (1 oz each)	8 (1 oz each)	12 (1 oz each)
sugar	1½ t	2 t	1 T
skillet	7- or 8-inch	9- or 10-inch	10-inch

Quick Shortcakes

 MAKES 5 SERVINGS, 1 SHORTCAKE EACH

Preheat oven to 400°F. Using *1 package (5 ounces) refrigerated buttermilk flaky biscuits (5 biscuits)*, separate biscuits. Melt *2½ teaspoons unsalted margarine;* dip biscuits into margarine, being sure to use all of margarine, then sprinkle each with *½ teaspoon granulated sugar.* Transfer biscuits to baking sheet and bake until golden brown, about 10 minutes. Cool on wire rack.

Serving Suggestion—Split each shortcake in half horizontally. Spoon 1 tablespoon thawed frozen dairy whipped topping onto each bottom half; replace top halves and spoon ¼ cup berries (blueberries or raspberries) or ½ cup strawberries over each shortcake.

For Additional Servings Use

	8 servings	10 servings
biscuits	8 (1 oz each)	one 10-oz pkg (10 biscuits)
margarine	1 T + 1 t	1 T + 2 t
sugar	½ t each biscuit	½ t each biscuit

Sticky Raisin Buns

 MAKES 10 SERVINGS, 1 BUN EACH

These will keep in the refrigerator for several days; just warm in the oven to refresh.

1 tablespoon plus 2 teaspoons
  margarine
2 tablespoons thawed frozen
  concentrated orange juice (no
  sugar added)
1 tablespoon plus 2 teaspoons
  granulated brown sugar

½ teaspoon ground cinnamon
½ cup raisins
1 package (10 ounces) refrigerated
  buttermilk flaky biscuits (10
  biscuits)

Preheat oven to 350°F. In 8- or 9-inch round baking pan melt margarine; add juice, sugar, and cinnamon and stir to combine. Sprinkle raisins evenly over juice mixture. Separate biscuits and arrange in pan, over raisins; bake until biscuits are browned, 20 to 25 minutes. Remove pan from oven and top with 10-inch heatproof plate; invert biscuits onto plate and serve hot.

Strawberry Chiffon

MAKES 8 SERVINGS

1 envelope (four ½-cup servings)
  strawberry-flavored gelatin
1½ cups boiling water
4 cups strawberries
12 ounces vanilla dietary frozen
  dessert, softened slightly

1 egg white (at room temperature)
½ cup thawed frozen dairy whipped
  topping

In heatproof 2-quart bowl combine gelatin and water, stirring until gelatin is completely dissolved; cover and refrigerate until syrupy, 15 to 20 minutes.

Set aside 8 strawberries for garnish; in blender container puree remaining berries. Stir pureed berries and frozen dessert into syrupy gelatin.

In mixing bowl, using electric mixer, beat egg white until stiff peaks form; using wire whisk, beat white into berry mixture. Divide chiffon into 8 parfait glasses; cover lightly and refrigerate until set, about 4 hours.

To serve, top each parfait with 1 tablespoon whipped topping and garnish with a reserved berry.

Wine-Poached Pears

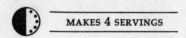 MAKES 4 SERVINGS

1¾ cups dry red wine
2 teaspoons granulated sugar
2-inch cinnamon stick

4 firm but ripe small pears, pared
(stems left on)

In saucepan large enough to hold pears in 1 layer combine wine, sugar, and cinnamon stick; bring to a boil over medium-high heat. Add pears, cover pan, and cook until pears are tender, 5 to 8 minutes, turning pears once during cooking.

Using slotted spoon, transfer each pear to a dessert dish; cook wine mixture, uncovered, until liquid is reduced by half. Remove and discard cinnamon stick and pour an equal amount of remaining liquid over each pear; serve at room temperature.

For Additional Servings Use

	6 servings	8 servings
wine	2½ c + 2 T	3½ c
sugar	1 T	1 T + 1 t
cinnamon sticks	one 2-inch	two 2-inch
pears	6 small	8 small

Peanut Butter Brittle

MAKES 4 SERVINGS

1 tablespoon each granulated sugar
and light corn syrup
1½ teaspoons water

2 tablespoons chunky-style peanut
butter
½ teaspoon baking soda, sifted

In metal measuring cup, or other small flameproof container, combine sugar, corn syrup, and water; cook over medium-low heat, stirring constantly, until mixture comes to a boil and sugar is dissolved. Reduce heat to low and let simmer, stirring occasionally, until mixture is reduced slightly and thickened, about 15 minutes (watch very carefully so that mixture does not burn). Add peanut butter and cook, stirring constantly, until peanut butter is melted and thoroughly combined; sprinkle with baking soda and stir until soda is completely absorbed (mixture will puff slightly).

Pour peanut butter mixture onto smooth cutting board; let stand until slightly cooled. Using rolling pin, roll mixture into a 6-inch square; cut into 4 equal portions and transfer to wire rack. Let stand until completely hardened. Wrap in wax paper to store. (Peanut Butter Brittle can be frozen if desired.) At serving time each piece may then be broken into smaller pieces.

For Additional Servings Use

	6 servings	*8 servings*	*12 servings*
sugar and syrup	1 T + 1½ t each	2 T each	3 T each
water	2¼ t	1 T	1 T + 1½ t
peanut butter	3 T	¼ c	⅓ c + 2 t
baking soda	¾ t	1 t	1½ t
Method: roll mixture into a	9 x 6-inch rectangle	12 x 6-inch rectangle	12 x 9-inch rectangle

Treat Yourself Like Company

Soup
Cream of Asparagus Soup

Sandwich
Monte Cristo Sandwich

Entrées
Oriental Salad
"Waldorf" Chicken Salad
Huevos Rancheros (South-of-the-Border Ranch-Style Eggs)
Spiced Vegetable-Egg Bake
"Lemon-Butter"-Baked Sole
Scampi Supreme
Chicken Cordon Bleu
Chicken with Hot Peanut Sauce
Curried Eggplant and Lamb Stew
Lamb Patty in Mustard Gravy
Curried Livers in Wine Sauce
Mexican Liver

Side Dish
Asparagus with Sesame "Butter"

Desserts
Glazed Coconut-Fruit Kabobs
Pineapple-Yogurt Broil

Sauces and Syrup
Apple Syrup
Pineapple Topping
Blueberry Topping
Chocolate Topping

You take extra steps to make a meal special when guests are coming—and you undoubtedly enjoy that special attention as much as they do. So why not treat *yourself* like company when guests aren't coming?

Cooking for one offers its own unique opportunities to be innovative, but it also has built-in challenges. It's tempting to skip meals when you're not responsible for the nourishment of others, and this can be disastrous to your weight-control efforts. Preparing the proper amount for one may seem like a hurdle because so many items are packaged in portions greater than one serving, or must be purchased in larger quantities in order to get the best value for your dollar. But it isn't necessary always to limit yourself to preparing single meals. If you purchase more than can be used for one meal, prepare extra portions to refrigerate or freeze for days when you don't feel like cooking, or to use for impromptu entertaining.

In addition to cooking for one, you probably do all the shopping and cleaning up, too, and often, this must be worked into a hectic schedule. But remembering to give yourself a little special treatment, even if it means extra effort, can make it all a labor of love and not just a labor.

Here are some tips that will help make cooking for one easier and more economical.

• Use resealable plastic bags or storage containers to store leftovers. Containers come in different sizes for storing small or large quantities; the bags have the advantage of being airtight. Resealable bags designed specifically for freezing are also available.

• Select foods that are easy to prepare for one portion, such as ground beef or veal. Since they can be preportioned, wrapped, and frozen, you can buy the larger economy-priced packages and still only prepare one portion at a time. Boneless chicken breasts, chops, or small steaks also make easy servings for one. Freeze in single-serving portions.

• Take advantage of the broiler and skillet. They are excellent for preparing fast meals in small quantities.

• Learn about proper storage of fresh vegetables so that you can enjoy them with every meal and still take advantage of in-season savings. Most fresh vegetables need only be blanched, then portioned and frozen in moisture- and vapor-resistant materials.

131

• Menu-planning is essential in order to make cooking for one easy, economical, and interesting. Remember that it's just as important to plan ahead for yourself as it is for company.

AVOID SHOPPING HAZARDS

Shopping for one need not be a problem if you organize. A shopping list helps avoid the pitfalls of haphazard over-buying or impulse buying. To complete your list, draw up a menu plan for the week. Plan it around the foods you like, the items you have on hand, and what's on "special" (check the newspaper and supermarket fliers). Organize your shopping list by categories, the way the store you shop in is arranged, so that you can avoid taking extra steps to get something you missed in Aisle #2 when you're already in Aisle #5. A weekly list also saves you the hassle of last-minute dashes to the store.

If you don't like to decide beforehand what you want, but prefer to make that decision in the supermarket, you can make this preference work for you. Prepare a partial list, organized into categories, but decide on quanties beforehand (e.g., "vegetables—five portions; meat—three portions; poultry—two portions"). You can then decide what to purchase when you see what's available, and still shop sensibly. Just be sure to take your list with you; don't trust to memory.

Learn to read labels. Private brands (items sold under the supermarket's own brand name or names) may be similar or identical in quality to those that are nationally advertised. However, since the supermarket brands generally aren't heavily publicized, they are usually less expensive. The savings can be substantial, making it more feasible to buy small sizes if you prefer. Be aware that supermarkets may have more than one private brand, and each has its own standard of quality. Frequently, the highest quality private brand is similar, if not identical, to the national one. Ask the supermarket manager which private brand is the store's "premium."

The supermarket is a great convenience, since most items can be purchased under one roof, but it can also be a trap. You may spend more money than necessary and purchase foods you don't really need. Enter the supermarket armed with the knowledge necessary for avoiding these traps, and you'll exit with only what you need—including the satisfaction of being a wise shopper.

P.S. Don't forget, having a "company attitude" toward yourself also applies to eating with any family members. Treating *them* like VIPs will also increase your enjoyment of the meal.

Cream of Asparagus Soup

 MAKES 1 SERVING, ABOUT 1 CUP

6 asparagus spears (fresh or frozen),
   cut into pieces
¾ cup water
1 packet instant chicken broth and
   seasoning mix
¼ bay leaf
Dash each pepper and ground
   thyme

2 teaspoons reduced-calorie
   margarine
2¼ teaspoons all-purpose flour
½ cup evaporated skimmed milk (at
   room temperature)

If using fresh asparagus, trim away woody ends. In small saucepan combine asparagus, water, broth mix, and seasonings; bring to a boil. Reduce heat to low and let simmer until asparagus are tender, 5 to 8 minutes; remove from heat and let cool.

Remove and discard bay leaf; transfer asparagus and cooking liquid to work bowl of food processor or blender container and process until pureed; set aside.

In same saucepan (which has been wiped clean) heat margarine over low heat until bubbly and hot; add flour and stir to combine. Using wire whisk, gradually stir in milk and cook, stirring constantly, until mixture is smooth and thickened; stir in asparagus puree and heat (*do not boil*).

For Additional Servings Use

	2 servings	3 servings	4 servings
asparagus	12 spears	18 spears	24 spears
water	1½ c	2¼ c	3 c
broth mix	2 pkt	3 pkt	4 pkt
bay leaves	½	½	1
pepper and thyme	dash each	dash each	⅛ t each
margarine	1 T + 1 t	2 T	2 T + 2 t
flour	1 T + 1½ t	2 T + ¾ t	3 T
milk	1 c	1½ c	2 c

Monte Cristo Sandwich

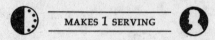

MAKES 1 SERVING

May be garnished with parsley sprigs and dill pickle slices.

1 large egg, beaten
¼ cup skim milk
1 teaspoon grated Parmesan cheese
Dash freshly ground pepper

1 ounce each sliced boiled ham and
    sliced Swiss cheese
2 slices white bread
1 teaspoon margarine

In shallow bowl combine egg, milk, Parmesan cheese, and pepper and set aside. Place ham, then Swiss cheese on 1 slice of bread; top with remaining slice of bread. Dip sandwich into egg mixture, turning several times until as much liquid as possible has been absorbed.

In small nonstick skillet heat margarine until bubbly and hot; add sandwich, pouring any remaining egg mixture over bread. Cook over low heat, turning once, until brown and crisp on both sides; serve immediately.

For Additional Servings Use

	2 servings	3 servings	4 servings
eggs	2 large	3 large	4 large
milk	½ c	¾ c	1 c
Parmesan cheese	2 t	1 T	1 T + 1 t
pepper	⅛ t	⅛ t	¼ t
ham and Swiss cheese	2 oz each	3 oz each	4 oz each
bread	4 slices	6 slices	8 slices
margarine	2 t	1 T	1 T + 1 t
skillet	9-inch	12-inch	12-inch

Oriental Salad

MAKES 1 SERVING

---

2 ounces julienne-cut roast beef (thin strips)*
½ cup cooked long-grain rice
1 egg, scrambled without fat
¼ cup diagonally sliced celery
1 tablespoon chopped scallion (green onion)
1 tablespoon teriyaki sauce

1½ teaspoons each dry sherry and peanut or vegetable oil
⅛ teaspoon each garlic powder and honey
Dash each powdered mustard and ground ginger
4 iceberg, romaine, or loose-leafed lettuce leaves

In salad bowl combine first 5 ingredients and toss; cover and refrigerate for at least 30 minutes. In small bowl combine remaining ingredients except lettuce; cover and refrigerate until ready to serve.

Stir dressing and pour over rice mixture; toss to coat all ingredients. Serve on bed of lettuce leaves.

* Julienne-cut cooked pork or cooked and skinned chicken may be substituted for the roast beef.

For Additional Servings Use

	2 servings	3 servings	4 servings
beef	4 oz	6 oz	8 oz
rice	1 c	1½ c	2 c
eggs	2	3	4
celery	½ c	¾ c	1 c
scallions and teriyaki sauce	2 T each	3 T each	¼ c each
sherry and oil	1 T each	1 T + 1½ t each	2 T each
garlic powder	¼ t	¼ t	½ t
honey	¼ t	¼ t + ⅛ t	½ t
mustard and ginger	dash each	dash each	⅛ t each
lettuce	8 leaves	12 leaves	16 leaves

"Waldorf" Chicken Salad

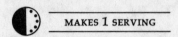 MAKES 1 SERVING

An interesting and tasty way to use up leftover chicken.

4 ounces chilled skinned and boned cooked chicken, cut into cubes
¼ cup diced celery
½ small McIntosh or Red Delicious apple, cored and cut into cubes
6 large seedless green grapes, cut lengthwise into halves

2 tablespoons plain lowfat yogurt
1½ teaspoons mayonnaise
½ packet (about ½ teaspoon) instant chicken broth and seasoning mix
1 teaspoon sunflower seed

In salad bowl combine first 4 ingredients. In small bowl combine yogurt, mayonnaise, and broth mix, mixing well; pour over salad and toss to coat thoroughly. Sprinkle salad with sunflower seed.

For Additional Servings Use

	2 servings	3 servings	4 servings
chicken	8 oz	12 oz	1 lb
celery	½ c	¾ c	1 c
apples	1 small	1½ small	2 small
grapes	12 large	18 large	24 large
yogurt	¼ c	⅓ c + 2 t	½ c
mayonnaise	1 T	1 T + 1½ t	2 T
broth mix	1 pkt	1½ pkt	2 pkt
sunflower seed	2 t	1 T	1 T + 1 t

Huevos Rancheros
(South-of-the-Border Ranch-Style Eggs)

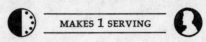 MAKES 1 SERVING

1 egg
1 serving Salsa (see page 221)
1 corn tortilla (6-inch diameter),
  toasted

1 ounce sharp Cheddar cheese,
  shredded

Spray small nonstick skillet with nonstick cooking spray and heat (to test, sprinkle drop of water into skillet; if water sizzles, pan is hot enough). Break egg into a cup, being careful not to break yolk, then slide carefully into skillet; cook over low heat for 3 to 4 minutes or until done to taste. If Salsa has been refrigerated, heat in small saucepan while egg is cooking.

Place tortilla on flameproof plate and slide cooked egg onto tortilla; spoon Salsa over white portion of egg and sprinkle cheese over yolk. Broil until cheese is melted.

Variation—Omit Cheddar cheese. Proceed as directed but sprinkle egg yolk with 1 teaspoon grated Parmesan cheese.

For Additional Servings Use

	2 servings	3 servings	4 servings
eggs	2	3	4
Salsa	2 servings	3 servings	4 servings
tortillas	2	3	4
Cheddar cheese	2 oz	3 oz	4 oz
Variation:			
Parmesan cheese	2 t	1 T	1 T + 1 t

Spiced Vegetable-Egg Bake

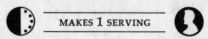

MAKES 1 SERVING

1 teaspoon margarine
½ garlic clove, crushed
½ cup well-drained cooked chopped
  broccoli (fresh or frozen)
1 teaspoon all-purpose flour
½ cup skim milk (at room
  temperature)

1 ounce Gruyère or Swiss cheese,
  shredded
⅛ teaspoon salt
Dash each pepper and ground
  nutmeg
1 large egg

Preheat oven to 350°F. In small nonstick skillet heat margarine until bubbly and hot; add garlic and sauté for 1 minute. Remove and discard garlic clove. Add broccoli to skillet and cook over medium heat, stirring constantly, for 1 to 2 minutes; sprinkle with flour and stir to combine. Stirring constantly, gradually add milk and continue cooking until mixture thickens. Remove skillet from heat; add cheese, salt, pepper, and nutmeg and stir until thoroughly combined.

Spray 10-ounce custard cup with nonstick cooking spray and spoon broccoli mixture into cup; make a well or depression in center of mixture. Break egg into small bowl, then carefully slide into well; bake 10 to 12 minutes or until egg is done to taste.

For Additional Servings Use

	2 servings	*3 servings*	*4 servings*
margarine	2 t	1 T	1 T + 1 t
garlic	1 clove	1½ cloves	2 cloves
broccoli	1 c	1½ c	2 c
flour	2 t	1 T	1 T + 1 t
milk	1 c	1½ c	2 c
cheese	2 oz	3 oz	4 oz
salt	¼ t	¼ t	½ t
pepper and nutmeg	⅛ t each	⅛ t each	¼ t each
eggs	2 large	3 large	4 large

"Lemon-Butter"-Baked Sole

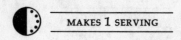 MAKES 1 SERVING

Fish can be dipped and dredged several hours before cooking; place pre-pared fillet on baking sheet, cover with plastic wrap, and refrigerate until ready to bake.

1 sole fillet, 5 ounces

1½ teaspoons each margarine, melted, and freshly squeezed lemon juice

1 tablespoon plus 1½ teaspoons all-purpose flour

1½ teaspoons chopped fresh parsley

⅛ teaspoon salt

Dash each pepper and paprika

Garnish: lemon wedge and parsley sprigs

Preheat oven to 375°F. Rinse fish in cold water, pat dry with paper towel, and set aside.

In small bowl combine margarine and lemon juice. On sheet of wax paper, or on a paper plate, thoroughly combine flour, chopped parsley, salt, and pepper. Dip fish into margarine mixture, then dredge in flour mixture; transfer to nonstick baking sheet and drizzle any remaining margarine mixture over fish. Sprinkle with paprika. Bake until fish is golden brown and flakes easily when tested with a fork, 15 to 20 minutes. If crisper texture is desired, broil baked fish for 1 minute. Serve garnished with lemon wedge and parsley sprigs.

For Additional Servings Use

	2 servings	3 servings	4 servings
sole fillets	2 (5 oz each)	3 (5 oz each)	4 (5 oz each)
margarine and lemon juice	1 T each	1 T + 1½ t each	2 T each
flour	3 T	¼ c + 1½ t	⅓ c + 2 t
chopped parsley	1 T	1 T	2 T
salt	¼ t	¼ t	½ t
pepper	dash	dash, or to taste	⅛ t
paprika	dash each fillet	dash each fillet	dash each fillet

Scampi Supreme

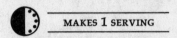 MAKES 1 SERVING

Festive fare in less than 15 minutes.

¾ teaspoon each margarine, melted, and olive oil
½ garlic clove, minced
Dash each salt and pepper
5 ounces shelled and deveined large shrimp

1½ teaspoons chopped fresh parsley
Garnish: 2 lemon wedges

Preheat broiler. In shallow individual flameproof casserole combine margarine, oil, garlic, salt, and pepper; add shrimp and toss to coat. Spread shrimp in single layer and broil for 3 to 4 minutes; turn shrimp over and broil until firm and lightly browned, 3 to 4 minutes longer. Sprinkle with parsley and garnish with lemon wedges.

For Additional Servings Use

	2 servings	3 servings	4 servings
margarine and oil	1½ t each	2¼ t each	1 T each
garlic	1 clove	1½ cloves	2 cloves
salt	⅛ t	⅛ t	¼ t
pepper	dash	dash	⅛ t
shrimp	10 oz	15 oz	1¼ lb
parsley	1 T	1 T	2 T

Chicken Cordon Bleu

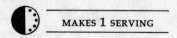

MAKES 1 SERVING

1 teaspoon margarine, divided
1 skinned and boned chicken breast
   (4 ounces), pounded to ⅛-inch
   thickness

½ ounce each sliced boiled ham and
   sliced Swiss cheese
2¼ teaspoons plain dried bread
   crumbs

In small skillet heat half of the margarine over medium heat until bubbly and hot; add chicken and cook briefly on each side (just until no longer pink). Transfer chicken to plate and top with ham, then cheese; starting from narrow end, roll chicken to enclose filling. Secure with toothpick and transfer to shallow individual baking dish; set aside.

Preheat oven to 400°F. In same skillet heat remaining margarine over low heat until bubbly and hot; add crumbs and stir to combine. Sprinkle crumb mixture evenly over chicken roll and bake until cheese is melted, 2 to 3 minutes; remove toothpick and serve.

For Additional Servings Use

	2 servings	3 servings	4 servings
margarine	2 t	1 T	1 T + 1 t
chicken breasts	2 (4 oz each)	3 (4 oz each)	4 (4 oz each)
ham and cheese	1 oz each	1½ oz each	2 oz each
bread crumbs	1 T +1½ t	2 T + ¾ t	3 T
skillet	small	9-inch	10-inch

Chicken with Hot Peanut Sauce

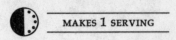

MAKES 1 SERVING

1 teaspoon peanut oil

1½ teaspoons each minced fresh garlic and minced pared ginger root

¼ cup prepared instant chicken broth and seasoning mix (prepared according to packet directions)

2 tablespoons dry sherry

1 tablespoon plus 1½ teaspoons smooth peanut butter

1½ teaspoons each soy sauce and rice wine vinegar

½ teaspoon Chinese sesame oil

Dash each ground and crushed red pepper

2 ounces skinned and boned cooked chicken breast, thinly sliced

¾ cup cooked vermicelli (very thin spaghetti), hot

1½ teaspoons minced scallion (green onion)

In small saucepan heat peanut oil over high heat; add garlic and ginger root and sauté briefly, about 30 seconds. Add remaining ingredients except chicken, vermicelli, and scallion and bring to a boil. Reduce heat to low and cook, stirring constantly, until sauce is smooth and thickened, about 3 minutes; add chicken and stir to combine. Serve over hot vermicelli and sprinkle with scallion.

For Additional Servings Use

	2 servings	3 servings	4 servings
peanut oil	2 t	1 T	1 T + 1 t
garlic and ginger	1 T each	1 T + 1½ t each	2 T each
broth	½ c	¾ c	1 c
sherry	¼ c	⅓ c + 2 t	½ c
peanut butter	3 T	¼ c + 1½ t	⅓ c + 2 t
soy sauce and vinegar	1 T each	1 T + 1½ t each	2 T each
sesame oil	1 t	1½ t	2 t
ground and crushed pepper	dash each	dash each	dash each, or to taste
chicken	4 oz	6 oz	8 oz
vermicelli	1½ c	2¼ c	3 c
scallions	1 T	1 T + 1½ t	2 T

Curried Eggplant and Lamb Stew

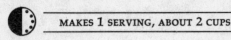

MAKES 1 SERVING, ABOUT 2 CUPS

Since lamb and eggplant are a natural pair, this is an excellent way to use up that leftover roast.

½ teaspoon olive or vegetable oil
¼ cup diced onion
½ garlic clove, minced
¾ cup cubed pared eggplant
   (1-inch cubes)
½ cup drained canned whole
   tomatoes, chopped

¼ teaspoon curry powder
⅛ teaspoon oregano leaves
Dash salt
4 ounces boned cooked lamb, cut
   into 1-inch cubes
1½ teaspoons chopped fresh
   parsley

In 1-quart saucepan heat oil; add onion and garlic and sauté until softened. Add eggplant and sauté for 2 minutes; add tomatoes, curry powder, oregano, and salt and bring to a boil. Reduce heat, cover, and let simmer for 15 minutes; add lamb, cover, and let simmer until thoroughly heated, about 10 minutes longer. Serve sprinkled with parsley.

For Additional Servings Use

	2 servings	3 servings	4 servings
oil	1 t	1½ t	2 t
onions	½ c	¾ c	1 c
garlic	1 clove	1½ cloves	2 cloves
eggplant	1½ c	2¼ c	3 c
tomatoes	1 c	1½ c	2 c
curry powder	½ t	½ t, or to taste	1 t
oregano leaves	¼ t	¼ t	½ t
salt	⅛ t	⅛ t	¼ t
lamb	8 oz	12 oz	1 lb
parsley	1 T	1 T	2 T

Lamb Patty in Mustard Gravy

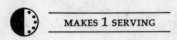

MAKES 1 SERVING

1 lamb patty, 5 ounces
Dash pepper
1 teaspoon vegetable oil
¼ cup diced onion
3 tablespoons water

1 teaspoon each red wine and
Dijon-style mustard
¼ packet (about ¼ teaspoon)
instant beef broth and seasoning
mix

Preheat broiler. Sprinkle lamb with pepper; transfer to rack in broiling pan and broil, turning once, until done to taste.

In small nonstick skillet heat oil over medium-high heat; add onion and sauté until lightly browned. Stir in water, wine, mustard, and broth mix; cook until liquid is reduced by half. Reduce heat to low, add broiled patty, and let simmer until meat is heated, about 1 minute longer.

For Additional Servings Use

	2 servings	*3 servings*	*4 servings*
lamb patties	2 (5 oz each)	3 (5 oz each)	4 (5 oz each)
pepper	dash	dash	⅛ t
oil	2 t	1 T	1 T + 1 t
onions	½ c	¾ c	1 c
water	⅓ c	½ c + 1 T	¾ c
wine and mustard	2 t each	1 T each	1 T + 1 t each
broth mix	½ pkt (about ½ t)	¾ pkt (about ¾ t)	1 pkt
skillet	small	9-inch	9-inch

Curried Livers in Wine Sauce

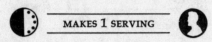

MAKES 1 SERVING

Delicious over noodles or rice.

1 teaspoon peanut or vegetable oil
½ medium green bell pepper,
    seeded and cut into 1-inch pieces
¼ cup diced onion
½ small garlic clove, minced, or
    dash garlic powder
5 ounces chicken livers
¼ teaspoon curry powder

2 tablespoons dry white wine
2 tablespoons prepared instant
    chicken broth and seasoning mix
    (prepared according to packet
    directions), at room temperature
½ teaspoon cornstarch
Dash each salt and pepper

In small nonstick skillet heat oil; add green pepper, onion, and fresh garlic and sauté until vegetables are softened (if garlic powder is used, add with curry powder). Add livers and cook, turning occasionally, until livers are browned, 5 to 7 minutes.

Sprinkle mixture with curry powder (and, if used, garlic powder), then add wine and bring to a boil. In small cup combine broth and cornstarch, stirring to dissolve cornstarch; add to liver mixture and cook, stirring occasionally, until sauce is slightly thickened. Season with salt and pepper and serve.

For Additional Servings Use

	2 servings	3 servings	4 servings
oil	2 t	1 T	1 T + 1 t
green peppers	1 medium	1½ medium	2 medium
onions	½ c	¾ c	1 cup
garlic	½ medium clove or ⅛ t powder	½ medium clove or ⅛ t powder	1 medium clove or ¼ t powder
livers	10 oz	15 oz	1¼ lb
curry powder	½ t	¾ t	1 t
wine and broth	¼ c each	⅓ c plus 2 t each	½ c each
cornstarch	1 t	1½ t	2 t
salt and pepper	⅛ t each	⅛ t each	⅛ to ¼ t each
skillet	8-inch	10-inch	12-inch

Mexican Liver

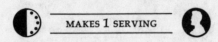 MAKES 1 SERVING

If south-of-the-border seasonings please your palate, you'll say "Si, si" to this 30-minute taste treat.

2 teaspoons all-purpose flour
1 teaspoon chili powder
5 ounces sliced beef liver, cut into
   2-inch-long strips
1 teaspoon vegetable oil
2 tablespoons chopped onion

¼ cup each chopped canned whole
   tomatoes and drained canned
   whole-kernel corn
¼ teaspoon salt
Dash pepper

In shallow dish, or on sheet of wax paper, combine flour and chili powder; dredge liver strips in mixture to coat, being sure to use all of mixture.

   In small nonstick skillet heat oil over high heat; add onion and sauté until translucent, about 3 minutes. Reduce heat to medium, add liver, and cook, turning once, until lightly browned on all sides; stir in tomatoes, corn, salt, and pepper. Reduce heat to low, cover pan, and let simmer for 10 minutes.

For Additional Servings Use

	2 servings	3 servings	4 servings
flour	1 T + 1 t	2 T	2 T + 2 t
chili powder	2 t	1 T	1 T + 1 t
liver	10 oz	15 oz	1¼ lb
oil	2 t	1 T	1 T + 1 t
onions	¼ c	⅓ c + 2 t	½ c
tomatoes and corn	½ c each	¾ c each	1 c each
salt	½ t	¾ t	1 t
pepper	dash	dash	dash, or to taste
skillet	9-inch	10-inch	12-inch

Asparagus with Sesame "Butter"

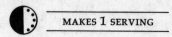 MAKES 1 SERVING

A wonderful accompaniment to Veal Patties in Parsley Sauce (see page 173).

6 asparagus spears, woody ends
   removed
¼ teaspoon salt
1 teaspoon each margarine and
   lemon juice

¾ teaspoon sesame seed
Garnish: parsley sprigs and 1 thin
   lemon slice

In saucepan large enough to hold asparagus in 1 layer arrange spears; sprinkle with salt, add water to cover, and bring to a boil. Reduce heat and let simmer until cut ends of spears are tender, 5 to 8 minutes; drain. Transfer asparagus to a warm plate; set aside and keep warm.

In small metal measuring cup, or other small flameproof container, combine margarine, lemon juice, and sesame seed; cook over low heat, stirring occasionally, until margarine is melted and seeds are golden. Spoon mixture evenly over asparagus spears. Garnish with parsley sprigs and lemon slice.

For Additional Servings Use

	2 servings	*3 servings*	*4 servings*
asparagus	12 spears	18 spears	24 spears
salt	½ t	¾ t	1 t
margarine and lemon juice	2 t each	1 T each	1 T + 1 t each
sesame seed	1½ t	2¼ t	1 T

Glazed Coconut-Fruit Kabobs

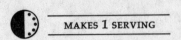 MAKES 1 SERVING

¼ cup canned pineapple chunks
(no sugar added)/ drain and
reserve juice
10 small seedless green grapes

1½ teaspoons reduced-calorie
orange marmalade (16 calories
per 2 teaspoons)
1 teaspoon shredded coconut

Onto each of two 12-inch wooden skewers, thread ½ of the pineapple chunks and 5 grapes, alternating ingredients; transfer kabobs to flameproof dish that is just large enough to hold them in 1 layer.

In 1-cup metal measure, or other small flameproof container, combine reserved juice and marmalade and heat until marmalade is melted; spoon mixture evenly over fruit. Sprinkle fruit on each skewer with ½ teaspoon coconut and broil until coconut is browned, 1 to 2 minutes.

For Additional Servings Use

	2 servings	*3 servings*	*4 servings*
pineapple	½ c	¾ c	1 c
grapes	20 small	30 small	40 small
marmalade	1 T	1 T + 1½ t	2 T
coconut	2 t	1 T	1 T + 1 t
skewers	4	6	8

Pineapple-Yogurt Broil

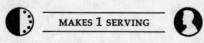

MAKES 1 SERVING

Try this 5-minute delicacy for yourself, your family, and your guests.

**½ cup canned pineapple chunks
(no sugar added)
¼ cup plain lowfat yogurt**

**½ teaspoon each vanilla extract and
granulated brown sugar**

Preheat broiler. In blender container process pineapple until smooth; pour into 6-ounce flameproof custard cup. In small bowl combine yogurt and extract; spoon mixture over fruit. Sprinkle yogurt mixture with sugar and broil 3 inches from heat source until sugar is melted, bubbly, and slightly crisp, about 3 minutes; serve immediately.

For Additional Servings Use

	2 servings	3 servings	4 servings
pineapple	1 c	1½ c	2 c
yogurt	½ c	¾ c	1 c
vanilla and sugar	1 t each	1½ t each	2 t each

Apple Syrup

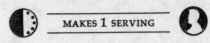

MAKES 1 SERVING

Pare, core, and thinly slice *1 small apple*. In small nonstick saucepan combine apple slices with *dash lemon juice* and toss; drizzle with *1½ teaspoons low-calorie pancake syrup (14 calories per tablespoon)*. Cover pan and cook over low heat until apple slices are very soft; serve warm.

For Additional Servings Use

	2 servings	3 servings	4 servings
apples	2 small	3 small	4 small
lemon juice	⅛ t	⅛ t	¼ t
pancake syrup	1 T	1 T + 1½ t	2 T

Pineapple Topping

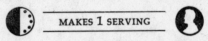

MAKES 1 SERVING

In metal 1-cup measure, or other small flameproof container, heat *¼ cup canned crushed pineapple (no sugar added)*. Dissolve *¼ teaspoon cornstarch* in *1½ teaspoons water*; add dissolved cornstarch and *½ teaspoon granulated sugar* to pineapple and bring mixture to a boil. Cook, stirring constantly, until thickened, about 2 minutes; pour into a small cup or bowl and let cool. Serve at room temperature or cover and refrigerate until chilled.

For Additional Servings Use

	2 servings	3 servings	4 servings
pineapple	½ c	¾ c	1 c
cornstarch	½ t	¾ t	1 t
water	1 T	1 T	2 T
sugar	1 t	1½ t	2 t

Blueberry Topping

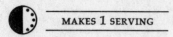

MAKES 1 SERVING

This topping and Pineapple Topping are both delicious with Freezer French Toast (see page 187), dietary frozen dessert, and plain lowfat yogurt.

½ cup fresh blueberries (or frozen, no sugar added)
1 tablespoon water

1 teaspoon granulated sugar
¼ teaspoon cornstarch, dissolved in 1½ teaspoons water

In metal 1-cup measure, or other small flameproof container, combine berries, water, and sugar; bring mixture to a boil. Stir in dissolved cornstarch and cook, stirring constantly, until mixture thickens, about 2 minutes; pour into small cup or bowl and let cool. Serve at room temperature or cover and refrigerate until chilled.

For Additional Servings Use

	2 servings	3 servings	4 servings
blueberries	1 c	1½ c	2 c
water	2 T	3 T	¼ c
sugar	2 t	1 T	1 T + 1 t
cornstarch	½ t, dissolved in 1 T water	¾ t, dissolved in 1 T water	1 t, dissolved in 2 T water

Chocolate Topping

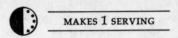

MAKES 1 SERVING

Delicious with dietary frozen dessert.

1 teaspoon each unsweetened cocoa
and granulated sugar
¼ teaspoon cornstarch

¼ cup evaporated skimmed milk
⅛ teaspoon vanilla extract

In metal 1-cup measure, or other small flameproof container, combine cocoa, sugar, and cornstarch; gradually stir in milk. Stirring constantly, bring mixture to a boil and continue cooking until thickened, about 2 minutes; stir in vanilla. Pour into small cup or bowl and cover with plastic wrap to prevent skin from forming; let cool and serve at room temperature or refrigerate and serve chilled.

For Additional Servings Use

	2 servings	*3 servings*	*4 servings*
cocoa and sugar	2 t each	1 T each	1 T + 1 t each
cornstarch	½ t	¾ t	1 t
milk	½ c	¾ c	1 c
vanilla	¼ t	¼ t	½ t

Appliance Appeal

◆◆

Microwave Recipes
Artichoke-Cheese Pie (appetizer or entrée)
Stuffed Apple (entrée)
Marinated Cod Teriyaki (entrée)
Salmon Loaf (entrée)
Chicken Rosé (entrée)
Spiced Lamb Pilaf (entrée)
Yogurt Hollandaise (sauce)
Cauliflower Provençale (side dish)
Wine Custard (dessert)

Pressure Cooker Recipes
Rabbit Stew in White Wine Sauce (entrée)
Southern Stew (entrée)
Vegetable Risotto (side dish)
Brown Sugar Custard (dessert)

Blender Recipes
Cream of Celery Soup (soup)
Buttermilk-Cheese Dressing (dip or salad dressing)
Strawberry Milk Shake (beverage)
Honeydew Squash (beverage)

Processor Recipes
Creamy Cauliflower Soup (soup)
Easy Vegetable-Barley Soup (soup)
Veal Patties in Parsley Sauce (entrée)
Potato-Vegetable Puree (side dish)

More and more households today have a microwave oven, a pressure cooker, a blender, or a food processor; this chapter offers recipes that make use of these popular convenience appliances.

The pressure cooker and the microwave oven make it possible to convert formerly long-cooking dishes into fast and fabulous meals. Because the microwave oven takes only about one fourth the time required by a conventional oven, hour-long recipes can now be cooked in a matter of minutes, and chilled or frozen dishes, prepared in advance, can be warmed up quickly. The pressure cooker, too, cuts down on cooking time because the pressure of the accumulated steam produces a higher degree of heat than cooking under normal pressure conditions.

The food processor and the blender save work on the preparation end by reducing such time-consuming tasks as blending, grinding, chopping, crumbing, grating, kneading, mixing, liquefying, pureeing, shredding, and slicing to the simple flick of a switch.

The information that follows will help you give these valuable time-saving tools the proper care and use so that they can help you expand your repertoire of impressive meals.

MICROWAVE OVEN

A conventional oven produces heat so that not only the food but the utensils and even the oven become very hot. A microwave oven, on the other hand, produces electromagnetic waves that cause the molecules in the food to vibrate, producing friction, which then results in heat; only the *food* becomes hot, not the dishes—nor the kitchen (an obvious boon on hot days).

This convenience appliance not only offers a vastly different cooking technique, it also uses less energy than does a conventional oven because it works so much faster. Cleaning up is cut in half since foods can be prepared directly on the serving plate. (Just be sure not to use plates with metal trim and to check manufacturer's directions regarding cookware.) The oven can be cleaned easily with a damp paper towel.

However, although a microwave oven may be a delightful addition to your kitchen, it should not be considered a replacement for the conventional oven. Because the two cooking methods are so different, the results differ considerably, too. Microwaved foods do not crisp (unless cooked on a special utensil made for that purpose). They do not brown (unless the unit has a browning element). Foods don't necessarily cook evenly and may require stirring or turning during the heating process, nor do tough cuts of meat become tender; they require a slower form of cooking.

PRESSURE COOKER

Like microwave cooking, pressure cooking also markedly cuts down the preparation time. Pressure cookers are available in both electric and non-electric forms. In the electric version, the quantity of heat used to produce steam is regulated, and once the desired degree is reached, it is controlled *automatically*. The nonelectric type, however, must be watched closely. The manufacturer's directions should explain in detail the correct way to use your pressure cooker. Both types come in 4-quart and 6-quart sizes.

Tips for Successful Pressure Cooking

- Be sure to use the *exact* amounts of liquid specified in recipes.
- Don't fill the pressure cooker more than two-thirds full.
- Be sure the cover is locked securely.
- Keep the pressure regulator *unclogged*. (The regulator, which is on the vent pipe, stabilizes the amount of pressure produced.) Because clogging is a problem, it is not advisable to pressure-cook items that froth, such as applesauce, cereals, cranberries, pasta, pearl barley, rhubarb, or split peas.
- Begin timing as soon as the regulator has a steady rocking motion, which indicates that the desired pressure (15 pounds) has been reached. With a nonelectric pressure cooker it may be necessary to turn down the heat so that the regulator does not move excessively, an indication that too much steam is being generated.
- Be careful not to overcook. Remember: one minute of pressure cooking is equal to approximately three minutes of regular cooking.
- For safety's sake, allow the pressure to drop before removing cover. This can be done by removing the pot from the heat and allowing it to stand for about five minutes, or by placing the pot in cold water. (However, with an electric pressure cooker be sure to check the manufacturer's directions before placing it in water.)

BLENDER

In addition to blending, crushing ice, chopping, grinding, liquefying, and pureeing, the blender also incorporates air, making it perfect for frothy foods such as milk shakes.

Tips for Blender Usage

- Cut foods into small pieces and don't overload the container.
- Before starting, make sure that the container is firmly in place and the lid is on securely.
- When chopping, add a few small pieces at a time, and empty the container often.
- Beware of overblending, unless you want a puree.
- Use a rubber scraper to push food down.
- Never put piping-hot foods (especially liquids) into a blender. (They may shoot right up.)

FOOD PROCESSOR

A high scorer on the versatility scale, this portable motor-driven appliance has revolutionized the preparation of many dishes. In a relatively short period of time, the food processor has become one of the most popular and useful pieces of equipment in the kitchen. It blends, chops, makes crumbs, grates, kneads, mixes, purees, shreds, and slices quickly and easily. Food processors usually come equipped with standard basic blades (blender, chopper, shredder, slicer); additional blades can be purchased for most units to expand their versatility. *Be sure to use the appropriate blade for the desired task.*

In addition to its many uses, the food processor has the added advantage of being easy to clean because the blades can be removed. They are, however, very sharp—so be extra cautious when handling them.

NOTE: With all appliances, always follow the manufacturer's directions. They give specifics about the use, care, and safety of the appliance as well as information about warranties.

Artichoke-Cheese Pie

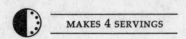

MAKES 4 SERVINGS

¼ cup minced onion
1 tablespoon margarine, divided
1 garlic clove, minced
4 large eggs
¼ teaspoon salt
⅛ teaspoon each oregano leaves,
basil leaves, and pepper

1½ cups chopped cooked frozen
artichoke hearts (9-ounce
package), divided
3 tablespoons plain dried bread
crumbs
4 ounces Swiss cheese, shredded
1 tablespoon chopped fresh parsley

1. In custard cup combine onion, 2 teaspoons margarine, and the garlic; microwave on High for 2 minutes.

2. In medium bowl beat eggs with seasonings; stir in onion mixture, ¾ cup chopped artichokes, and all of the bread crumbs.

3. Grease 7-inch glass pie plate with remaining teaspoon margarine; pour egg mixture into plate and top with remaining ¾ cup artichokes.

4. Fill glass baking dish that is large enough to hold pie plate with about 1 inch hot water; set pie plate into dish and microwave on High for 6 minutes. Sprinkle pie with cheese and parsley and microwave on High until cheese is melted, 2 to 3 minutes longer; let stand for 5 minutes before cutting.

Stuffed Apple

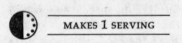

MAKES 1 SERVING

2 ounces boiled ham, minced
1 ounce Swiss cheese, minced
1 tablespoon minced celery

1 teaspoon mayonnaise
¼ teaspoon Dijon-style mustard
1 small Golden Delicious apple

In small bowl combine all ingredients except apple, mixing well. Core apple; cut into quarters, only about ¾ of the way down, leaving bottom intact. Set apple into a custard cup and fill with ham mixture; cover lightly with wax paper or plastic wrap and microwave on High for 2 minutes.

Marinated Cod Teriyaki

 MAKES 2 SERVINGS

2 tablespoons each teriyaki sauce
  and water
1 tablespoon plus 1 teaspoon dry
  sherry

1 garlic clove, minced
¼ teaspoon ground ginger
10 ounces cod fillets

In small bowl combine teriyaki sauce, water, sherry, garlic, and ginger.
Arrange fillets in 8 x 8-inch glass baking dish and pour teriyaki mixture
over fillets; turn fish over to coat other side. Cover dish; refrigerate for 1
hour. Microwave marinated fillets, uncovered, on High until fish flakes
easily when tested with a fork, 4 to 5 minutes.

Salmon Loaf

 MAKES 4 SERVINGS

12 ounces skinned and boned
  drained canned salmon
½ cup evaporated skimmed milk
2 slices white bread, made into fine
  crumbs
2 eggs, slightly beaten
¼ cup each minced celery and
  scallions (green onions)

2 teaspoons chopped fresh dill
½ teaspoon grated lemon peel
¼ teaspoon thyme leaves
⅛ teaspoon each salt and pepper
1 tablespoon margarine, melted,
  divided
Garnish: thin lemon slices, cut
  into halves, and dill sprigs

In medium bowl combine all ingredients except margarine and garnish; add
2 teaspoons margarine and, using a fork, mix well. Grease 8½ x 4½ x
2½-inch glass loaf pan with remaining teaspoon margarine; spoon in salmon mixture and smooth top. Microwave on Medium-High for about 18
minutes (center should be firm). Let stand for 5 minutes, then invert loaf
onto a serving platter; garnish with lemon slices and dill.

Chicken Rosé

MAKES 2 SERVINGS
---

2 teaspoons all-purpose flour
½ teaspoon salt, divided
⅛ teaspoon pepper
1½ pounds chicken parts, skinned*
¼ cup minced onion
2 teaspoons vegetable oil
1 garlic clove, minced

1 medium green bell pepper, seeded
   and cut into 1-inch squares
1 cup quartered mushrooms
½ cup canned crushed tomatoes
¼ cup rosé wine
¼ teaspoon thyme leaves
2 teaspoons chopped fresh parsley

On sheet of wax paper combine flour, ¼ teaspoon salt, and the pepper; dredge chicken parts in flour mixture, turning to coat all sides.

In shallow 2-quart glass baking dish combine onion, oil, and garlic and microwave on Medium-High for 2 minutes; add chicken and green pepper and microwave on Medium-High for 5 minutes. Stir mixture, then add mushrooms, tomatoes, wine, thyme, and remaining ¼ teaspoon salt; cover with plastic wrap and microwave on Medium-High for 20 minutes, stirring twice during cooking. Uncover and cook until chicken is tender, about 5 minutes longer. Serve sprinkled with parsley.

* 1½ pounds chicken parts will yield about 8 ounces cooked meat.

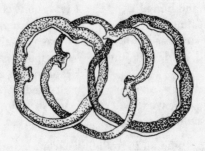

Spiced Lamb Pilaf

 MAKES 1 SERVING

Dress up leftover lamb with fruit and spices for a quick and easy treat.

¼ cup diced celery
2 tablespoons diced onion
1 teaspoon margarine
1 cup water
1 ounce uncooked regular long-grain
  rice
1 tablespoon raisins

1 packet instant chicken broth and
  seasoning mix
Dash each ground cinnamon,
  ground allspice, and ground
  cloves
4 ounces boned cooked lamb, cut
  into 1-inch cubes

In shallow 1-quart glass-ceramic casserole combine celery, onion, and margarine; microwave on High for 5 minutes. Stir in water, rice, raisins, broth mix, and spices; cover and microwave on High for 5 minutes. Rotate casserole and stir mixture; cover and microwave on Medium for 10 minutes. Add lamb and microwave, uncovered, on Medium for 3 minutes.

Yogurt Hollandaise

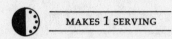 MAKES 4 SERVINGS, ABOUT ⅓ CUP EACH

Delicious with cooked chicken or cooked green vegetables.

2 tablespoons all-purpose flour
1 tablespoon plus 1 teaspoon
  margarine
2 large eggs, beaten
1 cup plain lowfat yogurt

¼ teaspoon salt
⅛ teaspoon white pepper
½ teaspoon lemon juice
¼ teaspoon Dijon-style mustard
Dash ground red pepper

In 1-quart glass measure combine flour and margarine; microwave on High for 1 minute, then stir. Add eggs and mix until thoroughly combined; gradually add yogurt, stirring until well blended. Add salt and white pepper and microwave on High for 2 minutes; stir. Microwave on High for 1 minute longer; stir in remaining ingredients and serve immediately.

Cauliflower Provençale

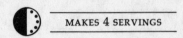 MAKES 4 SERVINGS

2 packages (10 ounces each) frozen cauliflower (about 4 cups)*
¼ cup boiling water
½ teaspoon salt, divided
¼ cup minced onion
1 tablespoon olive oil
1 garlic clove, minced

1 cup canned crushed tomatoes
8 pitted black olives, sliced
¼ teaspoon each basil leaves and Worcestershire sauce
⅛ teaspoon pepper
Garnish: 1 tablespoon chopped fresh parsley

In 8 x 8-inch glass baking dish combine cauliflower, water, and ¼ teaspoon salt; microwave on High for 5 to 7 minutes. Drain, cover, and let stand for 2 minutes. Remove cauliflower from dish and set aside.

In same dish combine onion, oil, and garlic and microwave on High for 2 minutes; stir in tomatoes, olives, basil, Worcestershire, pepper, and remaining ¼ teaspoon salt. Cover and microwave on High for 8 minutes, stirring once during cooking; add cauliflower, cover, and cook on High for 2 minutes longer. Serve sprinkled with parsley.

* 4 cups fresh florets may be substituted for the frozen; use 2 cups boiling water instead of ¼ cup and microwave for 7 minutes. Continue as directed.

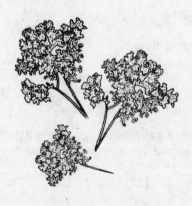

Wine Custard

 MAKES 4 SERVINGS, ABOUT ½ CUP EACH

3 tablespoons all-purpose flour
2 tablespoons granulated sugar
Dash salt (optional)
2 cups skim milk

2 large eggs
2 tablespoons dry Marsala wine
1 teaspoon vanilla extract

In 2- or 2½-quart glass bowl combine flour, sugar, and, if desired, salt; using wire whisk or a fork, stir in milk and combine thoroughly. Microwave on High until thickened, 7 to 10 minutes, stirring 3 times during cooking process.

In small bowl lightly beat together eggs and wine; stir in ½ cup hot milk mixture. Slowly pour egg mixture into remaining milk mixture, stirring rapidly to prevent lumping; microwave on High until thick, 1 to 2 minutes. Remove custard from oven and let cool slightly; stir in vanilla and let stand for 5 minutes (custard will continue to cook while standing). Divide cooled custard into 4 dessert dishes and serve immediately, or cover and refrigerate until chilled.

Rabbit Stew in White Wine Sauce

MAKES 4 SERVINGS

1 tablespoon plus 1 teaspoon
  vegetable oil, divided
1½ pounds rabbit, cut into pieces
½ cup chopped onion
1 garlic clove, minced
1 medium green bell pepper, seeded
  and cut into 1-inch squares
1 cup sliced mushrooms
2 teaspoons all-purpose flour

3 medium tomatoes, blanched,
  peeled, seeded, and chopped
½ cup white wine
¼ cup water
1 packet instant chicken broth and
  seasoning mix
¼ teaspoon each thyme leaves, salt,
  and pepper
2 teaspoons chopped fresh parsley

1. In 4-quart pressure cooker heat 1 tablespoon oil; add rabbit, a few pieces at a time, and cook until evenly browned on all sides. Set rabbit pieces aside.

2. Add remaining teaspoon oil to cooker and heat; add onion and garlic and sauté until onion is soft. Add green pepper and mushrooms and continue sautéing until pepper is tender-crisp; sprinkle vegetable mixture with flour and cook, stirring constantly, for 2 minutes longer. Stir in tomatoes and wine and bring to a boil; add water, broth mix, thyme, salt, pepper, and browned rabbit and stir to combine.

3. Close cover securely; place pressure regulator firmly on vent pipe and heat until regulator begins to rock gently. Cook at 15 pounds pressure for 15 minutes.

4. Hold cooker under running cold water to bring pressure down.* Transfer rabbit to serving dish and cook sauce over high heat until slightly thickened, about 2 minutes; pour over rabbit and sprinkle with parsley.

* If using an electric pressure cooker, follow manufacturer's directions for reducing pressure.

Southern Stew

MAKES 4 SERVINGS

1¼ pounds boneless sirloin steak
2 teaspoons vegetable oil
1 cup sliced onions
2 garlic cloves, minced
1½ cups canned crushed tomatoes
1 teaspoon salt
½ teaspoon chili powder

⅛ teaspoon ground red pepper
1 cup thinly sliced green cabbage
8 ounces drained canned chick-peas
(garbanzo beans)
¼ cup chopped red or green bell
pepper
2 tablespoons chopped fresh parsley

On rack in broiling pan broil steak for 5 minutes on each side; cut into 2-inch pieces and set aside.

In 4-quart pressure cooker heat oil over medium heat; add onions and garlic and sauté, stirring occasionally, until onions are translucent. Add beef, tomatoes, salt, chili powder, and ground pepper; close cover securely and place pressure regulator firmly on vent pipe. Heat until regulator begins to rock gently; cook at 15 pounds pressure for 20 minutes. Let pressure drop of its own accord.

Add cabbage, chick-peas, and bell pepper to cooker; close cover again and cook at 15 pounds pressure for 2 minutes. Let pressure drop of its own accord; stir in parsley.

Vegetable Risotto

 MAKES 2 SERVINGS

2 teaspoons vegetable oil
2 tablespoons diced onion
1 garlic clove, minced
½ cup chopped mushrooms
½ cup diced zucchini (½-inch dice)
1 medium green bell pepper, seeded
and cut into ½-inch squares

1 medium tomato, blanched, peeled,
seeded, and chopped
2 ounces uncooked regular
long-grain rice
⅔ cup water
1 packet instant chicken broth and
seasoning mix

In 4-quart pressure cooker heat oil; add onion and garlic and sauté until onion is softened. Add mushrooms and zucchini and toss to combine; add green pepper and tomato and sauté for 3 minutes. Add rice and stir to combine; stir in water and broth mix. Close cover securely; place pressure regulator firmly on vent pipe and heat until regulator begins to rock gently. Cook at 15 pounds pressure for 5 minutes.

Let pressure drop of its own accord. Open cooker and let stand uncovered for 5 minutes. Using a fork, toss risotto lightly before serving.

Brown Sugar Custard

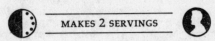

MAKES 2 SERVINGS

1 cup skim milk
1 tablespoon firmly packed light
  brown sugar

1 large egg, lightly beaten
1 teaspoon vanilla extract
1 cup water

In small saucepan combine milk and sugar and heat to just below the boiling point; let cool. Add egg and vanilla and stir well to combine; into each of two 6-ounce custard cups pour half of mixture. Using foil, cover each cup tightly.

Pour water into 4-quart pressure cooker; place rack in cooker and set custard cups on rack. Close cover securely and place pressure regulator firmly on vent pipe. Heat until regulator begins to rock gently; cook at 15 pounds pressure for 4 minutes. Immediately hold cooker under running cold water to bring pressure down.* Serve custard at room temperature or refrigerate until chilled.

* If using an electric pressure cooker, follow manufacturer's directions for reducing pressure.

Cream of Celery Soup

MAKES 2 SERVINGS, ABOUT 1 CUP EACH

2 teaspoons unsalted margarine
2 cups diced celery (about 4
  large ribs)
½ cup diced onion
1 packet instant chicken broth and
  seasoning mix

1 tablespoon plus 1½ teaspoons
  all-purpose flour
1 cup skim milk (at room
  temperature)
Dash white pepper

In 1-quart nonstick saucepan melt margarine; add celery, onion, and broth mix and stir until combined. Cover and let simmer until vegetables are tender, 10 to 15 minutes.

Sprinkle flour over vegetable mixture and cook, stirring constantly, for 1 minute; gradually stir in milk and continue to cook, stirring constantly, until mixture thickens (*do not boil*). Remove from heat and let cool slightly.

Pour half of soup into blender container and process on low speed until smooth; return pureed mixture to saucepan and cook, stirring, until thoroughly combined and heated.

For Additional Servings Use

	3 servings	4 servings	6 servings
margarine	1 T	1 T + 1 t	2 T
celery	3 c	4 c	6 c
onions	¾ c	1 c	1½ c
broth mix	1½ pkt	2 pkt	3 pkt
flour	2 T + ¾ t	3 T	¼ c + 1½ t
milk	1½ c	2 c	3 c
pepper	dash	⅛ t	⅛ t, or to taste

Buttermilk-Cheese Dressing

 MAKES 2 SERVINGS, ABOUT 3 TABLESPOONS EACH

This dressing will keep for about 3 days in the refrigerator.

¼ cup buttermilk (made from skim milk)
2 tablespoons plus 2 teaspoons cottage cheese
1½ teaspoons chopped fresh parsley

1 teaspoon lemon juice
½ teaspoon Dijon-style mustard
Dash each salt, ground cumin, white pepper, and ground coriander

In blender container combine all ingredients and process for 1 minute; transfer to 1-cup container, cover, and refrigerate until ready to use.

For Additional Servings Use

	3 servings	4 servings	6 servings
buttermilk	⅓ c + 2 t	½ c	¾ c
cottage cheese	¼ c	⅓ c	½ c
parsley	2¼ t	1 T	1 T + 1½ t
lemon juice	1½ t	2 t	1 T
mustard	¾ t	1 t	1½ t
salt and cumin	dash each	⅛ t each	⅛ t each
white pepper and coriander	dash each	dash each	dash each

Strawberry Milk Shake

MAKES 1 SERVING, ABOUT 1 CUP

½ cup strawberries
1 tablespoon plus 1 teaspoon
   instant nonfat dry milk powder
3 ounces vanilla dietary frozen
   dessert

¼ cup skim milk
1 teaspoon granulated sugar

In blender container combine berries and milk powder and process until berries are crushed; add remaining ingredients and process until smooth.

For Additional Servings Use

	2 servings	3 servings	4 servings
strawberries	1 c	1½ c	2 c
milk powder	2 T + 2 t	¼ c	⅓ c
frozen dessert	6 oz	9 oz	12 oz
skim milk	½ c	¾ c	1 c
sugar	2 t	1 T	1 T + 1 t

Honeydew Squash

MAKES 2 SERVINGS, ABOUT ½ CUP EACH

Chill two champagne cocktail glasses. In blender container combine *1 cup very ripe honeydew chunks* and *½ cup chilled orange juice (no sugar added)* and process until smooth; divide mixture into chilled glasses and *garnish each with a lemon slice.* Serve immediately.

For Additional Servings Use

	3 servings	4 servings	6 servings
honeydew	1½ cups	2 cups	3 cups
orange juice	¾ cup	1 cup	1½ cups
lemon slices	3	4	6

Creamy Cauliflower Soup

MAKES 2 SERVINGS, ABOUT 1 CUP EACH

2 cups cauliflower florets
  or 1 package (10 ounces)
  frozen cauliflower
2 tablespoons chopped onion
1¼ cups water, divided
2 teaspoons each margarine and
  all-purpose flour

1 packet instant chicken broth and
  seasoning mix
⅛ teaspoon ground celery seed
Dash white pepper
Garnish: 1½ teaspoons chopped
  fresh parsley

1. In 1-quart saucepan add cauliflower and onion to ½ cup boiling water; return water to a boil. Reduce heat, cover, and let simmer until florets are tender, about 10 minutes (if frozen cauliflower is used, cook with onion and ½ cup water but follow package directions for timing). Remove from heat and let cool slightly. Pour vegetables and liquid into work bowl of food processor and process until smooth; set aside.

2. In same saucepan heat margarine until bubbly and hot; add flour and cook, stirring constantly, for 1 minute. Stir in broth mix and remaining water and bring to a boil. Reduce heat and cook, stirring constantly, until mixture is smooth and thickened. Add pureed vegetables and seasonings to saucepan; cook over low heat, stirring constantly, until thoroughly combined and heated. Pour into soup bowls and sprinkle each portion with ¾ teaspoon parsley.

For Additional Servings Use

	3 servings	*4 servings*	*6 servings*
cauliflower	3 c or 1½ pkg frozen	4 c or 2 pkg frozen	6 c or 3 pkg frozen
water	1¾ c	2½ c	3¾ c
onions	3 T	¼ c	⅓ c + 2 t
margarine and flour	1 T each	1 T + 1 t each	2 T each
broth mix	1½ pkt	2 pkt	3 pkt
celery seed	⅛ t	¼ t	¼ t
pepper	dash	⅛ t	⅛ t, or to taste
parsley	2¼ t	1 T	1 T + 1½ t
Method: Step 1—use process	¾ c water as directed	1 c water as directed	1½ c water in 2 batches

Easy Vegetable-Barley Soup

MAKES 4 SERVINGS, ABOUT 1 CUP EACH

Any leftover soup can be frozen for future use.

1 cup coarsely chopped green
  cabbage
½ cup coarsely chopped onion
½ cup each sliced celery, carrot,
  and zucchini
½ cup each cut green beans and
  canned whole tomatoes
1 tablespoon plus 1 teaspoon
  margarine

½ cup sliced mushrooms
2¼ cups water
1 cup cooked medium barley
3 packets instant beef broth and
  seasoning mix
1 small bay leaf
Dash each thyme leaves, salt, and
  freshly ground pepper

In work bowl of food processor process cabbage until finely chopped but
not pureed; transfer to large bowl. Repeat procedure with onion, celery,
carrot, zucchini, green beans, and tomatoes, processing each vegetable
separately.

In 2-quart saucepan heat margarine until bubbly and hot; add chopped
vegetables and mushrooms and cook over medium heat, stirring occasionally, until cabbage begins to wilt, about 10 minutes. Add remaining ingredients and bring to a boil. Reduce heat, cover, and let simmer for 30
minutes, stirring occasionally. Remove and discard bay leaf before serving.

For Additional Servings Use

	6 servings	8 servings
cabbage	1½ c	2 c
onions, celery, carrots, zucchini, green beans, and tomatoes	¾ c each	1 c each
margarine	2 T	2 T + 2 t
mushrooms	¾ c	1 c
water	3⅓ c	1 qt + ½ c
barley	1½ c	2 c
broth mix	4½ pkt	6 pkt
bay leaves	1 small	1 medium
thyme leaves, salt, and pepper	dash each	⅛ t each

Veal Patties in Parsley Sauce

MAKES 2 SERVINGS

½ cup evaporated skimmed milk, divided
1 slice white bread, torn into pieces
1 tablespoon margarine, divided
¼ cup diced onion
8 ounces ground veal
1 egg
¼ teaspoon salt

⅛ teaspoon pepper
Dash each ground nutmeg and ground allspice
1 tablespoon chopped fresh parsley, divided
¾ cup water and 1 packet instant chicken broth and seasoning mix
1 teaspoon all-purpose flour

In food processor combine half the milk with bread and process for about 30 seconds; let stand for 5 minutes. In small skillet heat ⅓ of the margarine until bubbly and hot; add onion and sauté until softened. Add onion, veal, egg, salt and spices to processor and process until smooth; add ⅓ the parsley and process to combine. Refrigerate covered for 15 minutes.

Using moist hands, shape veal mixture into 4 patties. In 9-inch skillet heat remaining margarine; add patties and cook, turning once, until evenly browned. Add water and broth mix, cover, and let simmer for 15 minutes, turning patties once. Remove patties from pan and keep warm; reserve pan juices. Combine flour with remaining milk, stirring to dissolve. Stir into pan juices; stirring constantly, bring to a simmer and cook until thickened. Stir in remaining parsley; serve over patties.

For Additional Servings Use

	4 servings	*6 servings*
milk	1 c	1½ c
bread	2 slices	3 slices
margarine	2 T	3 T
onions	½ c	¾ c
veal	1 lb	1 lb 7 oz
eggs	2	3
salt	½ t	¾ t
pepper	¼ t	¼ t, or to taste
nutmeg and allspice	⅛ t each	⅛ t each
parsley	2 T	3 T
water	1½ c	2¼ c
broth mix	2 pkt	3 pkt
flour	2 t	1 T
skillet	12-inch	12-inch

Potato-Vegetable Puree

MAKES 2 SERVINGS, ABOUT 1¼ CUPS EACH

2 teaspoons margarine
½ cup diced onion
¼ cup each diced carrot and celery
6 ounces pared potatoes, sliced
1 cup shredded green cabbage
¾ cup water
½ cup canned crushed tomatoes

1 packet instant chicken broth
  and seasoning mix
¼ teaspoon salt
½ bay leaf
Dash each thyme leaves and
  white pepper

In 1-quart saucepan heat margarine over medium heat until bubbly and hot; add onion, carrot, and celery and sauté, stirring occasionally, until onion is translucent. Add remaining ingredients and stir to combine. Reduce heat to low, cover pan, and let simmer, stirring occasionally, until vegetables and potatoes are tender, about 20 minutes. Remove from heat and let cool slightly; remove and discard bay leaf.

Pour mixture into work bowl of food processor and process until smooth;* return to saucepan and heat.

* Mixture may also be pureed in blender container. If using a blender, process no more than 2 cups of potato mixture at a time.

For Additional Servings Use

	3 servings	*4 servings*	*6 servings*
margarine	1 T	1 T + 1 t	2 T
onions	¾ c	1 c	1½ c
carrots and celery	⅓ c + 2 t each	½ c each	¾ c each
potatoes	9 oz	12 oz	1 lb 2 oz
cabbage	1½ c	2 c	3 c
water	1 c + 2 T	1½ c	2¼ c
tomatoes	¾ c	1 c	1½ c
broth mix	1½ pkt	2 pkt	3 pkt
salt	¼ t	½ t	¾ t
bay leaves	½	1	1
thyme leaves and pepper	dash each	dash each	dash to ⅛ t each
Method: process	as directed	as directed	in 2 batches

Freeze for the Future

—◆◆◆—

Basic Pastry Shell
Basic Pot Pie Dough
Basic Crêpes
Ham 'n' Cabbage Crêpe Filling
Chicken-Mushroom Crêpe Filling
Seafood Crêpe Filling
Italian Bread Four Ways

Breakfast Entrée
Freezer French Toast

Entrées
Turkey Pot Pie
Tuna Pot Pie
Beef Pot Pie
Veal Chili Pot Pie

Sauces
Béchamel (White Sauce)
Fresh Tomato Sauce

Desserts and Snacks
Raisin Biscuits
Peanut Butter Muffins
Tropical Muffins
Lace Cookie Cones
Pineapple Upside-Down Cake
Tortoni
Rum-Raisin "Ice Cream"
Vanilla Fudge Swirl
Mango Sherbet

The freezer is an indispensable ally in easing both your budget and your schedule, as well as allowing you some flexibility in menu planning. With adequate freezer space, you can prepare and store partial or even complete meals in advance for swift warming on rush-hour days. And the freezer also enables you to take advantage of supermarket specials and in-season produce to be frozen for use later.

Don't overlook another time-saver—freeze the welcome "extras" that can perk up your dishes and make the difference between drab and delightful. A few ideas follow:

Prefer fresh herbs? With the help of the freezer, you can always have the taste of fresh herbs. Buy herbs in quantity in season (or grow your own). Rinse well, blot dry, and package—either chopped or whole—in resealable plastic freezer bags. Seal, label, and freeze. Break off only the amount you need when cooking and return the rest to the freezer.

Relish the taste of fresh lemon or lemon juice? Squeeze the lemon for juice, grate the peel, and freeze both, separately, in premeasured amounts. When a recipe calls for either of these items, you will have them on hand in fresh form.

Like to flavor with margarine? Cream margarine with garlic, onion, or parsley; pack in small cups and freeze. When thawed, the margarine can be used to flavor broiled fish and poultry.

Have gourmet-style mushrooms in minutes. For another fast taste-enhancer, cook a combination of chopped mushrooms and shallots with wine (measured amounts, of course); then freeze in small containers for use in mushroom dishes, omelets, sauces, soups, etc.

SUCCESSFUL FREEZER STORAGE

The passwords for freezer storage are *planning* and proper *preparation.* Here are some essential guidelines.

• Temperature should be kept at 0°F. Check periodically with a freezer-refrigerator thermometer (an indispensable kitchen tool).

• Freeze high-quality products only, for the best results.

Recommended Storage Times for Frozen Fish, Meat, and Poultry*

FISH

Most fish	up to 6 months
Fish with high oil content (e.g., bluefish, mackerel, etc.)	up to 3 months

MEATS

Beef	6 to 12 months
Lamb and veal	6 to 9 months
Pork (including fresh ham)	3 to 6 months
Pork, ground	1 to 3 months
Ground beef, lamb, veal	3 to 4 months
Variety meats (e.g., liver)	3 to 4 months
Cooked meats	2 to 3 months

POULTRY

Chicken and turkey	up to 6 months
Giblets	up to 3 months
Cooked chicken and turkey	up to 2 months

* Uncooked, unless otherwise specified.

• Prepare foods correctly before freezing. Most fresh vegetables should be blanched (briefly scalded). Meat surfaces should be wiped with paper towels; fish should be rinsed in cold water, then patted dry with paper towels.

• Proper wrapping is essential to prevent freezer-burn or "off" odors. Products should be wrapped in moisture- and vapor-resistant materials, such as heavy-duty aluminum foil, plastic freezer bags, transparent freezer wrap, or plastic freezer containers with self-sealing lids. Wrap foods securely, pressing all air from the package. (A good tip when wrapping chops, patties, steaks, etc., is to place a double sheet of wax paper between each item. They will then separate easily.)

• Label each package by name, weight or number of servings, and the date it was frozen. Place behind or beneath foods already in the freezer, so that you use the *oldest* products first.

• Leave space for air to circulate when storing unfrozen items. Pack compactly *after* they are frozen.

• Keep foods frozen. Partial thawing may result in loss of quality. To avoid this problem purchase frozen items *last* when shopping, and get them into your home freezer as quickly as possible. (If you have other errands, do them *before* purchasing frozen foods.)

• Know which foods should *not* be frozen. These include cake batter, custard pie fillings, gelatin salads, luncheon meats, mayonnaise, salad dressings, and sausages, as well as cooked potatoes. (A tip for freezing stew: prepare and freeze stew without potatoes; when stew is to be served, thaw, reheat, and add *freshly cooked* potatoes.)

To avoid possible deterioration and spoilage, fish, meats, and poultry should not be stored longer than the times recommended on page 178.

ENERGY SAVERS

The freezer doesn't have to be a drain on your energy budget if you follow these few easy tips:

• Don't open the door more often than necessary.

• Don't store more food than can freeze within 24 hours. (The maximum amount of unfrozen food that should be put into the freezer at any one time is three pounds for each cubic foot of space.)

• Try to keep the freezer at least two-thirds full at all times.

THAWING TIPS

Allow enough time for thawing when preparing dishes. Small pieces of frozen meat and some frozen cooked entrées do not require thawing before warming, but most frozen foods do. As a general rule, breads, cakes, cookies, and unbaked pastry should be thawed at *room temperature*. Margarine, meat, poultry, and seafood should be defrosted in the *refrigerator* (to avoid possible spoilage while thawing). Concentrated juices should also be thawed in the refrigerator, so they won't become too warm.

By using your freezer wisely to meet your needs, you'll avoid being caught short, and, best of all, even on your most rushed days, you'll have interesting items to liven up your menus.

Basic Pastry Shell

MAKES 2 SHELLS, 4 or 8 SERVINGS EACH

*Prepare ahead and freeze for use with Yogurt-Caraway Quiche and
Lemon Meringue Pie recipes (see pages 106 and 305).*

1½ cups all-purpose flour   **⅓ cup margarine**
½ teaspoon salt   **½ cup plain lowfat yogurt**

In mixing bowl combine flour and salt; with pastry blender, or 2 knives
used scissors-fashion, cut in margarine until mixture resembles coarse
meal. Add yogurt and mix thoroughly. Form dough into 2 equal balls;
cover each with plastic wrap and chill for about 1 hour.

Roll each ball between 2 sheets of wax paper, forming 2 circles, one
about ⅛ inch thick, the other about ¼ inch thick. Fit the ⅛-inch-thick
circle into an 8-inch quiche dish, the other into a 7-inch flameproof pie
plate; flute edges if desired. Wrap in moisture- and vapor-resistant wrapping, label, and freeze for future use.*

* If shell is going to be used immediately, rather than frozen, prick bottom and sides
in several places with the tines of a fork.

For Additional Servings Use

	3 shells	4 shells	6 shells
flour	2¼ c	3 c	4½ c
salt	¾ t	1 t	1½ t
margarine	½ c	⅔ c	1 c
yogurt	¾ c	1 c	1½ c

Basic Pot Pie Dough

MAKES 2 SERVINGS

Prepare ahead and use as directed in pot pie recipes.

⅓ cup plus 2 teaspoons all-purpose
    flour
Dash salt

1 tablespoon plus 1 teaspoon
    margarine
2 tablespoons plain lowfat yogurt

In mixing bowl combine flour and salt; with pastry blender, or 2 knives used scissors-fashion, cut in margarine until mixture resembles coarse meal. Add yogurt and mix thoroughly.

Form dough into 2 equal balls; cover each with plastic wrap and chill for 30 to 40 minutes (may be kept in refrigerator for up to 3 days); or wrap in plastic freezer wrap and freeze until ready to use. If dough has been frozen, thaw completely in refrigerator before using.

Variations:

1. *Cheddar Dough*—Add 1 ounce shredded Cheddar cheese to dry ingredients and proceed as directed.

2. *Pastry Dough*—Omit salt from basic dough recipe. Proceed as directed, but form dough into 1 ball; cover and chill for at least 1 hour.

For Additional Servings Use

	3 servings	*4 servings*	*6 servings*
flour	½ c + 1 T	¾ c	1 c + 2 T
salt	dash	⅓ t	⅛ t
margarine	2 T	2 T + 2 t	¼ c
yogurt	3 T	¼ c	⅓ c + 2 t
Method: form dough into	3 equal balls	4 equal balls	6 equal balls
Variations: Cheddar Dough— add	1½ oz cheese	2 oz cheese	3 oz cheese
Pastry Dough— form dough into	3 equal balls	2 equal balls	3 equal balls

Basic Crêpes

MAKES 4 SERVINGS, 2 CRÊPES EACH

Prepare ahead and keep in freezer for use in recipes calling for crêpes (see Ham 'n' Cabbage Crêpes, page 110, Chicken-Mushroom Crêpes, page 109, Seafood Crêpes, page 111, and Orange "Cream" Crêpes, page 304; thaw at room temperature for 10 to 15 minutes before using.

1 cup skim milk	**2 large eggs**
¾ cup all-purpose flour	**⅛ teaspoon salt**

In blender container combine all ingredients and process until smooth; let stand for 15 to 20 minutes.

Lightly spray an 8-inch nonstick skillet with nonstick cooking spray and heat (to test, sprinkle skillet with drop of water; if water sizzles, skillet is hot enough). Pour ⅛ of batter into skillet and quickly swirl batter so that it covers entire bottom of pan; cook over medium-high heat until edges and underside are dry. Using pancake turner, carefully turn crêpe over; cook other side briefly just to dry, about 30 seconds. Slide crêpe onto a plate and let cool. Repeat procedure 7 more times, using remaining batter and making 7 more crêpes.

To freeze, stack cooled crêpes, using 2 sheets of wax paper (or 1 sheet folded in half) between each to separate; wrap stack in moisture- and vapor-resistant wrapping and label. Freeze for future use.

For Additional Servings Use

	6 servings	8 servings
milk	1½ c	2 c
flour	1 c + 2 T	1½ c
eggs	3 large	4 large
salt	⅛ t	¼ t
Method: prepare a total of	12 equal crêpes	16 equal crêpes

Ham 'n' Cabbage Crêpe Filling

MAKES 4 SERVINGS

Prepare ahead and freeze for a 20-minute company dinner (see Ham 'n' Cabbage Crêpes, page 110); let frozen filling thaw overnight in refrigerator.

1 tablespoon plus 1 teaspoon
   margarine
1 cup diced onions
1 garlic clove, minced
1 cup julienne-cut carrots
   (matchstick pieces)

4 cups finely shredded green
   cabbage
10 ounces julienne-cut boiled ham
   (matchstick pieces)
¼ teaspoon pepper
1 cup water

In 12-inch skillet heat margarine until bubbly and hot; add onions and garlic and sauté until onions are translucent, 2 to 3 minutes. Add carrots and sauté for 3 minutes; add cabbage, ham, and pepper and sauté until cabbage is wilted, about 5 minutes. Stir in water and bring to a boil. Reduce heat and let simmer, stirring occasionally, until almost all liquid has evaporated, 5 to 10 minutes. Let cool, then divide evenly into plastic freezer bags, label, and freeze for future use.

For Additional Servings Use

	6 servings	8 servings
margarine	2 T	2 T + 2 t
onions	1½ c	2 c
garlic	2 cloves	2 cloves
carrots	1½ c	2 c
cabbage	6 c	8 c
ham	15 oz	1¼ lb
pepper	¼ t, or to taste	½ t
water	1½ c	2 c
pan	3-qt saucepan	4-qt saucepan

Chicken-Mushroom Crêpe Filling

MAKES 4 SERVINGS

Prepare ahead and keep in freezer for an elegant company dinner in 20 minutes (see Chicken-Mushroom Crêpes, page 109); let frozen filling thaw overnight in refrigerator.

1 tablespoon plus 1 teaspoon
  margarine
½ cup diced onion
1 cup sliced mushrooms
3 tablespoons all-purpose flour
1½ cups water
2 packets instant chicken broth and
  seasoning mix

12 ounces skinned and boned cooked
  chicken, cut into ½-inch cubes
½ teaspoon each salt and crushed
  thyme leaves
¼ teaspoon white pepper
1 cup frozen tiny peas

In 2-quart saucepan heat margarine until bubbly and hot; add onion and sauté until softened, 1 to 2 minutes. Add mushrooms and sauté for 3 minutes; add flour and cook, stirring constantly, for 3 minutes longer.

Remove pan from heat and gradually stir in water; add broth mix, return to heat, and bring to a boil. Reduce heat and let simmer for 5 minutes. Add chicken and seasonings and simmer 3 minutes longer; stir in peas and cook until tender, about 3 more minutes. Let cool, then divide evenly into plastic freezer bags, label, and freeze for future use.

For Additional Servings Use

	6 servings	8 servings
margarine	2 T	2 T + 2 t
onions	¾ c	1 c
mushrooms	1½ c	2 c
flour	¼ c + 1½ t	⅓ c + 2 t
water	2¼ c	3 c
broth mix	3 pkt	4 pkt
chicken	1 lb 2 oz	1½ lb
salt and thyme leaves	¾ t each	1 t each
pepper	¼ t, or to taste	½ t
peas	1½ c	2 c

Seafood Crêpe Filling

MAKES 4 SERVINGS

Prepare ahead and freeze for that extra-special impressive but simple dinner (see Seafood Crêpes, page 111); let frozen filling thaw overnight in the refrigerator.

1 tablespoon plus 1 teaspoon
    margarine
¼ cup minced celery
2 tablespoons minced shallots or
    onion
2 cups sliced mushrooms
2 tablespoons lemon juice

1 tablespoon plus 1 teaspoon dry
    sherry
6 ounces each drained canned crab
    meat and shrimp, chopped
½ teaspoon salt
⅛ teaspoon white pepper

In 12-inch skillet heat margarine over medium heat until bubbly and hot; add celery and shallots (or onion) and sauté until vegetables are soft, about 3 minutes. Add mushrooms, lemon juice, and sherry and cook, stirring occasionally, until most of the liquid has evaporated, about 5 minutes. Stir in seafood and seasonings and cook until heated. Let cool, then divide evenly into plastic freezer bags, label, and freeze for future use.

For Additional Servings Use

	6 servings	8 servings
margarine	2 T	2 T + 2 t
celery	⅓ c + 2 t	½ c
shallots or onions	3 T	¼ c
mushrooms	3 c	4 c
lemon juice	3 T	¼ c
sherry	2 T	2 T + 2 t
crab meat and shrimp	9 oz each	12 oz each
salt	¾ t	1 t
pepper	¼ t	¼ t, or to taste
pan	2-qt saucepan	3-qt saucepan

Italian Bread Four Ways

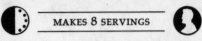

MAKES 8 SERVINGS

Use *one 8-ounce loaf Italian bread* with one of the following spreads:

Onion Spread

½ cup minced onion
2 tablespoons plus 2 teaspoons
   margarine, softened

Garlic-Herb "Butter"

2 tablespoons plus 2 teaspoons
   margarine, softened
¼ teaspoon each oregano leaves
   and basil leaves
⅛ teaspoon each garlic powder and
   onion powder
Dash each salt and crushed red
   pepper

Cheese Spread

¼ cup grated Parmesan cheese
2 tablespoons plus 2 teaspoons
   margarine, softened
⅛ teaspoon each paprika and
   prepared mustard

Anchovy "Butter"

2 tablespoons plus 2 teaspoons
   margarine, softened
1 tablespoon plus 1 teaspoon
   drained canned mashed anchovies
1 teaspoon lemon juice

In small bowl combine ingredients for desired spread, stirring until smooth. Cut loaf of bread in half lengthwise and spread mixture evenly over surface of one cut side. Place bread halves together and wrap entire loaf in heavy-duty foil; freeze.

When ready to use, preheat oven to 350°F.; bake wrapped frozen loaf until bread is hot and spread is melted, 20 to 30 minutes. Slice into 8 equal portions.

Freezer French Toast

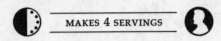

MAKES 4 SERVINGS

Can be frozen for up to 2 weeks.

4 eggs, lightly beaten
2 tablespoons evaporated skimmed
milk
2 teaspoons vanilla extract

4 slices white bread
2 teaspoons vegetable oil or
margarine

In shallow bowl combine eggs, milk, and vanilla. Dip bread slices into egg mixture, coating all sides; let bread soak in mixture until as much liquid as possible has been absorbed.

In 12-inch nonstick skillet, over medium-high heat, heat oil (or margarine); add bread and pour an equal amount of any remaining egg mixture over each slice. Reduce heat and cook until bread is browned on underside; turn slices and brown other side. Transfer toast to a baking sheet; cool slightly, then freeze. Once frozen, wrap toast slices individually or stack and wrap, using 2 sheets of wax paper between each slice to separate. To serve, reheat in toaster or in 350°F. oven.

Serving Suggestions
Just before serving:
1. Top each heated slice with 1 portion Apple Syrup (see page 150).
2. Top each heated slice with 2 teaspoons reduced-calorie fruit-flavored spread (16 calories per 2 teaspoons).
3. Pour 1 tablespoon low-calorie pancake syrup (14 calories per tablespoon) over each heated slice.

For Additional Servings Use

	6 servings	*8 servings*	*12 servings*
eggs	6	8	12
milk	3 T	¼ c	⅓ c + 2 t
vanilla	1 T	1 T + 1 t	2 T
bread	6 slices	8 slices	12 slices
oil or margarine	1 T*	1 T + 1 t*	2 T*

* A 12-inch skillet will accommodate only 4 slices of bread. Therefore, when preparing toast in larger quantities, the browning procedure will have to be repeated 2 or 3 times according to the number of slices of bread being used; each time the skillet is used, heat ½ teaspoon oil (or margarine) per slice of bread to be browned.

Turkey Pot Pie

MAKES 2 SERVINGS, 1 POT PIE EACH

---

2 teaspoons all-purpose flour
¾ cup water
1 packet instant chicken broth and
  seasoning mix
1 medium carrot (3 to 4 ounces),
  thinly sliced
1 tablespoon chopped onion

8 ounces skinned and boned cooked
  turkey, diced
½ cup frozen peas
¼ teaspoon poultry seasoning
Dash pepper
Chilled Basic Pot Pie Dough (see
  page 181)

Advance Preparation

1. In 2-quart saucepan dissolve flour in water; add broth mix and bring to a boil. Add carrot and onion. Reduce heat to low, cover, and cook until carrot slices are tender, about 10 minutes.

2. Add remaining ingredients except dough; cook uncovered, stirring occasionally, for 5 minutes. Divide mixture evenly into two individual casseroles.

3. Roll 1 ball of dough between 2 sheets of wax paper, forming a circle slightly larger than top of casserole. Lift dough onto 1 filled dish. Using a fork, press edges of dough to rim of dish; gently pierce top of dough to allow steam to escape. Repeat procedure; pies can now be wrapped and frozen for future use.

Final Preparation: Preheat oven to 375°F. Bake on baking sheet until crust is lightly browned, 40 to 45 minutes (if pies have not been frozen, bake for 30 to 35 minutes).

For Additional Servings Use

	3 servings	4 servings	6 servings
flour	1 T	1 T + 1 t	2 T
water	1 c + 2 T	1½ c	2¼ c
broth mix	1½ pkt	2 pkt	3 pkt
carrots	1½ medium	2 medium	3 medium
onions	1 T + 1½ t	2 T	3 T
turkey	12 oz	1 lb	1½ lb
peas	¾ c	1 c	1½ c
poultry seasoning	¼ t	½ t	¾ t
pepper	dash	⅛ t	⅛ t, or to taste
dough	3 servings	4 servings	6 servings

Tuna Pot Pie

MAKES 2 SERVINGS, 1 POT PIE EACH

---

1 teaspoon margarine
½ cup chopped scallions (green onions) or onion
¼ cup chopped pimientos
1 cup sliced mushrooms
2 teaspoons all-purpose flour
½ cup prepared instant chicken broth and seasoning mix (prepared according to package directions)

¼ cup each dry sherry and evaporated skimmed milk
1 ounce Cheddar cheese, shredded
2 tablespoons chopped fresh parsley
6 ounces drained canned solid white tuna, flaked
Chilled Basic Pot Pie Dough (see page 181)

Advance Preparation

1. In 9-inch skillet heat margarine over medium heat until bubbly and hot; add scallions (or onion) and pimientos and sauté briefly, about 3 minutes. Add mushrooms and cook, stirring constantly, until most of the liquid has evaporated.

2. Sprinkle flour over vegetables and stir to combine; gradually stir in broth and sherry and cook, stirring constantly, until thickened. Stir in milk, cheese, and parsley and bring to a simmer (*do not boil*); add tuna and stir until thoroughly combined. Divide evenly into two individual casseroles.

3. Follow Step 3 in Turkey Pot Pie recipe (page 188).

Final Preparation: See Turkey Pot Pie recipe.

For Additional Servings Use

	3 servings	4 servings	6 servings
margarine	1½ t	2 t	1 T
scallions or onions	¾ c	1 c	1½ c
pimientos	⅓ c + 2 t	½ c	¾ c
mushrooms	1½ c	2 c	3 c
flour	1 T	1 T + 1 t	2 T
broth	¾ c	1 c	1½ c
sherry and milk	⅓ c + 2 t each	½ c each	¾ c each
cheese	1½ oz	2 oz	3 oz
parsley	3 T	¼ c	⅓ c
tuna	9 oz	12 oz	1 lb 2 oz
dough	3 servings	4 servings	6 servings
skillet	10-inch	12-inch	3-qt saucepan

Beef Pot Pie

MAKES 2 SERVINGS, 1 POT PIE EACH

1 teaspoon vegetable oil
½ cup chopped onion
1 garlic clove, minced
6 ounces broiled beef for stew
   (½-inch cubes)
¾ cup water
½ cup each diced carrot, celery, and
   mushrooms
1 teaspoon tomato paste

1 packet instant beef broth and
   seasoning mix
1 small bay leaf
1 whole clove
⅛ teaspoon ground thyme
Dash pepper
2 teaspoons all-purpose flour
Chilled Cheddar Dough (see
   page 181)

Advance Preparation

1. In 2-quart saucepan heat oil over medium heat; add onion and garlic and sauté until onion is translucent, about 5 minutes. Add remaining ingredients except flour and dough. Cover pan, reduce heat to low, and cook until meat is fork-tender, about 45 minutes.

2. Sprinkle flour over beef mixture and stir to dissolve; cook uncovered, stirring occasionally, until thickened. Remove and discard bay leaf and clove. Divide mixture into two individual casseroles. Follow Step 3 in Turkey Pot Pie recipe (page 188).

Final Preparation: See Turkey Pot Pie recipe.

For Additional Servings Use

	3 servings	4 servings	6 servings
oil	1½ t	2 t	1 T
onions	¾ c	1 c	1½ c
garlic	1½ cloves	2 cloves	3 cloves
beef	9 oz	12 oz	1 lb 2 oz
water	1 c + 2 T	1½ c	2¼ c
carrots, celery, and mushrooms	¾ c each	1 c each	1½ c each
tomato paste	1½ t	2 t	1 T
broth mix	1½ pkt	2 pkt	3 pkt
bay leaves	1 small	1½ small	2 small
cloves	1	2	2
thyme	⅛ t	¼ t	¼ t
pepper	dash	⅛ t	⅛ t, or to taste
flour	1 T	1 T + 1 t	2 T
dough	3 servings	4 servings	6 servings

Veal Chili Pot Pie

MAKES 2 SERVINGS, 1 POT PIE EACH

1 teaspoon vegetable oil
½ cup each chopped onion and
    chopped green bell pepper
2 garlic cloves, minced
10 ounces ground veal
1½ teaspoons chili powder
½ teaspoon each oregano leaves
    and ground cumin

Dash each salt and hot sauce
3 ounces drained canned pinto beans
½ cup canned crushed tomatoes
1 tablespoon plus 1 teaspoon
    tomato paste
Chilled Basic Pot Pie Dough (see
    page 181)

Advance Preparation

1. In 10-inch nonstick skillet heat oil over medium heat; add onion, green pepper, and garlic and sauté until onion is translucent, about 5 minutes.

2. Add veal and seasonings to vegetables and cook, stirring constantly, until meat loses its pink color, about 3 minutes.

3. Add beans, tomatoes, and tomato paste and cook, stirring occasionally, for 5 to 8 minutes longer. Divide mixture evenly into two individual casseroles.

4. Follow Step 3 in Turkey Pot Pie recipe (page 188).

Final Preparation: See Turkey Pot Pie recipe.

For Additional Servings Use

	3 servings	4 servings	6 servings
oil	1½ t	2 t	1 T
onions and peppers	¾ c each	1 c each	1½ c each
garlic	3 cloves	4 cloves	6 cloves
veal	15 oz	1¼ lb	1 lb 14 oz
chili powder	2¼ t	1 T	1 T + 1½ t
oregano leaves and cumin	½ t each	¾ t each	1 t each
salt and hot sauce	dash each	⅛ t each	⅛ to ¼ t each
beans	4½ oz	6 oz	9 oz
tomatoes	¾ c	1 c	1½ c
tomato paste	2 T	2 T + 2 t	¼ c
dough	3 servings	4 servings	6 servings
skillet	12-inch	12-inch	4-qt saucepan

Béchamel (White Sauce)

 MAKES 4 SERVINGS, ABOUT ½ CUP EACH

Handy to have in the freezer for use in other dishes. If you plan on pre-paring a recipe that calls for Béchamel, earlier that day transfer the required number of portions of frozen sauce to the refrigerator and let thaw; the Béchamel will be ready when you are.

2 tablespoons margarine
3 tablespoons all-purpose flour
2 cups skim milk, heated

⅛ teaspoon salt
Dash white pepper
Dash ground nutmeg (optional)

In 1-quart saucepan heat margarine until bubbly and hot; add flour and cook over low heat, stirring constantly, for 3 minutes.

Remove pan from heat; using small wire whisk, gradually stir in milk and continue stirring until mixture is smooth. Add remaining ingredients and cook over medium heat, stirring constantly, until sauce is thickened. Reduce heat to low and cook for 10 minutes longer, stirring occasionally. Let cool, then divide evenly into freezer containers, label, and freeze for future use.

For Additional Servings Use

	6 servings	*8 servings*	*12 servings*
margarine	3 T	¼ c	⅓ c + 2 t
flour	¼ c + 1½ t	⅓ c + 2 t	½ c + 1 T
milk	3 c	1 qt	1½ qt
salt	⅛ t	¼ t	¼ t, or to taste
pepper	dash	⅛ t	⅛ t, or to taste
nutmeg (optional)	dash	⅛ t	⅛ t, or to taste

Fresh Tomato Sauce

MAKES ABOUT 1 QUART

There is nothing like the flavor of homemade tomato sauce. This sauce may be frozen for up to 3 months or refrigerated for up to 2 weeks.

2½ pounds very ripe plum tomatoes, cut into halves
½ cup firmly packed fresh basil leaves

3 garlic cloves, cut into halves
1 teaspoon salt
Dash freshly ground pepper

In 2-quart saucepan combine all ingredients; cover and bring to a boil. Reduce heat and let simmer for 15 to 20 minutes.

Remove sauce from heat and let cool. Remove skin and other solids by pressing mixture through a food mill or coarse sieve into a large bowl. Divide into ¼-cup, ½-cup, and 1-cup freezer containers, label, and freeze; when ready to use, thaw only the amount needed.

For Additional Servings Use

	2 quarts	3 quarts	4 quarts
tomatoes	5 lb	7½ lb	10 lb
basil leaves	¾ c	¾ c	1 c
garlic	4 cloves	5 cloves	6 cloves
salt	2 t	2 t, or to taste	1 T
pepper	⅛ t	⅛ to ¼ t	¼ t

Raisin Biscuits

 MAKES 4 SERVINGS, 1 BISCUIT EACH

A quick-energy snack for people-on-the-go. Also a favorite with children.

1½ ounces bran flakes with raisins
cereal
⅓ cup plus 2 teaspoons self-rising
flour
2 tablespoons raisins

1 tablespoon firmly packed brown
sugar
¼ cup skim milk
1 tablespoon margarine, melted

Preheat oven to 400°F. In a small bowl combine cereal, flour, raisins, and brown sugar, stirring with a fork until well mixed; add milk and margarine and stir until thoroughly combined.

Spray a baking sheet with nonstick cooking spray. Drop batter by heaping tablespoonsful onto sheet, making 4 equal biscuits and leaving a space of about 2 inches between each. Bake until golden brown, 10 to 12 minutes. Remove biscuits to a wire rack and let cool. Serve immediately or wrap individually and freeze until ready to use; thaw or reheat as directed in Peanut Butter Muffins recipe, page 195.

Serving Suggestion—Just before serving, dust each biscuit with ¼ teaspoon confectioners' sugar (an easy method for doing this is to press sugar through a mesh tea strainer).

For Additional Servings Use

	6 servings	8 servings
cereal	2¼ oz	3 oz
flour	½ c + 1 T	¾ c
raisins	3 T	¼ c
sugar	1 T + 1½ t	2 T
milk	⅓ c + 2 t	½ c
margarine	1 T + 1½ t	2 T

Peanut Butter Muffins

MAKES 4 SERVINGS, 1 MUFFIN EACH

Frozen muffins can be thawed at room temperature or reheated in oven at 300°F. for about 10 minutes. Good as a breakfast entrée as well as a dessert or snack.

⅓ cup plus 2 teaspoons self-rising flour
1 tablespoon superfine sugar
¼ cup skim milk

1 egg, lightly beaten
3 tablespoons chunky-style peanut butter (at room temperature)
1 teaspoon margarine, melted

Preheat oven to 400°F. Into bowl sift together flour and sugar; add remaining ingredients and stir until combined (batter will be lumpy). *Do not beat or overmix.*

Spray four 2½-inch-diameter muffin pan cups with nonstick cooking spray; fill each with an equal amount of the batter (each cup will be about ⅔ full). Partially fill remaining cups with water (this will prevent pan from warping and/or burning); bake until muffins are golden brown, about 20 minutes. Remove muffins to wire rack and let cool (carefully drain off water before removing muffins from pan; remember, it will be boiling hot). Serve cooled muffins or wrap individually and freeze until ready to use.

Serving Suggestion—Just before serving, spread each muffin with 1 teaspoon reduced-calorie fruit-flavored spread (16 calories per 2 teaspoons).

For Additional Servings Use

	8 servings	12 servings
flour	¾ c	1 c + 2 T
sugar	2 T	3 T
milk	½ c	¾ c
eggs	2	3
peanut butter	⅓ c + 2 t	½ c + 1 T
margarine	2 t	1 T

Tropical Muffins

MAKES 12 SERVINGS, 1 MUFFIN EACH

It's handy to have these in the freezer when unexpected company drops in for coffee. Thaw or reheat as directed in Peanut Butter Muffins, page 195.

2¼ cups all-purpose flour
¼ cup granulated sugar
1 tablespoon double-acting baking powder
⅓ cup plus 2 teaspoons unsalted margarine

1½ cups canned crushed pineapple (no sugar added)
1 teaspoon vanilla extract
½ teaspoon imitation coconut flavor

Preheat oven to 375°F. In medium mixing bowl combine flour, sugar, and baking powder; with a pastry blender, or 2 knives used scissors-fashion, cut in margarine until mixture resembles coarse meal. Add remaining ingredients and stir just until mixture forms a sticky dough and leaves sides of bowl (*do not overmix*).

Spray twelve 2½-inch-diameter muffin pan cups with nonstick cooking spray; spoon an equal amount of pineapple mixture into each cup. Bake until muffins are golden brown, 30 to 35 minutes. Remove muffins to a wire rack and let cool. Serve immediately or wrap individually and freeze until ready to use.

Lace Cookie Cones

MAKES 6 SERVINGS, 1 CONE EACH

This recipe may be doubled.

2 tablespoons firmly packed light
  brown sugar
2 tablespoons margarine, melted
1 tablespoon light corn syrup

½ teaspoon vanilla extract
¼ cup plus 1½ teaspoons
  all-purpose flour

1. Preheat oven to 350°F. In small bowl combine sugar, margarine, syrup, and vanilla, stirring until smooth; add flour and stir until blended.

2. Lightly spray 14 x 17-inch nonstick baking sheet with nonstick cooking spray; using a 1-tablespoon measure and half of batter, drop batter onto sheet, forming 3 equal cookies and leaving a space of about 6 inches between each. Using your fingertips, carefully flatten each cookie into a ¼-inch-thick circle. Bake until golden brown, 5 to 6 minutes (batter will spread to form thin cookies, each about 5 inches in diameter).

3. Remove baking sheet from oven and let cookies cool until slightly firm, 1 to 2 minutes. Using a pancake turner, carefully remove cookies from sheet; shape each into a cone by wrapping it around the handle of a wooden spoon (if cookie becomes too firm to shape, reheat in oven for 15 to 20 seconds.) Transfer cones to wire rack, seam-side down; let cool.

4. Repeat Steps 2 and 3, using remaining batter and making 3 more cones.

5. Transfer cooled cones to a freezer container and freeze until ready to use (or store in an airtight container in the refrigerator).

Serving Suggestions
Just before serving:
1. Fill each cone with ¾ ounce vanilla dietary frozen dessert.
2. Lay each cone in a dessert dish and fill with ½ cup blueberries; top each portion of berries with 1 tablespoon thawed frozen dairy whipped topping.
3. Fill each cone with 2 tablespoons prepared whipped topping mix (8 calories per tablespoon).

Pineapple Upside-Down Cake

MAKES 8 SERVINGS

Have this in your freezer for those busy days when you'd like to serve a special dessert but just don't have time to fuss, or for unexpected drop-in-for-dinner (or coffee) company; to serve, let thaw at room temperature.

2 tablespoons plus 2 teaspoons unsalted margarine, divided

2 tablespoons granulated brown sugar

6 canned pineapple slices (no sugar added), drained

½ cup frozen pitted dark sweet cherries (no sugar added), thawed

1½ cups cake flour

1 tablespoon double-acting baking powder

¼ teaspoon salt

2 tablespoons granulated white sugar

2 large eggs

½ cup skim milk

1 teaspoon vanilla extract

1. Preheat oven to 350°F. Spray 8 x 8 x 2-inch baking pan with non-stick cooking spray. In small bowl combine 1 tablespoon plus 1 teaspoon margarine with the brown sugar; dot bottom of pan with mixture. Using paper towels, pat pineapple slices and cherries dry and arrange fruit in bottom of pan; set aside.

2. Onto sheet of wax paper or into small bowl sift together flour, baking powder, and salt; set aside.

3. In medium mixing bowl cream remaining 1 tablespoon plus 1 teaspoon margarine with white sugar; add eggs and, using electric mixer, beat until thoroughly combined. Add milk, then beat in sifted flour, ⅓ at a time, and continue beating until thoroughly combined; beat in vanilla.

4. Pour batter over fruit in baking pan; bake in middle of center oven rack for 35 to 40 minutes (until top is lightly browned and a cake tester, inserted in center, comes out clean).

5. Transfer pan to wire rack and let cake cool in pan; invert cake onto serving platter. Serve immediately or freeze for future use.

6. To freeze, cut cake in half, then cut each half into quarters; wrap each piece in plastic freezer wrap, label, and freeze for future use.

Tortoni

MAKES 4 SERVINGS, 1 TORTONI EACH

Easy to prepare and simple to serve . . . keep this on hand for a delicious dessert or snack.

1 tablespoon plus 1 teaspoon
  granulated sugar
1 tablespoon water
1 egg white (from large egg), at
  room temperature
Dash each salt and cream of tartar

¼ cup thawed frozen dairy
  whipped topping
⅛ teaspoon almond extract
2 graham crackers (2½-inch
  squares), made into fine crumbs

In small metal measuring cup, or other small flameproof container, combine sugar and water; cook over low heat until sugar is dissolved and becomes a thin syrup (coats spoon). Turn off heat but leave cup on burner to keep warm.

In small bowl beat egg white with salt and cream of tartar until stiff peaks form; continue beating and slowly pour sugar syrup into beaten white. Fold whipped topping and extract into egg white mixture.

Line each of 4 cups of a muffin pan with a 2½-inch-diameter paper baking cup or paper soufflé cup and spoon an equal amount of the whipped topping mixture into each; using a rubber scraper, gently level and smooth tops. Sprinkle each portion with an equal amount of the graham cracker crumbs. Cover pan with plastic wrap and place in freezer; freeze for at least 30 minutes before serving.*

* Tortoni can be kept for several weeks in the freezer. Once frozen, remove cups from muffin pan and wrap each individually in plastic wrap; return to freezer until ready to serve.

For Additional Servings Use

	8 servings	12 servings
sugar	2 T + 2 t	¼ c
water	2 T	3 T
egg whites (from large eggs)	2	3
salt and cream of tartar	⅛ t each	⅛ t each
whipped topping	½ c	¾ c
extract	¼ t	¼ t, or to taste
graham crackers	4	6

Rum-Raisin "Ice Cream"

MAKES 4 SERVINGS

In cup or small bowl soak ¼ *cup raisins* in warm water to cover until plumped. While raisins are soaking, in another bowl soften *12 ounces vanilla dietary frozen dessert*. Drain raisins and add to softened dessert along with *1 teaspoon rum extract;* stir to combine. Spoon half of mixture into each of 2 freezer-safe ice cream or dessert dishes; cover with plastic wrap and freeze until hard (or cover bowl, freeze until "ice cream" is hard, and scoop into dishes just before serving).

Serving Suggestions
Just before serving:
1. Sprinkle 1 teaspoon lightly toasted shredded coconut over each portion of "ice cream."
2. Top each portion of "ice cream" with 1 tablespoon thawed frozen dairy whipped topping.

For Additional Servings Use

	6 servings	8 servings
raisins	⅓ c + 2 t	½ c
frozen dessert	18 oz	24 oz
rum extract	1½ t	2 t

Vanilla Fudge Swirl

MAKES 4 SERVINGS, ABOUT ½ CUP EACH

In 2-quart mixing bowl soften *12 ounces vanilla dietary frozen dessert;* using an electric mixer at low speed, beat until smooth. Add *¼ cup reduced-calorie chocolate topping (16 calories per tablespoon)* and stir slightly through dessert to create a swirl effect (do not combine). Divide mixture into 4 freezer-safe parfait glasses; cover with plastic wrap and freeze until firm (or cover bowl with wrap, freeze until mixture is firm, and scoop into glasses just before serving). Top each portion with *1 tablespoon thawed frozen dairy whipped topping.*

For Additional Servings Use

	6 servings	*8 servings*
frozen dessert	18 oz	24 oz
chocolate topping	⅓ c + 2 t	½ c
whipped topping	1 tablespoon each serving	1 tablespoon each serving

Mango Sherbet

 MAKES 4 SERVINGS, ABOUT ¾ CUP EACH

2 very ripe small mangoes, pared,
    pitted, and cut into small pieces
½ cup evaporated skimmed milk
1 tablespoon plus 1 teaspoon
    granulated sugar

2 teaspoons lemon juice
¼ teaspoon vanilla extract

In blender container combine all ingredients and process until smooth. Divide mixture into 4 freezer-safe dessert dishes (or into 2 freezer trays); cover with plastic wrap and freeze until firm. Allow to soften slightly before serving. If trays are used, divide into dessert dishes just before serving.

For Additional Servings Use

	6 servings	8 servings
mangoes	3 small	4 small
milk	¾ c	1 c
sugar	2 T	2 T + 2 t
lemon juice	1 T	1 T + 1 t
vanilla	¼ t	½ t

Refrigerator Ready

◆◆

Entrées
Bacon and Egg Salad
Seasoned Bean 'n' Egg Salad
Tuna-Macaroni Salad
Curried Rice Salad

Salads and Salad Dressings
Potato-Egg Salad
Macaroni Salad
Confetti Rice Salad
Oriental Ginger Slaw
Spaghetti Squash Slaw
Fresh Mushroom Salad
Tomato-Onion Salad with Basil Dressing
Buttermilk-Herb Dressing
Sweet Herb Vinaigrette

Sauces
Salsa
Sweet and Sour Barbecue Sauce

Relishes
Mixed Fruit Chutney
Pepper Relish

Desserts and Snacks
Jellied Apple
Melon Mélange
Pineapple Cheesecake
Chocolate Fudge

Because advance preparation and on-hand staples are two keys to making quickly prepared but delicious meals, the refrigerator rates as one of the most essential of all appliances. It makes it possible for you to keep fresh staples on hand, to stock up on supermarket specials, and to prepare and store dishes ahead of time.

HEAD START

Whenever you're planning to prepare a meal from scratch, consider which of the ingredients you are preparing for today's dinner could be used at some future date. Then prepare extra to refrigerate or freeze. For instance, some of the most necessary but time-consuming cooking steps include chopping, weighing, measuring, etc., so take some time on unhurried days to prepare for future occasions, when having precut, premeasured foods readily available may be a boon to a harried schedule. For instance:

• Chop, mince, and dice various vegetables. Place measured amounts in airtight containers; cover, label, and refrigerate. The vegetables will be ready for use in casseroles, salads, soups, etc., and will markedly cut down preparation time.

• Peel and slice a melon, cut it into small pieces, place in an airtight container, and refrigerate for use in salads and desserts or for a snack. It can be stored for up to two days.

• Place fresh parsley or basil into a jar or glass of water, stem ends down. Cover the leaves with a plastic bag and refrigerate. The herb will keep for almost two weeks.

MAKE DOUBLE

You can also get twice as much mileage from your efforts by cooking double meals and refrigerating (or freezing) half. To avoid that leftover look, transform the second meal of chicken, meat, or seafood into an easy casserole or salad.

STORAGE

Life in the kitchen flows more smoothly if certain staples like skim milk, plain lowfat yogurt, eggs, cheeses, fruits, and vegetables are always on hand. To maintain freshness, it's important to know how to refrigerate these foods properly. When storing foods in the refrigerator, remember that the *back* of the shelves tends to stay colder and that areas under the light may be warmer.

For reasons of food safety, flavor, texture, and nutrition, arrange items in the refrigerator so that the oldest ones are used first. But remember that refrigeration only *retards* the growth of bacteria; it doesn't destroy them. Therefore, foods cannot be refrigerated for an indefinite period of time. *If the freshness of a food is questionable, discard it.*

When you are packaging foods (other than fresh produce) for refrigerator storage, wrap them securely in foil or plastic wrap, or put them into plastic containers, and cover. This helps avoid spillage and prevents the transfer of odors from one food to another. Uncovered foods also tend to dry out, particularly in a frost-free refrigerator. Label containers of foods that are not easily identifiable.

Milk products, meats, and any leftovers should be stored in the coldest area of the refrigerator. For this reason, it's best to avoid storing cheeses and margarine in the door compartments.

Eggs should be kept, broad-end up, in the cartons in which they are purchased or in the refrigerator egg compartment.

Fresh fruits and vegetables should be kept in the vegetable crisper (hydrator drawer), which provides the proper moisture and temperature control. The hydrator functions best if it is kept at least two-thirds full. If produce is refrigerated in a plastic bag, it should be open or perforated to allow circulation of air.

Most fruits keep from several days to a week; apples, grapefruit, oranges, and watermelon stay fresh for considerably longer. Even bananas can be stored in the refrigerator. The skin will turn black, but the fruit inside will remain fresh for three to six days. Fruits such as berries, grapes, and nectarines should be used as soon as possible.

It helps to have an assortment of fresh seasonal vegetables on hand; most will keep well in the crisper for at least a week.

Note: Some produce should *not* be refrigerated. This includes eggplant, sweet potatoes, and winter squash, which require a temperature of approximately 60°F. If the temperature falls below 50°F., the resultant chilling may injure these vegetables. Don't refrigerate onions, potatoes, or shallots, either. They should be kept in loosely woven or open-mesh bags and stored in a dark area at room temperature or slightly cooler.

EFFICIENCY

To serve you well, the refrigerator needs some special care from you. For optimum performance as well as energy conservation, keep these facts in mind.

• Refrigerator temperature should always be between 38° and 42°F.; compartments in which meat and fish are stored should be 35° to 40°F. Check periodically with a freezer-refrigerator thermometer.

• Cleanliness counts. The refrigerator should be kept as clean as possible, both inside and out. This includes the motor and refrigerating unit, which should be kept free of lint and dirt.

• Gaskets (the rubber insulation around the door) should be *pliable* in order to prevent air from seeping into the refrigerator and affecting the temperature. If the gaskets become too hard, their rigidity causes gaps to develop and lowers the efficiency of your appliance.

• Proper air circulation requires "breathing room." Don't cover the shelves or stack foods, since this inhibits the circulation of air within the unit.

• Cool foods before refrigerating. Putting hot foods into your refrigerator makes it work harder and can adversely affect foods you are trying to keep well chilled.

Bacon and Egg Salad

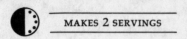 MAKES 2 SERVINGS

4 ounces diced cooked Canadian-
style bacon
2 eggs, hard-cooked and chopped
½ cup diced celery
2 tablespoons chopped scallion
(green onion)
1 tablespoon mayonnaise

1 teaspoon each lemon juice and
Dijon-style mustard
Dash each salt and pepper
4 chilled iceberg, romaine, or
loose-leafed lettuce leaves
6 chilled cherry tomatoes, cut into
halves

In 1-quart bowl combine all ingredients except lettuce and tomatoes; cover and refrigerate until chilled.

On serving platter arrange lettuce leaves; spoon bacon mixture onto lettuce and surround with cherry tomatoes.

For Additional Servings Use

	3 servings	4 servings	6 servings
bacon	6 oz	8 oz	12 oz
eggs	3	4	6
celery	¾ c	1 c	1½ c
scallions	3 T	¼ c	⅓ c + 2 t
mayonnaise	1 T + 1½ t	2 T	3 T
lemon juice and mustard	1½ t each	2 t each	1 T each
salt and pepper	dash each	⅛ t each	⅛ t each
lettuce	6 leaves	8 leaves	12 leaves
cherry tomatoes	9	12	18

Seasoned Bean 'n' Egg Salad

MAKES 2 SERVINGS

6 ounces drained canned white
  kidney beans (cannellini beans)
4 pitted black olives, sliced
1 tablespoon each minced red onion,
  chopped fresh parsley, and
  lemon juice
2 teaspoons chopped pimiento

1 teaspoon olive oil
Dash each garlic powder, salt,
  pepper, and crumbled mint flakes
1 cup shredded lettuce, chilled
2 large eggs, hard-cooked and
  chilled
1 medium tomato, chilled

In bowl combine beans, olives, onion, parsley, lemon juice, pimiento, oil, and seasonings, mixing well; cover and chill for at least 30 minutes.

To serve, chill 2 salad plates; line each chilled plate with ½ cup shredded lettuce and top each portion with an equal amount of bean mixture. Cut each egg into 6 wedges and the tomato into 12 wedges; alternate 6 egg and tomato wedges around each portion of bean mixture.

For Additional Servings Use

	3 servings	4 servings	6 servings
kidney beans	9 oz	12 oz	1 lb 2 oz
olives	6	8	12
onions, parsley, and lemon juice	1 T + 1½ t each	2 T each	3 T each
pimientos	1 T	1 T + 1 t	2 T
oil	1½ t	2 t	1 T
garlic powder, salt, pepper, and mint flakes	dash each	⅛ t each	⅛ t each, or to taste
lettuce	1½ c	2 c	3 c
eggs	3 large	4 large	6 large
tomatoes	1½ medium, cut into 18 wedges	2 medium, each cut into 12 wedges	3 medium, each cut into 12 wedges

Tuna-Macaroni Salad

MAKES 2 SERVINGS

---

2 cups broccoli florets
2 eggs
1 medium tomato, chilled
1½ cups cooked small shell
   macaroni, chilled
4 ounces drained canned tuna, flaked

8 thin red onion rings
4 pitted black olives, cut into
   halves
2 servings Buttermilk-Herb
   Dressing (see page 219)

Advance Preparation

In 1-quart saucepan bring to a boil just enough water to cover broccoli; add broccoli and let boil until tender-crisp, 6 to 8 minutes (if preferred, broccoli can be steamed for 8 to 10 minutes). Drain florets and transfer to container; cover and refrigerate until chilled.

In small saucepan place eggs in enough cold water to cover eggs by about 1 inch; over high heat bring water just to a boil. Cover pan and remove from heat; let stand for about 17 minutes. Remove eggs from water and refrigerate until chilled.

Final Preparation

Remove shells from eggs and cut each egg into quarters. Cut tomato into 8 equal wedges.

In large serving bowl combine broccoli, macaroni, tuna, and onion rings and toss lightly; decoratively arrange tomato wedges, egg quarters, and olive halves over mixture. Serve with dressing on the side.

For Additional Servings Use

	3 servings	4 servings	6 servings
broccoli	3 c	4 c	6 c
eggs	3	4	6
tomatoes	1½ medium, cut into 12 wedges	2 medium, each cut into 8 wedges	3 medium, each cut into 8 wedges
macaroni	2¼ c	3 c	4½ c
tuna	6 oz	8 oz	12 oz
red onions	12 rings	16 rings	24 rings
olives	6	8	12
dressing	3 servings	4 servings	6 servings

Curried Rice Salad

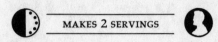

MAKES 2 SERVINGS

Turn that leftover chicken into a delicious meal-in-minutes.

1 cup buttermilk (made from skim milk)
1 tablespoon mayonnaise
1 teaspoon granulated sugar
½ teaspoon curry powder
¼ teaspoon salt
Dash white pepper
8 ounces skinned and boned cooked chicken, diced

1 cup cooked long-grain rice
½ cup chopped tomato
¼ cup chopped red bell pepper
1 tablespoon each chopped scallion (green onion) and chopped fresh parsley

In medium bowl combine first 6 ingredients; add remaining ingredients and toss lightly. Cover and refrigerate until chilled.

For Additional Servings Use

	3 servings	4 servings	6 servings
buttermilk	1½ c	2 c	3 c
mayonnaise	1 T + 1½ t	2 T	3 T
sugar	1½ t	2 t	1 T
curry powder	¾ t	1 t	1½ t
salt	¼ t	½ t	¾ t
pepper	dash	⅛ t	⅛ to ¼ t
chicken	12 oz	1 lb	1½ lb
rice	1½ c	2 c	3 c
tomatoes	¾ c	1 c	1½ c
red peppers	⅓ c + 2 t	½ c	¾ c
scallions and parsley	1 T + 1½ t each	2 T each	3 T each

Potato-Egg Salad

MAKES 2 SERVINGS

6 ounces peeled cooked potatoes,
   cooled and cut into cubes
1 egg, hard-cooked and diced
¼ cup diced celery
1 tablespoon each minced onion and
   chopped fresh parsley

2 tablespoons plain lowfat yogurt
1 tablespoon mayonnaise
½ teaspoon cider vinegar
¼ teaspoon salt
Dash each pepper and paprika

In bowl combine potatoes, egg, celery, onion, and parsley. In small bowl combine remaining ingredients, mixing thoroughly. Add yogurt mixture to potato mixture and toss gently to coat; cover and refrigerate until ready to serve. Toss again just before serving.

For Additional Servings Use

	4 servings	*6 servings*	*8 servings*
potatoes	12 oz	1 lb 2 oz	1½ lb
eggs	2	3	4
celery	½ c	¾ c	1 c
onions and parsley	2 T each	3 T each	¼ c each
yogurt	¼ c	⅓ c + 2 t	½ c
mayonnaise	2 T	3 T	¼ c
vinegar	1 t	1½ t	2 t
salt	½ t	¾ t	1 t
pepper and paprika	dash each	dash to ⅛ t each	⅛ t each

Macaroni Salad

¼ cup buttermilk (made from skim milk)
1 tablespoon mayonnaise
½ teaspoon granulated sugar
¼ teaspoon each salt and prepared mustard

Dash each garlic powder and pepper
1½ cups cooked elbow macaroni
¼ cup each chopped celery and tomato
2 tablespoons each chopped red bell pepper and scallion (green onion)

In bowl combine milk, mayonnaise, sugar, and seasonings, stirring until smooth and well mixed. Add remaining ingredients and toss to combine; cover and refrigerate until ready to serve (at least 1 hour).

For Additional Servings Use

	3 servings	4 servings	6 servings
buttermilk	⅓ c + 2 t	½ c	¾ c
mayonnaise	1 T + 1½ t	2 T	3 T
sugar	¾ t	1 t	1½ t
salt and mustard	¼ t each	½ t each	¾ t each
garlic powder and pepper	dash each	dash each	dash to ⅛ t each
macaroni	2¼ c	3 c	4½ c
celery and tomatoes	⅓ c + 2 t each	½ c each	¾ c each
red peppers and scallions	3 T each	¼ c each	⅓ c + 2 t each

Confetti Rice Salad

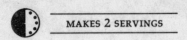

MAKES 2 SERVINGS

¼ cup each diced celery and green bell pepper
1 tablespoon each chopped pimiento and chopped fresh parsley
2 teaspoons minced red onion
1 teaspoon each olive oil and white wine vinegar

¼ teaspoon each salt, crumbled oregano leaves, and crumbled basil leaves
Dash pepper
1 cup cooked long-grain rice, chilled

In small bowl combine all ingredients except rice and toss until thoroughly mixed; add rice and toss to combine. Cover and refrigerate for at least 30 minutes before serving.

For Additional Servings Use _____

	3 servings	*4 servings*	*6 servings*
celery and green peppers	⅓ c + 2 t each	½ c each	¾ c each
pimientos and parsley	1 T + 1½ t each	2 T each	3 T each
onions	1 T	1 T + 1 t	2 T
oil and vinegar	1½ t each	2 t each	1 T each
salt, oregano leaves, and basil leaves	¼ t each	½ t each	¾ t each
pepper	dash	⅛ t	⅛ t, or to taste
rice	1½ c	2 c	3 c

Zucchini-
Pepper Slaw

Salmon Loaf

Sweet and Sour
Spinach-Mushroom
Salad

Spiced Orange Salad

Southern Stew

Mixed Fruit Chutney (left)

Pepper Relish (right)

Cran-Orange Relish (bottom)

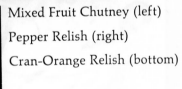

House Special Soup
(left)

Oven-Fried Chicken
with Orange-
Teriyaki Sauce (right)

Oriental Vegetable
Stir-Fry (bottom)

Shrimp and Linguini
with Basil-Caper Sauce (top)

Spaghetti Carbonara (left)

Creamy Pasta
with Broccoli (right)

Meat Loaf Wellington

Spaghetti Squash Slaw

Veal Patties
in Parsley Sauce

Asparagus with
Sesame "Butter"

Pizza Pie

Skillet Broccoli Soufflé

Rolled Stuffed Flounder Fillets

Tortoni (top left)

Peanut Butter Bonbons
(top right)

Chocolate Fudge (center)

"Orange-Crème"
Stuffed Prunes (bottom)

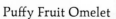

Puffy Fruit Omelet

Onion Popovers
Sesame Breadsticks (left)
Mexican Corn Bread (right)

Lace Cookie Cones
"Linzer Tart" Cookies (left)
Rugalach
(Raisin Crescents) (right)

Oriental Ginger Slaw

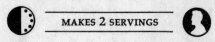

MAKES 2 SERVINGS

½ cup tomato juice
1 teaspoon each minced pared ginger
    root and teriyaki sauce
½ teaspoon granulated sugar

½ small garlic clove, mashed
1 tablespoon peanut or vegetable oil
2 cups shredded green cabbage
½ cup grated carrot

To prepare dressing, in blender container combine juice, ginger root, teriyaki sauce, sugar, and garlic and process until smooth. Remove center plastic cap from blender cover and, with motor running, slowly drizzle in oil, processing until well mixed.

In bowl combine cabbage and grated carrot; add dressing and toss well. Cover and chill until ready to serve.

For Additional Servings Use

	3 servings	4 servings	6 servings
tomato juice	¾ c	1 c	1½ c
ginger root	1 to 1½ t	2 t	2 t to 1 T
teriyaki sauce	1½ t	2 t	1 T
sugar	¾ t	1 t	1½ t
garlic	½ small clove	1 small clove	1½ small cloves
oil	1 T + 1½ t	2 T	3 T
cabbage	3 c	4 c	6 c
carrots	¾ c	1 c	1½ c

Spaghetti Squash Slaw

MAKES 4 SERVINGS

Squash can be baked in advance and refrigerated until ready to use.

2-pound spaghetti squash*
6 cherry tomatoes, cut into halves
½ cup diced red or green bell
  pepper
2 tablespoons chopped red onion or
  sliced scallion (green onion)

2 tablespoons each rice vinegar†
  and olive or vegetable oil
1 teaspoon salt
1 small garlic clove, mashed
½ teaspoon oregano leaves
Dash freshly ground pepper

Advance Preparation
Using the tines of a fork, pierce squash in several places; place in baking pan and bake at 350°F. until tender, about 1 hour. Use immediately or let cool slightly, then refrigerate until ready to use.

Final Preparation
Lay squash on its side; using a long sharp knife, horizontally cut off top ⅓ of squash. Discard seeds and scoop out pulp from top and bottom shells; transfer pulp to a large bowl and reserve bottom shell.

Add tomato, red (or green) pepper, and onion (or scallion) to pulp and toss to combine; add remaining ingredients and toss well. Spoon mixture into reserved shell; cover and chill overnight or at least 2 hours.

---

* A 2-pound spaghetti squash will yield about 3 cups cooked squash.
† Wine vinegar or cider vinegar can be substituted for the rice vinegar.

Fresh Mushroom Salad

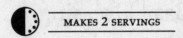

MAKES 2 SERVINGS

A good appetizer as well as a side dish.

1 tablespoon olive oil
1½ teaspoons lemon juice
¼ teaspoon each salt and oregano
   leaves
Dash pepper

2 cups sliced mushrooms
¼ cup thinly sliced scallions
   (green onions)
4 romaine lettuce leaves

In bowl thoroughly combine oil, lemon juice, and seasonings; add mushrooms and scallions and toss to coat. Cover bowl and refrigerate until chilled.

   To serve, chill a serving platter; line chilled platter with lettuce leaves. Toss salad again and serve on lettuce.

For Additional Servings Use

	3 servings	*4 servings*	*6 servings*
oil	1 T + 1½ t	2 T	3 T
lemon juice	2¼ t	1 T	1 T + 1½ t
salt and oregano leaves	¼ t each	½ t each	¾ t each
pepper	dash	dash	dash to ⅛ t
mushrooms	3 c	4 c	6 c
scallions	½ c + 2 t	½ c	¾ c
lettuce	6 leaves	8 leaves	12 leaves

Tomato-Onion Salad with Basil Dressing

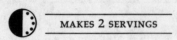 MAKES 2 SERVINGS

1 chilled large beefsteak tomato (about 9 ounces), cut into ¼-inch-thick slices
½ cup thinly sliced red onion
1 tablespoon olive oil
1½ teaspoons lemon juice or wine vinegar
1½ teaspoons finely chopped fresh basil or ½ teaspoon dried

½ garlic clove, minced
⅛ teaspoon salt
Dash pepper
Garnish: 1 tablespoon chopped fresh Italian (flat-leaf) parsley and 2 teaspoons thinly sliced scallion (green onion)

On round serving platter arrange tomato and onion slices in circular pattern, alternating and overlapping slices.

In small bowl thoroughly combine remaining ingredients except garnish; pour dressing over tomato and onion slices and sprinkle with parsley and scallion. Cover platter with plastic wrap and refrigerate until ready to serve.

For Additional Servings Use

	3 servings	4 servings	6 servings
tomatoes	1½ large	2 large	3 large
onions	¾ c	1 c	1½ c
oil	1 T + 1½ t	2 T	3 T
lemon juice or vinegar	2¼ t	1 T	1 T + 1½ t
basil	2¼ t fresh or ¾ t dried	1 T fresh or 1 t dried	1 T + 1½ t fresh or 1½ t dried
garlic	½ clove	1 clove	1½ cloves
salt	⅛ t	¼ t	¼ t, or to taste
pepper	dash	dash	⅛ t
parsley	1 T	2 T	2 T
scallions	1 T	1 T	2 T

Buttermilk-Herb Dressing

 MAKES 2 SERVINGS, ABOUT ½ CUP EACH

Good as a dip, too.

1 cup buttermilk (made from
  skim milk)
1 tablespoon each mayonnaise and
  lemon juice
½ teaspoon each salt, granulated
  sugar, and prepared mustard

¼ teaspoon each oregano leaves
  and basil leaves
½ garlic clove, minced, or ⅛
  teaspoon garlic powder
Dash pepper

In small bowl combine all ingredients, stirring well to mix thoroughly.
Transfer to container, cover, and refrigerate until ready to use. Stir again
just before serving.

For Additional Servings Use

	3 servings	*4 servings*	*6 servings*
buttermilk	1½ c	2 c	3 c
mayonnaise and lemon juice	1 T + 1½ t each	2 T each	3 T each
salt, sugar, and mustard	¾ t each	1 t each	1½ t each
oregano leaves and basil leaves	¼ t each	½ t each	¾ t each
garlic	½ clove or ⅛ t powder	1 clove or ¼ t powder	1½ cloves or ¼ t powder
pepper	dash	⅛ t	⅛ t, or to taste

Sweet Herb Vinaigrette

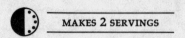

MAKES 2 SERVINGS

1 tablespoon olive oil
2 teaspoons white wine vinegar
1 teaspoon fresh basil leaves or
  ¼ teaspoon dried
½ teaspoon each lemon juice and
  Dijon-style mustard

¼ teaspoon granulated sugar
Dash each salt, pepper, garlic
  powder, and onion powder

In blender container combine all ingredients and process on low speed until thoroughly blended, scraping down sides of container as necessary. Transfer to jar that has tight-fitting cover or refrigerator container; cover and refrigerate until ready to use. Just before serving, shake or stir well.

For Additional Servings Use

	3 servings	4 servings	6 servings
oil	1 T + 1½ t	2 T	3 T
vinegar	1 T	1 T + 1 t	2 T
basil	1½ t fresh or ¼ t dried	2 t fresh or ½ t dried	1 T fresh or ¾ t dried
lemon juice and mustard	¾ t each	1 t each	1½ t each
sugar	¼ t + ⅛ t	½ t	¾ t
salt, pepper, garlic powder, and onion powder	dash each	⅛ t each	⅛ t each, or to taste

Salsa

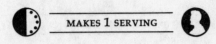

MAKES 1 SERVING

Our version of Mexican spicy tomato sauce. Try it with rice, tacos, or eggs as they do south of the border.

1 teaspoon vegetable oil
2 tablespoons each diced onion and
   green bell pepper
½ cup canned crushed tomatoes
½ teaspoon chopped canned green
   chili peppers

⅛ teaspoon garlic powder
Dash salt
1 to 2 drops hot sauce

In small saucepan heat oil over medium heat; add onion and bell pepper and sauté until onion is translucent. Reduce heat, add remaining ingredients, and let simmer until sauce thickens slightly, 5 to 6 minutes. Use immediately or let cool, transfer to container, cover, and refrigerate until ready to use.

For Additional Servings Use

	2 servings	3 servings	4 servings
oil	2 t	1 T	1 T + 1 t
onions and green peppers	¼ c each	⅓ c + 2 t each	½ c each
tomatoes	1 c	1½ c	2 c
chili peppers	½ t	¾ t	¾ t
garlic powder	⅛ t	¼ t	¼ t
salt	⅛ t	⅛ t	¼ t
hot sauce	to taste	to taste	to taste
Method:	When preparing more than 1 serving, it may take slightly longer for sauce to thicken; increase simmering time accordingly.		

Sweet and Sour Barbecue Sauce

 MAKES 2 SERVINGS, ABOUT ¼ CUP EACH

May be served warm or at room temperature. This is excellent with poultry, veal, beef, or fish.

½ cup canned sliced peaches (no sugar added)
1 tablespoon rice vinegar
2 teaspoons apricot preserves

1½ teaspoons teriyaki or soy sauce
½ teaspoon firmly packed brown sugar
⅛ teaspoon garlic powder

In blender container combine all ingredients and process until smooth. Pour mixture into small nonstick saucepan and bring to a boil. Reduce heat and cook, stirring occasionally, until thickened, about 5 minutes. Use immediately or let cool slightly, then transfer to container; cover and refrigerate for future use.

For Additional Servings Use

	3 servings	4 servings	6 servings
peaches	¾ c	1 c	1½ c
vinegar	1 T + 1½ t	2 T	3 T
preserves	1 T	1 T + 1 t	2 T
teriyaki or soy sauce	2¼ t	1 T	1 T + 1½ t
sugar	¾ t	1 t	1½ t
garlic powder	⅛ t	¼ t	¼ t

Mixed Fruit Chutney

 MAKES 2 SERVINGS, ABOUT 3 TABLESPOONS EACH

Delicious served warm or chilled with chicken or ham.

4 dried apricot halves, diced
2 tablespoons each raisins, diced
   onion, and water
1½ teaspoons firmly packed brown
   sugar

1 teaspoon cider vinegar
¼ teaspoon ground cinnamon
Dash salt

In small saucepan combine all ingredients and bring to a boil. Reduce heat, cover, and let simmer until apricots are tender and mixture thickens, 15 to 20 minutes. Serve immediately or let cool, transfer to container, cover, and refrigerate until ready to serve.

For Additional Servings Use

	3 servings	*4 servings*	*6 servings*
apricots	6 halves	8 halves	12 halves
raisins, onions, and water	3 T each	¼ c each	⅓ c + 2 t each
sugar	2¼ t	1 T	1 T + 1½ t
vinegar	1½ t	2 t	1 T
cinnamon	¼ t	½ t	¾ t
salt	dash	dash	dash, or to taste

Pepper Relish

 MAKES 2 SERVINGS, ABOUT 6 TABLESPOONS EACH *or* 4 SERVINGS,
ABOUT 3 TABLESPOONS EACH

Delicious with burgers and hot dogs or as a side dish.

½ cup each diced red and green
   bell peppers
¼ cup diced onion
1 teaspoon cider vinegar

½ teaspoon granulated sugar
½ bay leaf
¼ teaspoon salt
Dash pepper

In small saucepan combine all ingredients; bring to a slow boil over medium-low heat. Reduce heat to low, cover, and let simmer, stirring occasionally, until peppers are soft, about 15 minutes. Remove from heat and let cool. Transfer relish to container, cover, and refrigerate until chilled. Remove bay leaf before serving.

For Additional Servings Use

	3 servings, 6 T each, or 6 servings, 3 T each	4 servings, 6 T each or 8 servings, 3 T each	6 servings, 6 T each or 12 servings, 3 T each
bell peppers	¾ c each	1 c each	1½ c each
onions	⅓ c + 2 t	½ c	¾ c
vinegar	1½ t	2 t	1 T
sugar	¾ t	1 t	1½ t
bay leaves	½	1	1½
salt	¼ t	½ t	¾ t
pepper	dash	dash	dash to ⅛ t

Jellied Apple

MAKES 1 SERVING

This provides a nostalgic trip back to circuses and carnivals and is a treat for children of all ages.

1 small Red Delicious apple
2 teaspoons reduced-calorie grape spread (16 calories per 2 teaspoons)

1 honey-graham cracker (2½-inch square), made into fine crumbs
1 teaspoon shredded coconut

1. Insert an ice cream bar stick into stem end of apple and set aside.
2. In small metal measuring cup melt grape spread over low heat.
3. On sheet of wax paper, or on a paper plate, combine cracker crumbs and coconut. Brush melted spread over entire surface of apple, then roll apple in crumb mixture until well coated and all of mixture has been used.
4. Cover apple with plastic wrap and refrigerate until spread has hardened, at least 1 hour.

Melon Mélange

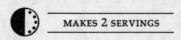 MAKES 2 SERVINGS

½ cup each watermelon and
  cantaloupe chunks
10 each small seedless green and
  red grapes

¼ cup dry white wine
½ teaspoon grenadine syrup
Garnish: mint sprigs

In small serving bowl combine all ingredients except garnish; cover and refrigerate for at least 2 hours. Serve garnished with mint sprigs.

For Additional Servings Use

	3 servings	*4 servings*	*6 servings*
watermelon and cantaloupe chunks	¾ c each	1 c each	1½ c each
green and red grapes	15 each	20 each	30 each
wine	⅓ c + 2 t	½ c	¾ c
grenadine syrup	¾ t	1 t	1½ t

Pineapple Cheesecake

MAKES 2 SERVINGS

3 graham crackers (2½-inch
    squares), made into crumbs
⅓ cup part-skim ricotta cheese
1 large egg
2 tablespoons plus 2 teaspoons
    instant nonfat dry milk powder
1 tablespoon plus 1½ teaspoons
    all-purpose flour

2 teaspoons margarine
1 teaspoon superfine sugar
½ teaspoon vanilla extract
¼ teaspoon grated lemon peel
½ cup canned crushed pineapple
    (no sugar added)

1. Preheat oven to 350°F. Spray two 6-ounce custard cups with non-stick cooking spray; sprinkle an equal amount of cracker crumbs into each, covering bottom and sides of cups, and set aside.

2. In blender container combine remaining ingredients except pineapple and process until smooth, scraping down sides of container as necessary. Stir pineapple into cheese mixture (*do not process*).

3. Divide pineapple mixture into custard cups and transfer cups to 8 x 8 x 2-inch baking pan; pour hot water into pan to a depth of about 1 inch. Bake until cheesecakes are set and lightly browned on top, 15 to 20 minutes.

4. Remove custard cups to wire rack and let cool; cover each with plastic wrap and refrigerate until chilled, at least 1 hour.

Serving Suggestion—Top each portion with 1 tablespoon thawed frozen dairy whipped topping.

For Additional Servings Use

	4 servings	6 servings	8 servings
graham crackers	6	9	12
cheese	⅔ c	1 c	1⅓ c
eggs	2 large	3 large	4 large
milk powder	⅓ c	½ c	⅔ c
flour	3 T	¼ c + 1½ t	⅓ c + 2 t
margarine	1 T + 1 t	2 T	2 T + 2 t
sugar	2 t	1 T	1 T + 1 t
vanilla	1 t	1½ t	2 t
lemon peel	½ t	¾ t	1 t
pineapple	1 c	1½ c	2 c

Chocolate Fudge

MAKES 6 SERVINGS, 4 PIECES EACH *or* 12 SERVINGS, 2 PIECES EACH

Once fudge has been cut into pieces, it may be left at room temperature for several hours; it will soften, but not melt.

1 cup reduced-calorie chocolate
   instant nonfat dry milk powder
1 tablespoon superfine sugar
1 teaspoon unsweetened cocoa
1½ teaspoons unflavored gelatin

⅓ cup water
¼ cup margarine
⅓ cup plus 2 teaspoons raisins
2 teaspoons sunflower seed

1. Line 7⅜ x 3⅝ x 2¼-inch loaf pan with 20-inch-long sheet of wax paper, allowing excess paper to extend over edges of pan; set aside.

2. In work bowl of food processor combine milk powder, sugar, and cocoa and process to a fine powder; transfer to small heatproof bowl and set aside.

3. In 1-cup metal measure, or small saucepan, sprinkle gelatin over water and let stand to soften; add margarine and cook over low heat, stirring constantly, until margarine is melted and gelatin is completely dissolved.

4. Pour gelatin mixture into cocoa mixture and stir to combine; stir in raisins and sunflower seed. Using rubber scraper, turn mixture into lined loaf pan, pressing mixture into all corners and smoothing surface. Fold excess paper over fudge to cover and refrigerate until firm, about 2 hours.

5. Using excess wax paper to lift, remove fudge from pan; cut into 24 equal pieces. Transfer fudge to serving platter, cover with plastic wrap, and refrigerate until ready to serve.

No-Cook Creations

❖❖❖

Breakfast Entrée
Banana Split Breakfast

Appetizers
Lox 'n' Horseradish Sauce Appetizer
Quick Liverwurst Pâté
Lime-Dressed Melon Delight
Spiced Orange Salad

Salads
Italian Tomato-Cheese Salad
Tossed Green Salad with Herb Dressing
Tomato-Cucumber Salad with Parsley Dressing
Sweet and Sour Corn Salad
Tabouli
Honeyed Fruit and Carrot Salad
Fruited Coleslaw
Zucchini-Pepper Slaw

Relishes & Toppings
Cran-Orange Relish
"Crème Fraîche"

Desserts and Snacks
Ginger "Ice Cream"
Cheese-Filled Pears
Coconut-Berry Parfait
Mixed Fruit Ambrosia
Peanut Butter Bonbons

Beverages
Coffee Cream
Strawberry Fizz
Tutti-Fruiti Milk Shake

This section includes recipes for no-cook appetizers, salads, drinks, and desserts—all tasty dishes that you can prepare without having to light your oven or range: a cool idea, particularly in hot weather.

Of the many dishes that lend themselves to no-cook cookery, none is as versatile as the salad. Salads have gone beyond the traditional mixed greens with a dressing, although such a salad, properly prepared, can add just the right touch to many meals. Today's salads offer various combinations of raw vegetables and fruits, and a wide variety of other foods, including leftovers.

Here are a few basic guidelines.

• All ingredients should be fresh and of good quality. In making your selections, think about color as well as flavor and texture, since salads should look colorful and attractive.

• Unlike most vegetables, salad greens should be washed before storing. Rinse thoroughly under running cold water; then drain well in a colander or on paper towels. Greens that are especially sandy or gritty, such as spinach and watercress, should be rinsed several times.

• Keep lettuce refrigerated. Store in the crisper, or keep loosely wrapped in paper towels in a securely closed plastic bag. The lettuce should keep fresh for three to five days.

• Wrap washed and drained watercress loosely in paper towels and store in a securely closed plastic bag in the coldest part of the refrigerator.

• Fresh spinach does *not* store well, so use it as soon as possible.

• Salads should always be served well chilled. It's best to add the dressing just before serving, so that the greens aren't wilted and soggy. (See *Guests Are Coming* for suggestions about dressings.)

• If leaves are not being left whole as a bed, *tear* the greens into bite-size, irregular pieces. (Never *cut* greens if they are to be stored.)

• Prepare greens as close to mealtime as possible. If this isn't convenient, tear them up in advance, place in a bowl of ice water, and refrigerate until serving time; the ice water will keep them crisp. Be sure to drain them well before serving. Greens should be thoroughly dry so that the dressing will cling evenly.

• To prevent cut fruits or white vegetables from turning brown after slicing, cut them with a stainless steel knife and sprinkle the slices lightly with lemon juice.

Leafy green salads, a combination of raw leafy green vegetables, are usually served as an accompaniment. For added interest, try to combine greens that have different textures, flavors, and colors. There's a wide variety to choose from: lettuces such as Bibb, Boston, iceberg, loose-leafed, romaine; chicory, endive (Belgian and curly); escarole; spinach; green, red, and savoy cabbage. You can also experiment with less well-known greens such as beet and mustard greens, Swiss chard, and turnip greens.

Vegetable salads combine raw vegetables cut into various shapes. Try mixing two or more of the following: bell peppers, broccoli, cabbage, carrots, cauliflower, cucumbers, mushrooms, onions, radishes, scallions, tomatoes, and zucchini.

Fruit salads are usually made from cut or sectioned fresh, canned, or dried fruits mixed with a dressing and served on a lettuce liner.

Cooked salads offer an opportunity to use up leftover meats, poultry, seafood, rice, pasta, and vegetables, and are often hearty enough to be an entrée. Use a substantial dressing to bind the salad together.

Combination salads usually contain two or more different types of ingredients; for example, greens and other vegetables may be mixed with eggs, olives, pickles, poultry, relishes, etc. Chef's salads and tossed garden salads fall into this category.

Gelatin salads have an unflavored or fruit-flavored gelatin base, to which a wide variety of fruits, vegetables, and other foods can be added. This versatile salad may be used as a side dish, an entrée, or a beautiful shimmering dessert. To chill gelatin quickly, substitute ice for half the water; gelatin will also chill faster in a large metal bowl. Once the gelatin begins to jell (becomes syrupy), add the ingredients; make sure they are well drained so they do not dilute the gelatin. Don't add *fresh* figs, papaya, or pineapple because they prevent the gelatin from congealing; however, these same fruits in canned form may be used.

The secret to serving a beautifully shaped gelatin salad lies in the unmolding. These few simple tips can help you to succeed every time:

• Dip the tip of a round-bladed knife or spatula (either metal or plastic) into hot water; then slide it around edge of the mold to loosen the mixture.

• Dip the entire mold into warm (not hot) water for about 10 seconds, being careful not to melt the gelatin. Lift the mold from the water and shake gently to loosen the mixture.

• Invert a platter on top of the mold; quickly invert the mold and platter together. Using both hands, carefully lift off mold.

Whatever you make, don't be afraid to be innovative. By blending in a little of your own imagination, you can quickly and easily prepare a dish that's filling, nutritious, attractive, and tasty.

Banana Split Breakfast

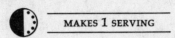 MAKES 1 SERVING

½ medium banana, peeled and cut in half lengthwise
½ teaspoon lemon juice
⅓ cup cottage cheese

2 teaspoons reduced-calorie strawberry spread (16 calories per 2 teaspoons), melted
½ teaspoon sunflower seed

On small plate arrange banana quarters and brush each with ¼ teaspoon lemon juice; spoon cheese into bowl between banana quarters. Pour melted spread over cheese and sprinkle with sunflower seed.

For Additional Servings Use

	2 servings	*3 servings*	*4 servings*
bananas	1 medium	1½ medium	2 medium
lemon juice	1 t	1½ t	2 t
cheese	⅔ c	1 c	1⅓ c
strawberry spread	1 T + 1 t	2 T	2 T + 2 t
sunflower seed	1 t	1½ t	2 t

Lox 'n' Horseradish Sauce Appetizer

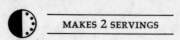 MAKES 2 SERVINGS

Can be prepared ahead and refrigerated until ready to serve.

1 tablespoon prepared horseradish
2 tablespoons plain lowfat yogurt
4 iceberg, romaine, or loose-leafed
   lettuce leaves
2 ounces thinly sliced lox (smoked
   salmon)

2 teaspoons diced red onion
2 pitted black olives, sliced
Garnish: 2 each radish roses, lemon
   wedges, and dill or parsley sprigs

Advance Preparation

On cloth towel mound horseradish; squeeze out as much moisture as possible. Crumble horseradish into small bowl; add yogurt and stir to combine. Cover and refrigerate until ready to serve.

Line each of 2 salad plates with 2 lettuce leaves; top each portion of lettuce with 1 ounce lox, 1 teaspoon onion, and 1 sliced olive and garnish each serving with a radish rose, lemon wedge, and dill or parsley sprig. Cover with plastic wrap and refrigerate until ready to serve (if serving immediately after preparation, chill salad plates before using).

Final Preparation

Just before serving, top each portion of lox with an equal amount of horseradish sauce.

For Additional Servings Use

	3 servings	4 servings	6 servings
horseradish	1 T + 1½ t	2 T	3 T
yogurt	3 T	¼ cup	⅓ c + 2 t
lettuce	6 leaves	8 leaves	12 leaves
lox	3 oz	4 oz	6 oz
onions	1 T	1 T + 1 t	2 T
olives	3	4	6

Quick Liverwurst Pâté

 MAKES 2 SERVINGS, ABOUT ¼ CUP EACH

3 ounces liverwurst
1½ teaspoons each pickle relish
  and mayonnaise
Dash each onion powder and
  garlic powder

2 iceberg, romaine, or loose-leafed
  lettuce leaves
12 saltine crackers

In small bowl, using a fork, mash liverwurst into smooth paste; add relish, mayonnaise, and seasonings and combine thoroughly. Line serving plate with lettuce leaves; mound pâté in center of lettuce and surround with crackers. Cover lightly and chill until ready to serve.

For Additional Servings Use

	3 servings	*4 servings*	*6 servings*
liverwurst	4½ oz	6 oz	9 oz
relish and mayonnaise	2¼ t each	1 T each	1 T + 1½ t each
onion and garlic powders	dash each	dash each	dash to ⅛ t each
lettuce	3 leaves	4 leaves	6 leaves
saltine crackers	18	24	36

Lime-Dressed Melon Delight

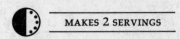 MAKES 2 SERVINGS

1 small cantaloupe, cut in half and
    seeded
2 tablespoons freshly squeezed lime
    juice
2 teaspoons vegetable oil
1 teaspoon grated lime peel

¼ teaspoon salt
Dash pepper
4 iceberg, romaine, or loose-leafed
    lettuce leaves
2 lime slices, twisted

Using melon-baller, scoop pulp from cantaloupe shells, reserving shells (or scoop out pulp with spoon, then cut pulp into bite-size chunks); place fruit in medium bowl and set aside.

In small bowl combine remaining ingredients except lettuce and lime slices; pour lime mixture over fruit and toss well to coat. Line each of 2 salad plates with 2 lettuce leaves and top with a melon shell; divide fruit mixture into shells and garnish each portion with a lime slice.

For Additional Servings Use

	3 servings	4 servings	6 servings
cantaloupes	1½ small	2 small	3 small
lime juice	3 T	¼ c	⅓ c + 2 t
oil	1 T	1 T + 1 t	2 T
lime peel	1½ t	2 t	1 T
salt	¼ t	½ t	¾ t
pepper	dash	⅛ t	⅛ t, or to taste
lettuce	6 leaves	8 leaves	12 leaves
lime slices	3	4	6

Spiced Orange Salad

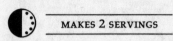 MAKES 2 SERVINGS

2 small oranges, peeled and sliced
  crosswise
6 thin red onion rings
2 tablespoons lemon juice
1 tablespoon olive oil

1 small garlic clove, minced
¼ teaspoon each salt and pepper
3 pitted black olives, sliced
1 tablespoon chopped fresh parsley

In bowl combine all ingredients except olives and parsley; toss well. Cover and refrigerate until chilled. Just before serving, toss again; on serving plate decoratively arrange orange mixture and garnish with olives and parsley.

For Additional Servings Use

	3 servings	*4 servings*	*6 servings*
oranges	3 small	4 small	6 small
onions	9 rings	12 rings	18 rings
lemon juice	3 T	¼ c	⅓ c + 2 t
oil	1 T + 1½ t	2 T	3 T
garlic	1 small clove	1 small clove	2 small cloves
salt and pepper	¼ t each	½ t each	¾ t each
olives	5	6	9
parsley	1 T	2 T	3 T

Italian Tomato-Cheese Salad

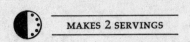 MAKES 2 SERVINGS

12 cherry tomatoes, cut into halves
1 ounce mozzarella cheese, cut into
   cubes
4 pitted black olives, sliced

1½ teaspoons Italian salad dressing
¼ teaspoon salt
2 large iceberg, romaine, or
   loose-leafed lettuce leaves

In bowl combine all ingredients except lettuce; toss lightly to coat with dressing. Cover and refrigerate until chilled. Serve on lettuce leaves.

For Additional Servings Use

	3 servings	*4 servings*	*6 servings*
cherry tomatoes	18	24	36
cheese	1½ oz	2 oz	3 oz
olives	6	8	12
dressing	2¼ t	1 T	1 T + 1½ t
salt	¼ t	½ t	¾ t
lettuce	3 leaves	4 leaves	6 leaves

Tossed Green Salad with Herb Dressing

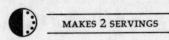

MAKES 2 SERVINGS

As a time-saving device, garlic cloves can be minced ahead of time and stored in resealable plastic bags in the refrigerator.

1 tablespoon plus 1½ teaspoons
   red wine vinegar
1 tablespoon water
1 teaspoon olive oil

⅛ teaspoon each basil leaves and
   minced fresh garlic
Dash each salt and pepper
2½ cups torn chilled salad greens

In jar that has tight-fitting cover combine all ingredients except greens; cover and shake well. In salad bowl arrange greens; pour dressing over greens and toss to coat. Serve immediately.

For Additional Servings Use

	3 servings	*4 servings*	*6 servings*
vinegar	2 T + ¾ t	3 T	¼ c + 1½ t
water	1 T + 1½ t	2 T	3 T
oil	1½ t	2 t	1 T
basil leaves and garlic	⅛ t each	¼ t each	¼ t each
salt	dash	⅛ t	⅛ t
pepper	dash	dash	dash to ⅛ t
salad greens	3¾ c	5 c	7½ c

Tomato-Cucumber Salad with Parsley Dressing

MAKES 2 SERVINGS

1 medium tomato, thinly sliced (about ⅛-inch-thick slices)
½ medium cucumber, scored and thinly sliced (about 12 slices)
1 tablespoon chopped fresh parsley
2 teaspoons vegetable oil

1½ teaspoons each lemon juice and rice vinegar
¼ teaspoon each salt, powdered mustard, and paprika
Dash pepper

On serving plate arrange about ⅔ of the tomato slices in circular pattern around edge of plate, overlapping slices; top with smaller circle of half of the cucumber slices, overlapping slices. Partially top cucumber slices with smaller circle of remaining tomato slices, edging tomatoes toward center of plate; top tomatoes with remaining cucumber slices.

In small bowl combine remaining ingredients, stirring well to blend; pour over salad. Cover with plastic wrap and refrigerate for at least 1 hour.

For Additional Servings Use

	3 servings	*4 servings*	*6 servings*
tomatoes	1½ medium	2 medium	3 medium
cucumbers	¾ medium (about 18 slices)	1 medium (about 24 slices)	1½ medium (about 36 slices)
parsley	1 T + 1½ t	2 T	3 T
oil	1 T	1 T + 1 t	2 T
lemon juice and vinegar	2¼ t each	1 T each	1 T + 1½ t each
salt, mustard, and paprika	¼ t each	½ t each	¾ t each
pepper	dash	dash	dash to ⅛ t

Sweet and Sour Corn Salad

MAKES 2 SERVINGS

This is good as a relish also.

1 cup drained canned whole-kernel corn
½ cup diced celery
6 cherry tomatoes, cut into halves
2 tablespoons sliced scallion (green onion)
1 tablespoon mayonnaise

2 teaspoons cider vinegar
¼ teaspoon each salt and granulated sugar
Dash pepper
4 iceberg, romaine, or loose-leafed lettuce leaves

In bowl combine all ingredients except lettuce, mixing well; cover and refrigerate for at least 1 hour.

To serve, line each of 2 salad plates with 2 lettuce leaves; toss salad again and spoon an equal amount of mixture over each portion of lettuce.

For Additional Servings Use

	3 servings	4 servings	6 servings
corn	1½ c	2 c	3 c
celery	¾ c	1 c	1½ c
cherry tomatoes	9	12	18
scallions	3 T	¼ c	⅓ c + 2 t
mayonnaise	1 T + 1½ t	2 T	3 T
cider vinegar	1 T	1 T + 1 t	2 T
salt	¼ t	½ t	¾ t
sugar	¼ t + ⅛ t	½ t	¾ t
pepper	dash	⅛ t	⅛ t, or to taste
lettuce	6 leaves	8 leaves	12 leaves

Tabouli

MAKES 2 SERVINGS

2 ounces uncooked cracked wheat (bulgur)
1/3 cup warm water
1/4 cup lemon juice
2 medium tomatoes, diced
1/2 cup each chopped scallions (green onions) and diced green bell pepper
1/4 cup chopped fresh parsley

1 tablespoon olive oil
1/2 teaspoon salt
1/2 teaspoon mint flakes (optional)
1/8 teaspoon each ground cumin and ground coriander
Dash pepper
8 romaine lettuce leaves
Garnish: mint sprigs and 1/2 lemon slice

In 1-quart bowl combine cracked wheat, water, and lemon juice; cover and refrigerate until all liquid is absorbed, about 1 hour.

Add remaining ingredients except lettuce to cracked wheat mixture and stir to combine; line serving dish with lettuce leaves and spoon tabouli over lettuce. Garnish with mint sprigs and lemon slice.

For Additional Servings Use

	3 servings	4 servings	6 servings
cracked wheat	3 oz	4 oz	6 oz
water	1/2 c	2/3 c	1 c
lemon juice	1/3 c	1/2 c	3/4 c
tomatoes	3 medium	4 medium	6 medium
scallions and green peppers	3/4 c each	1 c each	1 1/2 c each
parsley	1/3 c	1/2 c	3/4 c
oil	1 T + 1 1/2 t	2 T	3 T
salt	3/4 t	1 t	1 1/2 t
mint flakes (optional)	1/2 t	1 t	1 1/4 t
cumin and coriander	1/8 t each	1/4 t each	1/4 t each, or to taste
pepper	dash	1/8 t	1/4 t
lettuce	12 leaves	16 leaves	24 leaves

Honeyed Fruit and Carrot Salad

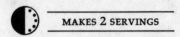 MAKES 2 SERVINGS

2 cups shredded carrots
1 small apple, cored and diced
1 large pitted prune, diced
1 tablespoon raisins, chopped

1 teaspoon sunflower seed, chopped
1 tablespoon plus 1½ teaspoons
  lemon juice
½ teaspoon honey

In serving bowl combine carrots, fruits, and sunflower seed. In small bowl mix lemon juice with honey; pour over salad and toss well.

For Additional Servings Use

	3 servings	*4 servings*	*6 servings*
carrots	3 c	4 c	6 c
apples	1½ small	2 small	3 small
prunes	2 large	2 large	3 large
raisins	1 T	2 T	3 T
sunflower seed	1½ t	2 t	1 T
lemon juice	2 T	3 T	¼ c
honey	¾ t	1 t	1½ t

Fruited Coleslaw

 MAKES 2 SERVINGS

2 tablespoons thawed frozen dairy
   whipped topping
2 teaspoons mayonnaise
1 teaspoon each granulated sugar
   and lemon juice
⅛ teaspoon salt
1 small orange, peeled and
   sectioned

2 cups shredded green cabbage
1 small red apple (Delicious or
   McIntosh), cored and diced
12 large seedless green grapes, cut
   into halves, or 20 small
4 iceberg, romaine, or loose-leafed
   lettuce leaves

In small bowl combine whipped topping, mayonnaise, sugar, lemon juice, and salt, mixing well. Cut orange sections into halves and, in medium bowl, combine with cabbage, apple, and grapes; pour mayonnaise mixture over fruit mixture and toss until well coated. Serve on bed of lettuce leaves.

For Additional Servings Use

	3 servings	*4 servings*	*6 servings*
whipped topping	3 T	¼ c	⅓ c + 2 t
mayonnaise	1 T	1 T + 1 t	2 T
sugar and lemon juice	1½ t each	2 t each	1 T each
salt	⅛ t	¼ t	¼ t
oranges	1½ small	2 small	3 small
cabbage	3 c	4 c	6 c
apples	1½ small	2 small	3 small
grapes	18 large or 30 small	24 large or 40 small	36 large or 60 small
lettuce	6 leaves	8 leaves	12 leaves

Zucchini-Pepper Slaw

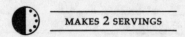

MAKES 2 SERVINGS

2 cups coarsely grated zucchini
⅛ teaspoon salt
½ medium red bell pepper, seeded
  and diced (¼-inch dice)
2 tablespoons diced red onion

½ teaspoon lemon juice
Dash pepper
2 servings Buttermilk-Cheese
  Dressing (see page 169)

Set colander into sink or a 2-quart mixing bowl; add zucchini and salt and toss well. Place a plate onto zucchini and weight with a 1-pound can; let stand 15 minutes to drain.

Remove weight and press zucchini to remove any remaining liquid. In salad bowl combine zucchini, red pepper, onion, lemon juice, and pepper; toss until well mixed. Add dressing and toss to coat.

For Additional Servings Use

	3 servings	4 servings	6 servings
zucchini	3 c	4 c	6 c
salt	⅛ t	¼ t	¼ t
red peppers	¾ medium	1 medium	1½ medium
onions	3 T	¼ c	⅓ c + 2 t
lemon juice	¾ t	1 t	1½ t
pepper	dash	dash	dash to ⅛ t
dressing	3 servings	4 servings	6 servings

Cran-Orange Relish

 MAKES 2 SERVINGS, ABOUT 3 TABLESPOONS EACH

Delicious with turkey, chicken, and ham.

½ cup cranberries
1 tablespoon thawed frozen
concentrated orange juice (no
sugar added)

2 teaspoons orange marmalade
1 teaspoon granulated sugar

In blender container combine all ingredients and process until pureed, scraping down sides of container as necessary. Serve immediately or refrigerate until ready to use.

For Additional Servings Use

	3 servings	4 servings	6 servings
cranberries	¾ c	1 c	1½ c
orange juice	1 T + 1½ t	2 T	3 T
marmalade	1 T	1 T + 1 t	2 T
sugar	1½ t	2 t	1 T

"Crème Fraîche"

MAKES 2 SERVINGS, 3 TABLESPOONS EACH *or* 4 SERVINGS,
1½ TABLESPOONS EACH

This is ideal for serving over fresh fruit and will keep for up to 5 days in the refrigerator.

In small container combine ¼ *cup plain lowfat yogurt* with 2 *tablespoons thawed frozen dairy whipped topping;* cover and refrigerate until ready to serve.

For Additional Servings Use

	3 servings, 3 T each or 6 servings, 1½ T each	4 servings, 3 T each or 8 servings, 1½ T each	6 servings, 3 T each or 12 servings, 1½ T each
yogurt	⅓ c + 2 t	½ c	¾ c
whipped topping	3 T	¼ c	⅓ c + 2 t

Ginger "Ice Cream"

 MAKES 2 SERVINGS

In blender container combine 6 *ounces vanilla dietary frozen dessert* and ¼ *teaspoon grated peeled ginger root* and process until smooth; spoon half of mixture into each of 2 freezer-safe dessert dishes. Cover with plastic wrap and freeze until ready to serve.

For Additional Servings Use

	3 servings	4 servings	6 servings
frozen dessert	9 oz	12 oz	18 oz
ginger root	¼ t	¼ t	½ t

Cheese-Filled Pears

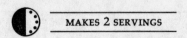

MAKES 2 SERVINGS

2 very ripe small pears, cut
  lengthwise into halves and cored
1 teaspoon lemon juice
2 ounces Gorgonzola or Danish blue
  cheese (at room temperature)

1 tablespoon margarine (at room
  temperature)
1 teaspoon sunflower seed, toasted
Garnish: mint sprigs and twisted
  lemon slices

Brush cut side of each pear half with ¼ teaspoon lemon juice; place halves,
cut-side up, on each of two salad plates.

In small bowl combine cheese and margarine, mixing until thoroughly
blended; fill a pastry bag that is fitted with star tip with cheese mixture.
Pipe out an equal amount of mixture into cored section of each pear half.
Sprinkle each half with ¼ teaspoon sunflower seed; serve immediately or
cover with plastic wrap and refrigerate until ready to serve. Serve each
portion garnished with mint and lemon.

For Additional Servings Use

	3 servings	4 servings	6 servings
pears	3 small	4 small	6 small
lemon juice	1½ t	2 t	1 T
cheese	3 oz	4 oz	6 oz
margarine	1 T + 1½ t	2 T	3 T
sunflower seed	1½ t	2 t	1 T

Coconut-Berry Parfait

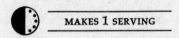 MAKES 1 SERVING

A simple but elegant-looking treat; ideal for a special breakfast.

½ cup blueberries
¼ cup plain lowfat yogurt
½ teaspoon each granulated sugar, vanilla extract, and lemon juice

¾ ounce crunchy nutlike cereal nuggets
1 teaspoon shredded coconut

Set aside 1 blueberry for garnish; spoon remaining berries into a parfait glass. In small bowl combine yogurt, sugar, vanilla, and lemon juice, mixing well; spoon over berries, reserving 1 tablespoon yogurt mixture for garnish. In small bowl combine cereal and coconut; sprinkle over yogurt mixture and top with reserved tablespoon yogurt mixture, then reserved blueberry.

For Additional Servings Use

	2 servings	3 servings	4 servings
blueberries	1 c	1½ c	2 c
yogurt	½ c	¾ c	1 c
sugar, vanilla, and lemon juice	1 t each	1½ t each	2 t each
cereal	1½ oz	2¼ oz	3 oz
coconut	2 t	1 T	1 T + 1 t

Mixed Fruit Ambrosia

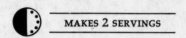

MAKES 2 SERVINGS

½ medium papaya, pared, seeded,
and cut into ½-inch cubes

¼ cup canned mandarin orange
sections (no sugar added)

10 small or 6 large seedless green
grapes, cut into halves

1 tablespoon plus 1½ teaspoons
lemon juice

1 teaspoon granulated sugar

¼ teaspoon rum extract

2 teaspoons shredded coconut

In bowl combine all ingredients except coconut, tossing to mix thoroughly.
Divide mixture into 2 sherbet glasses and sprinkle each portion with 1 teaspoon coconut.

For Additional Servings Use

	3 servings	*4 servings*	*6 servings*
papayas	¾ medium	1 medium	1½ medium
orange sections	⅓ c + 2 t	½ c	¾ c
grapes	15 small or 9 large	20 small or 12 large	30 small or 18 large
lemon juice	2 T	3 T	¼ c
sugar	1½ t	2 t	1 T
rum extract	¼ t	½ t	¾ t
coconut	1 T	1 T + 1 t	2 T

Peanut Butter Bonbons

 MAKES 2 SERVINGS, 4 BONBONS EACH

¾ ounce (⅓ cup less 1 teaspoon) cornflake crumbs, divided

2 tablespoons raisins, finely chopped

3 tablespoons chunky-style peanut butter

½ teaspoon superfine sugar

Measure 1½ teaspoons cornflake crumbs into a small bowl and set aside.

In another small bowl combine raisins with remaining crumbs; add peanut butter and, using a fork, mash until thoroughly combined. Using heaping teaspoonful of mixture at a time, form mixture with palms of hands into 1-inch balls (should yield 8 balls). Roll each ball in reserved cornflake crumbs, coating all sides. On a plate arrange coated balls in a single layer; cover lightly with plastic wrap and refrigerate until chilled.

Just before serving, roll each ball in sugar and place in a fluted candy paper liner.

For Additional Servings Use

	3 servings	4 servings	6 servings
cornflake crumbs	1⅛ oz (½ c less 1½ t)	1½ oz (½ c + 2 T)	2¼ oz (1 c less 1 T)
raisins	3 T	¼ c	⅓ c + 2 t
peanut butter	¼ c + 1½ t	⅓ c + 2 t	½ c + 1 T
sugar	¾ t	1 t	1½ t
Method: set aside	2¼ t crumbs	1 T crumbs	1 T + 1½ t crumbs
form into	12 balls	16 balls	24 balls

Coffee Cream

 MAKES 1 SERVING, ABOUT 1 CUP

2 tablespoons plus 2 teaspoons
   instant nonfat dry milk powder
1 teaspoon each instant coffee
   powder and superfine sugar
⅛ teaspoon vanilla extract

¼ cup water
3 ice cubes
1 tablespoon thawed frozen dairy
   whipped topping

Chill an 8-ounce glass. In blender container combine milk powder, coffee, sugar, and vanilla; add water and process at high speed until combined. With motor running add ice cubes, 1 at a time, processing until all ice is dissolved and mixture is thick and frothy. Add whipped topping and process just until combined. Pour into chilled glass and serve immediately.

For Additional Servings Use

	2 servings	3 servings	4 servings
milk powder	⅓ c	½ c	⅔ c
coffee powder and sugar	2 t each	1 T each	1 T + 1 t each
vanilla	¼ t	¼ t	½ t
water	½ c	¾ c	1 c
ice cubes	6	8	10
whipped topping	2 T	3 T	¼ c

Strawberry Fizz

 MAKES 1 SERVING, ABOUT 1 CUP

½ cup strawberries, reserve 1 for garnish
1½ ounces strawberry or vanilla dietary frozen dessert

¼ cup skim milk
¾ teaspoon granulated sugar
½ teaspoon vanilla extract
¼ cup chilled club soda

Chill a 10-ounce glass. In blender container combine all ingredients except reserved berry and soda and process for about 30 seconds; add soda and, using an on-off motion, process just until combined. Pour into chilled glass and garnish with reserved berry; serve immediately.

For Additional Servings Use

	2 servings	*3 servings*	*4 servings*
strawberries	1 c	1½ c	2 c
frozen dessert	3 oz	4½ oz	6 oz
milk	½ c	¾ c	1 c
sugar	1½ t	2¼ t	1 T
vanilla	1 t	1½ t	2 t
club soda	½ c	¾ c	1 c

Tutti-"Fruiti" Milk Shake

MAKES 2 SERVINGS, ABOUT 1 CUP EACH

½ cup canned crushed pineapple (no sugar added)

½ medium banana, peeled and cut into chunks

1 tablespoon thawed frozen concentrated orange juice (no sugar added)

1 cup buttermilk (made from skim milk)

¾ teaspoon granulated sugar

½ teaspoon vanilla extract

4 ice cubes

In blender container combine pineapple, banana, and orange juice and process until smooth; add milk, sugar, and vanilla and process until combined. Place 2 ice cubes in each of two 10-ounce glasses and pour an equal amount of shake into each glass; serve immediately.

Variation—Tutti-"Fruiti" Fizz—Use 12-ounce glasses and add ¼ cup club soda to each portion of shake.

For Additional Servings Use

	3 servings	*4 servings*
pineapple	¾ c	1 c
bananas	¾ medium	1 medium
orange juice	1 T + 1½ t	2 T
buttermilk	1½ c	2 c
sugar	1⅛ t	1½ t
vanilla	¾ t	1 t

Meal Mates

◆◆

Soups
Cream of Artichoke Soup
Creamy Tomato-Vegetable Soup
House Special Soup
Kidney Bean 'n' Ham Soup

Salads
Orzo 'n' Vegetable Salad Italienne
Sesame Three-Bean Salad
Sweet and Sour Spinach-Mushroom Salad
Vegetable-Cheddar Salad

Side Dishes
Braised Sweet and Sour Red Cabbage
Carrots au Gratin
Honeyed Pineapple Carrots
Cauliflower-Carrot Stir-Fry
Cauliflower Polonaise
Eggplant Provençale
Elegant Mushroom Sauté
Sautéed Tomatoes
Zucchini-Apple Sauté
Zucchini-Corn Sauté
Broccoli-Stuffed Potato
Parmesan-Topped Stuffed Potato
Italian-Style Scalloped Potatoes
Orange Rice
Mexican Corn Bread

Dessert
Raisin Bread Pudding

The mates to your main dishes should be selected as carefully as you choose accessories to complement your favorite clothes. When planning a menu, first select the basic entrée and then decide what soup, vegetables, salad, or dessert would accompany it most tastefully.

The tempting aroma of soup, whether as a first course or an entrée in itself, makes any meal more appetizing. If soup is to be a first course, for good overall balance to the meal the entrée should determine the type. A hearty entrée calls for a clear, light soup; if the main course is simple and light, a rich creamy soup is a good accompaniment. A clear soup can be a simple bouillon or a vegetable soup. Clear soups can also form the base of a hearty soup; to make a filling and delicious soup, simply add barley, meat or poultry, pasta, or rice to plain bouillon. Just be sure when adding ingredients to select combinations that blend together nicely. To avoid overcooking, add raw ingredients in the order of their cooking time (the longest-cooking ones first).

For a heavier vegetable soup, make a natural thickener by pureeing the vegetables and blending them back into the liquid. (It is important that vegetables be fully cooked to thicken the soup properly.) Vegetables with a high-starch content, such as legumes and potatoes, work extremely well, as do broccoli and cauliflower, but vegetables with little or no starch content, such as celery and onions, do not thicken well.

Creamed soup is another kind you might want to try. This is customarily a combination of a liquid, such as milk, a flavor-determining ingredient, such as a vegetable or meat, and a thickening agent, such as a mixture of flour and margarine.

Here are some tips for making tasty soups:

• Always use high-quality ingredients to make soup. Leftovers can add flavor, but a soup based entirely on leftover ingredients will not be as rich-tasting or as flavorful.

• Save the water in which vegetables have cooked, or the liquids drained from canned vegetables for use in making soups.

• In serving soup with sandwiches, use temperature contrasts as well as flavor contrasts to add interest. A hearty soup, such as bean or vegetable, is good with a cold sandwich, and a cold soup offers a nice contrast to a hot sandwich.

• Soup often tastes even better the next day, so don't hesitate to make more than you need for one meal. Many soups can be frozen for up to three months. However, it's not a good idea to freeze a soup that has been thickened with flour because it may separate. Soup can be either reheated straight from the freezer or thawed first in the refrigerator. All reheating should be done *gradually*.

Vegetables also set off the main dish, and should be selected with an eye to providing taste, texture, and color contrasts. Vegetables can be cooked in a variety of ways: steaming, boiling, stir-frying, sautéing, baking, and braising, as well as pressure cooking. (See the introduction to *Appliance Appeal* for tips about using pressure cookers.) The method you select should be determined by the vegetable you are cooking and the amount of time you have. Always keep in mind the importance of retaining as many nutrients as possible. Variety counts, too; no one cooking method is completely satisfactory for all vegetables.

Today, *steaming* is rapidly replacing boiling as the primary method of vegetable cookery. One of the swiftest methods, steaming also retains more valuable nutrients because they are not lost in any cooking liquids. Artichokes, asparagus, broccoli, brussels sprouts, cabbage, carrots, cauliflower, green beans, onions, peas, potatoes, summer squash, and turnips are especially suited to steaming. Steaming may take 4 to 15 minutes, depending on the vegetable. Guard against overcooking, as this results in changes in color, poor texture, and a loss of flavor and nutrients.

Boiling is a method that can be used with any vegetable that can be steamed (although steaming is usually preferable). For best results, use as little water as possible (barely cover the vegetable) and drain as soon as cooking is completed. Any vegetable kept in hot liquid continues to cook.

Sautéing and *stir-frying* are quick, easy methods of cooking in small amounts of fat, usually over high heat. The fat adds flavor and color. Although almost any vegetable can be cooked by either of these methods, mushrooms and onions are particularly good choices.

Baking, either in a covered casserole or without any cookware, takes the longest but has the advantage of conserving energy if you are also cooking another dish in the oven (and it frees you to do other tasks while both are cooking). It is an excellent method for eggplant, potatoes, squash, and tomatoes.

Braising is slow cooking in a minimal amount of liquid (as opposed to boiling, in which food is submerged) in a covered saucepan. Flavorful juices from the vegetable don't get lost in braising, and any liquid that remains after cooking can be reduced and served over the vegetables. This technique is very good for leeks, mushrooms, potatoes, and summer squash. An alternate method of braising is to parboil the vegetables first, then cook them uncovered in a small amount of liquid over low heat. The partially cooked vegetable soaks up the liquid as the cooking process is completed. Try this technique with brussels sprouts, cabbage, celery, leeks, lettuce, onions, and potatoes.

Whichever method you choose, be sure that all fresh vegetables are washed and thoroughly clean. If necessary, scrub them with a stiff vegetable brush. For even cooking and eye appeal, cut vegetables into uniform pieces. Most important of all, do not overcook: to be attractive and appetizing complements to your main dish vegetables should be prepared to just the right degree of "doneness."

For other soup, salad, vegetable, and dessert recipes, check the Index.

Cream of Artichoke Soup

 MAKES 2 SERVINGS, ABOUT 1 CUP EACH

2 teaspoons margarine
¼ cup chopped onion
½ garlic clove, minced
1 tablespoon plus 1½ teaspoons
   all-purpose flour
1 cup water
1 packet instant chicken broth and
   seasoning mix

¾ cup thawed and chopped frozen
   artichoke hearts
¼ cup evaporated skimmed milk
Dash each salt and pepper
1½ teaspoons chopped fresh parsley

In 1-quart nonstick saucepan heat margarine until bubbly and hot; add onion and garlic and sauté over medium-low heat until onion is soft. Sprinkle with flour and stir to combine. Using wire whisk, gradually stir in water, stirring until flour is completely dissolved; add broth mix. Reduce heat to low and cook, stirring occasionally, until mixture is thickened, about 5 minutes. Add artichokes and cook, stirring constantly, for 3 minutes longer. Add milk, salt, and pepper and cook until heated (*do not boil*). Serve each portion sprinkled with ¾ teaspoon parsley.

For Additional Servings Use

	3 servings	*4 servings*	*6 servings*
margarine	1 T	1 T + 1 t	2 T
onions	⅓ c + 2 t	½ c	¾ c
garlic	½ clove	1 clove	1½ cloves
flour	2 T + ¾ t	3 T	¼ c + 1½ t
water	1½ c	2 c	3 c
broth mix	1½ pkt	2 pkt	3 pkt
artichoke hearts	1 c + 2 T	1½ c	2¼ c
milk	⅓ c + 2 t	½ c	¾ c
salt and pepper	dash each	dash each	dash to ⅛ t each
parsley	2¼ t	1 T	1 T + 1½ t

Creamy Tomato-Vegetable Soup

 MAKES 2 SERVINGS, ABOUT 1 CUP EACH

2 teaspoons margarine
¼ cup each diced onion and celery
½ cup grated carrot
2 teaspoons all-purpose flour
1 packet instant beef broth and
  seasoning mix

1 cup tomato juice
1 tablespoon plus 1 teaspoon dry
  sherry
Dash pepper
½ cup evaporated skimmed milk

In 1-quart saucepan heat margarine over medium heat until bubbly and hot; add onion and celery and sauté until onion is translucent. Stir in carrot and sauté until vegetables are tender. Sprinkle vegetables with flour and broth mix and stir until coated; gradually stir in juice and sherry and, stirring occasionally, bring mixture to a boil. Reduce heat to low, add pepper, and let simmer until mixture thickens slightly, 2 to 3 minutes.

Remove pan from heat and gradually stir in milk; return to low heat and let simmer until flavors blend, about 2 minutes (*do not boil*).

For Additional Servings Use

	4 servings	*6 servings*	*8 servings*
margarine	1 T + 1 t	2 T	2 T + 2 t
onions and celery	½ c each	¾ c each	1 c each
carrots	1 c	1½ c	2 c
flour	1 T + 1 t	2 T	2 T + 2 t
broth mix	2 pkt	3 pkt	4 pkt
tomato juice	2 c	3 c	1 qt
sherry	2 T + 2 t	¼ c	⅓ c
pepper	dash	dash to ⅛ t	⅛ t
milk	1 c	1½ c	2 c

House Special Soup

 MAKES 4 SERVINGS, ABOUT 1 CUP EACH

½ cup cooked vermicelli (very thin spaghetti)

3 cups water

3 packets instant chicken broth and seasoning mix

4 ounces shelled and deveined cooked tiny shrimp*

1 cup shredded lettuce (romaine or loose-leafed)

½ cup drained canned whole-kernel corn

½ cup sliced mushrooms

2 tablespoons chopped scallion (green onion)

1 teaspoon cornstarch, dissolved in 1 tablespoon water

1 teaspoon teriyaki sauce

Cut vermicelli into 1-inch pieces and set aside. In 2-quart saucepan combine water and broth mix and bring to a boil; stir in vermicelli, shrimp, lettuce, corn, mushrooms, and scallion. Reduce heat and let simmer for 5 minutes; stir in dissolved cornstarch and teriyaki sauce and cook, stirring constantly, until thickened.

* Shredded cooked pork or skinned and shredded cooked chicken may be substituted for the shrimp.

For Additional Servings Use

	6 servings	8 servings
vermicelli	¾ c	1 c
water	1 qt + ½ c	1½ qt
broth mix	4½ pkt	6 pkt
shrimp	6 oz	8 oz
lettuce	1½ c	2 c
corn and mushrooms	¾ c each	1 c each
scallions	3 T	¼ c
cornstarch	1½ t, dissolved in 1 T water	2 t, dissolved in 2 T water
teriyaki sauce	1½ t	2 t

Kidney Bean 'n' Ham Soup

 MAKES 2 SERVINGS, ABOUT 1 CUP EACH

A hearty soup that can be a meal in itself. For a special treat, serve with Herbed Romano Sticks (see page 80).

2 teaspoons margarine
¼ cup each diced onion, celery, and carrot
½ packet (about ½ teaspoon) instant chicken broth and seasoning mix

¼ teaspoon oregano leaves
4 ounces diced boiled ham
1 cup canned crushed tomatoes
4 ounces drained canned red kidney beans
2 tablespoons to ¼ cup water

In 1-quart saucepan heat margarine until bubbly and hot; add onion, celery, carrot, broth mix, and oregano and stir to combine. Cover and cook over medium heat until vegetables are tender. Stir in remaining ingredients, adding water gradually until soup reaches desired consistency; cover and let simmer until thoroughly heated.

For Additional Servings Use

	3 servings	4 servings	6 servings
margarine	1 T	1 T + 1 t	2 T
onions, celery, and carrots	⅓ c + 2 t each	½ c each	¾ c each
broth mix	¾ pkt (about ¾ t)	1 pkt	1½ pkt
oregano leaves	¼ t	½ t	¾ t
ham	6 oz	8 oz	12 oz
tomatoes	1½ c	2 c	3 c
kidney beans	6 oz	8 oz	12 oz
water	3 T to ⅓ c	¼ to ½ c	⅓ to ¾ c

Orzo 'n' Vegetable Salad Italienne

MAKES 2 SERVINGS

1½ ounces uncooked orzo (tiny rice-shaped macaroni), cooked according to package directions and chilled
12 cherry tomatoes, cut into halves
½ cup julienne-cut green bell pepper (thin strips)
½ cup diagonally sliced celery

4 pitted black olives, sliced
1 tablespoon each olive oil, wine vinegar, and lemon juice
2 teaspoons grated Parmesan cheese
½ teaspoon each garlic powder and crushed basil leaves
¼ teaspoon salt
Dash pepper

In medium salad bowl combine all ingredients; toss well. Cover and chill for at least 1 hour. Just before serving, toss again.

For Additional Servings Use

	3 servings	*4 servings*	*6 servings*
orzo	2¼ oz	3 oz	4½ oz
cherry tomatoes	18	24	36
green peppers and celery	¾ c each	1 c each	1½ c each
olives	6	8	12
oil, vinegar, and lemon juice	1 T + 1½ t each	2 T each	3 T each
cheese	1 T	1 T + 1 t	2 T
garlic powder and basil leaves	½ t each	1 t each	1½ t each
salt	¼ t	½ t	¾ t
pepper	dash	⅛ t	⅛ t, or to taste

Sesame Three-Bean Salad

MAKES 2 SERVINGS, ABOUT 1¼ CUPS EACH

1 cup each cut green and wax beans (fresh, frozen, or drained canned*)

2 tablespoons each minced red onion, red wine vinegar, and water

4 ounces drained canned red kidney beans

1 tablespoon lemon juice

1 teaspoon each sesame seed, toasted, and Chinese sesame oil

¼ teaspoon each oregano leaves and salt

Dash pepper

In 1-quart saucepan combine green and wax beans, onion, vinegar, and water; bring to a boil. Cover and cook until beans are tender, about 10 minutes.*

Transfer bean mixture to a 1-quart bowl and add remaining ingredients; toss well, cover, and refrigerate until chilled, at least 1 hour (may be refrigerated overnight). Toss again just before serving.

* If canned beans are used, do not cook. Combine all ingredients in bowl; toss and chill as directed.

For Additional Servings Use

	3 servings	4 servings	6 servings
green and wax beans	1½ c each	2 c each	3 c each
onions, vinegar, and water	3 T each	¼ cup each	⅓ c + 2 t each
kidney beans	6 oz	8 oz	12 oz
lemon juice	1 T + 1½ t	2 T	3 T
sesame seed and oil	1½ t each	2 t each	1 T each
oregano leaves and salt	¼ t each	½ t each	¾ t each
pepper	dash	dash	dash to ⅛ t

Sweet and Sour
Spinach-Mushroom Salad

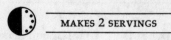 MAKES 2 SERVINGS

4 ounces fresh spinach
1 teaspoon vegetable oil
1½ teaspoons each red wine
   vinegar and lemon juice
¾ teaspoon granulated sugar
⅛ teaspoon salt

Dash pepper
½ teaspoon imitation bacon bits,
   crushed (optional)
½ cup thinly sliced mushrooms
¼ cup thinly sliced onion

Rinse spinach several times in cold water to remove all sand and grit. Trim off stems and tear leaves into uniform bite-size pieces (should yield about 2 cups); place on paper towels and set aside to dry.

In small nonstick saucepan heat oil over low heat; add vinegar, lemon juice, sugar, salt, and pepper and let simmer, stirring occasionally, until flavors blend, about 1 minute. Remove from heat and, if desired, stir in crushed bacon bits.

Transfer torn spinach to salad bowl; add mushrooms and onions and toss gently to combine. Serve with hot dressing.

For Additional Servings Use

	3 servings	*4 servings*	*6 servings*
spinach	6 oz	8 oz	12 oz
oil	1½ t	2 t	1 T
vinegar and lemon juice	2¼ t each	1 T each	1 T + 1½ t each
sugar	1⅛ t	1½ t	2¼ t
salt	⅛ t	¼ t	¼ to ½ t
pepper	dash	dash	⅛ t
bacon bits (optional)	¾ t	1 t	1½ t
mushrooms	¾ c	1 c	1½ c
onions	⅓ c + 2 t	½ c	¾ c

Vegetable-Cheddar Salad

MAKES 2 SERVINGS
---

2 cups broccoli florets, blanched
1 cup sliced mushrooms
2 ounces sharp Cheddar cheese,
 shredded
2 teaspoons sunflower seed

1 tablespoon each minced fresh
 chives,* lemon juice, and olive oil
¼ teaspoon each garlic powder and
 powdered mustard
⅛ teaspoon each salt and pepper

In salad bowl combine first 4 ingredients. In small bowl combine remaining ingredients; pour over salad and toss to coat. Cover and refrigerate for 1 hour.

* Freeze-dried chopped chives may be substituted for the minced fresh.

For Additional Servings Use

	3 servings	4 servings	6 servings
broccoli	3 c	4 c	6 c
mushrooms	1½ c	2 c	3 c
cheese	3 oz	4 oz	6 oz
sunflower seed	1 T	1 T + 1 t	2 T
chives, lemon juice, and oil	1 T + 1½ t each	2 T each	3 T each
garlic powder and powdered mustard	¼ t each	½ t each	¾ t each
salt and pepper	⅛ t each	¼ t each	¼ t each, or to taste

Braised Sweet and Sour Red Cabbage

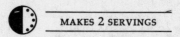 MAKES 2 SERVINGS

1 tablespoon plus 1 teaspoon
  reduced-calorie margarine,
  divided
1 small Golden Delicious apple,
  pared, cored, and shredded
¼ cup diced onion
2 cups shredded red cabbage

¼ cup dry red wine
2 tablespoons raisins
2 teaspoons white vinegar
1 teaspoon firmly packed dark
  brown sugar
¼ teaspoon salt

In 10-inch nonstick skillet heat half of the margarine over medium heat until bubbly and hot; add apple and onion and sauté, stirring occasionally, until onion is translucent, 1 to 2 minutes. Stir in remaining ingredients except margarine and reduce heat; cover and let simmer, stirring occasionally, for 15 to 20 minutes or until cabbage is done to taste (if mixture becomes too dry, add 1 to 2 tablespoons water). Transfer to a serving dish and stir in remaining margarine.

For Additional Servings Use

	3 servings	4 servings	6 servings
margarine	2 T	2 T + 2 t	¼ c
apples	1½ small	2 small	3 small
onions	⅓ c + 2 t	½ c	¾ c
cabbage	3 c	4 c	6 c
wine	⅓ c + 2 t	½ c	¾ c
raisins	3 T	¼ c	⅓ c + 2 t
vinegar	1 T	1 T + 1 t	2 T
sugar	1½ t	2 t	1 T
salt	¼ t	½ t	¾ t
skillet	10-inch	12-inch	3-qt saucepan

Carrots au Gratin

MAKES 2 SERVINGS

In the culinary world, the term "au gratin" refers to a dish that is prepared with cheese, butter, and bread crumbs and is browned in the oven or under a flame; we have substituted margarine for butter with great success.

1 tablespoon margarine, divided
2¼ teaspoons all-purpose flour
½ cup skim milk
2 cups cooked sliced fresh or
    frozen carrots

2 ounces Cheddar cheese, shredded
2 tablespoons plus ¾ teaspoon
    plain dried bread crumbs

In 1-quart saucepan heat half of the margarine until bubbly and hot; add flour and stir to combine. Gradually stir in milk and bring just to a boil. Reduce heat and cook, stirring constantly, until mixture is smooth and thickened. Add carrots and cheese and cook, stirring constantly, until cheese is melted; remove from heat.

Preheat oven to 375°F. Spray 2 individual au gratin dishes or 1½-cup casseroles with nonstick cooking spray.* Divide carrot mixture into dishes (or casseroles) and set aside.

In small nonstick skillet melt remaining margarine; add bread crumbs and stir until thoroughly combined and margarine has been absorbed. Sprinkle each portion of carrot mixture with an equal amount of crumb mixture and bake until topping is browned, 20 to 25 minutes.

* If preferred, one 2-cup casserole may be used.

For Additional Servings Use

	4 servings	6 servings	8 servings
margarine	2 T	3 T	¼ c
flour	1 T + 1½ t	2 T + ¾ t	3 T
milk	1 c	1½ c	2 c
carrots	4 c	6 c	8 c
cheese	4 oz	6 oz	8 oz
bread crumbs	¼ c + 1½ t	⅓ c + 1 T + 1¼ t	½ c + 1 T

Honeyed Pineapple Carrots

1 pound carrots
1 cup water
¼ teaspoon salt
½ cup canned crushed pineapple
  (no sugar added)

1 tablespoon margarine
1 teaspoon honey
½ teaspoon lemon juice
1 teaspoon cornstarch

Clean carrots and cut into ¼-inch-thick slices (should yield about 4 cups). In 1½-quart saucepan combine water and salt and bring to a boil; add carrots and return water to a boil. Reduce heat, cover, and let simmer until carrots are tender, 8 to 10 minutes. Remove from heat and drain water from saucepan, leaving carrots in pan.

Drain juice from the ½ cup pineapple into small cup or bowl and set aside; add crushed pineapple, margarine, honey, and lemon juice to carrots and cook over low heat until heated through. Dissolve cornstarch in reserved pineapple juice and stir into carrot mixture; cook, stirring constantly, until mixture thickens.

For Additional Servings Use

	3 servings	*4 servings*	*6 servings*
carrots	1½ lb	2 lb	3 lb
water	1½ c	2 c	3 c
salt	¼ t	½ t	¾ t
pineapple	¾ c	1 c	1½ c
margarine	1 T + 1½ t	2 T	3 T
honey	1½ t	2 t	1 T
lemon juice	¾ t	1 t	1½ t
cornstarch	1½ t	2 t	1 T

Cauliflower-Carrot Stir-Fry

 MAKES 2 SERVINGS

1½ teaspoons peanut or vegetable oil

½ teaspoon Chinese sesame oil

½ cup diagonally sliced carrot (⅛-inch-thick slices), blanched

½ garlic clove, minced, or ⅛ teaspoon garlic powder

⅛ teaspoon ground ginger

1 cup cauliflower florets, blanched

In small nonstick skillet combine oils and heat over medium-high heat; add carrot, garlic (or garlic powder), and ginger and stir-fry briefly, about 1 minute. Reduce heat, cover, and cook for about 3 minutes (carrot slices should still be crisp); add cauliflower and stir-fry until tender-crisp, about 5 minutes longer.

For Additional Servings Use

	3 servings	4 servings	6 servings
peanut or vegetable oil	2¼ t	1 T	1 T + 1½ t
sesame oil	¾ t	1 t	1½ t
carrots	¾ c	1 c	1½ c
garlic	½ clove or ⅛ t powder	1 clove or ¼ t powder	1½ cloves or ¼ t powder
ginger	⅛ t	⅛ t	¼ t
cauliflower	1½ c	2 c	3 c
skillet	9-inch	9- or 10-inch	10-inch

Cauliflower Polonaise

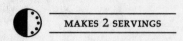 MAKES 2 SERVINGS

Polonaise is a culinary term meaning garnished with bread crumbs and chopped egg.

1 small head cauliflower (about 1 pound) or 2 packages (10 ounces each) frozen cauliflower	1 tablespoon margarine
	3 tablespoons seasoned dried bread crumbs
1 cup water	1 egg, hard-cooked and diced
½ teaspoon salt	

Break cauliflower into florets (should yield about 4 cups). In 2-quart saucepan combine water and salt and bring to a boil; add cauliflower and return water to a boil. Reduce heat, cover, and let simmer until tender-crisp, about 10 minutes (if frozen cauliflower is used, cook according to package directions); drain, transfer to a serving dish, and keep warm.

In small nonstick skillet melt margarine; add bread crumbs and stir until thoroughly combined and margarine has been absorbed. Sprinkle crumb mixture and diced egg over cauliflower and toss lightly.

For Additional Servings Use

	4 servings	6 servings	8 servings
cauliflower	2 small heads or 1 medium head (about 2 lb) or 4 pkg frozen	3 small heads or 1 large head (about 3 lb) or 6 pkg frozen	4 small heads or 2 medium heads (about 4 lb) or 8 pkg frozen
water	2 c	3 c	1 qt
salt	1 t	1½ t	2 t
margarine	2 T	3 T	¼ c
bread crumbs	⅓ c + 2 t	½ c + 1 T	¾ c
eggs	2	3	4

Eggplant Provençale

MAKES 2 SERVINGS

1½ teaspoons olive oil
1 teaspoon margarine
¼ cup diced onion
1 garlic clove, mashed with ¼
   teaspoon salt
2 cups pared and cubed eggplant
   (1-inch cubes)

1 medium tomato, blanched, peeled,
   and chopped
1 tablespoon chopped fresh basil or
   ½ teaspoon dried
Dash pepper

In 10-inch nonstick skillet combine oil and margarine and heat over medium heat until margarine is bubbly and hot; add onion and mashed garlic and sauté until onion is translucent. Add eggplant and cook, stirring occasionally, until lightly browned; stir in tomato and basil. Reduce heat to low, cover pan, and let simmer until eggplant is soft and mixture thickens slightly, 15 to 20 minutes.

For Additional Servings Use

	3 servings	4 servings	6 servings
oil	2¼ t	1 T	1 T + 1½ t
margarine	1½ t	2 t	1 T
onions	⅓ c + 2 t	½ c	¾ c
garlic	1 clove, with	2 cloves, with	3 cloves, with
	¼ t salt	½ t salt	½ t salt
eggplant	3 c	4 c	6 c
tomatoes	1½ medium	2 medium	3 medium
basil	1 T + 1½ t fresh	2 T fresh or	3 T fresh or
	or ½ t dried	1 t dried	1 t dried
pepper	dash	⅛ t	⅛ t
skillet	10-inch	12-inch	12-inch
Method: simmer	as directed	as directed	20 to 30 minutes

Elegant Mushroom Sauté

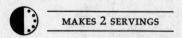

MAKES 2 SERVINGS

1 tablespoon margarine
4 cups sliced mushrooms
¼ cup sliced scallions (green
 onions)

1 tablespoon dry white wine
¼ teaspoon salt
⅛ teaspoon pepper

In 12-inch nonstick skillet heat margarine over high heat until bubbly and hot; add mushrooms and scallions and sauté, stirring occasionally, until vegetables are lightly browned and moisture has evaporated. Add wine and cook, stirring constantly, for 1 minute; sprinkle with salt and pepper.

For Additional Servings Use

	3 servings	*4 servings*	*6 servings*
margarine	1 T + 1½ t	2 T	3 T
mushrooms	6 c	8 c	12 c
scallions	⅓ c + 2 t	½ c	¾ c
wine	1 T + 1½ t	2 T	3 T
salt	¼ t	½ t	¾ t
pepper	⅛ t	¼ t	¼ t, or to taste
skillet	12-inch	12-inch	4-qt saucepan

Sautéed Tomatoes

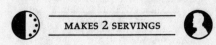

MAKES 2 SERVINGS

Make sure to dredge tomatoes in flour immediately before cooking; if allowed to stand, tomatoes will soak up flour and, when cooked, slices will become soggy.

3 tablespoons all-purpose flour
¼ teaspoon each salt and ground
   celery seed
⅛ teaspoon pepper

2 very ripe medium tomatoes, cut
   into ½-inch-thick slices
1 tablespoon margarine
1 cup shredded lettuce

On sheet of wax paper, or on a paper plate, combine flour and seasonings; dredge tomato slices in flour, coating both sides of each slice. In 12-inch nonstick skillet heat margarine over high heat until bubbly and hot; add tomatoes and sauté, turning once, until browned on both sides. Arrange lettuce on serving plate and top with sautéed tomato slices.

For Additional Servings Use

	3 servings	4 servings	6 servings
flour	¼ c + 1½ t	⅓ c + 2 t	½ c + 1 T
salt and celery seed	¼ t each	½ t each	¾ t each
pepper	⅛ t	¼ t	¼ t, or to taste
tomatoes	3 medium	4 medium	6 medium
margarine	1 T + 1½ t	2 T	3 T
lettuce	1½ c	2 c	3 c
Method: prepare in	2 batches	2 batches	3 batches

Zucchini-Apple Sauté

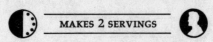

MAKES 2 SERVINGS

1 tablespoon plus 1 teaspoon
   margarine
4 cups sliced zucchini
½ cup thinly sliced onion
2 small apples, cored, pared, and
   thinly sliced

¼ teaspoon salt
Dash each ground cinnamon and
   freshly ground pepper

In 10-inch skillet heat margarine over medium heat until bubbly and hot; add zucchini and onion and sauté until zucchini is tender-crisp, about 4 minutes. Add remaining ingredients, cover, and cook just until apples soften slightly, about 5 minutes.

For Additional Servings Use

	3 servings	*4 servings*	*6 servings*
margarine	2 T	2 T + 2 t	¼ c
zucchini	6 c	8 c	12 c
onions	¾ c	1 c	1½ c
apples	3 small	4 small	6 small
salt	¼ t	½ t	¾ t
cinnamon and pepper	dash each	⅛ t each	⅛ t each, or to taste
skillet	12-inch	3-qt saucepan	5-qt saucepot or Dutch oven

Zucchini-Corn Sauté

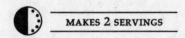

MAKES 2 SERVINGS

1 tablespoon plus 1 teaspoon olive
 oil
½ cup chopped onion
1 garlic clove, minced, or ¼
 teaspoon garlic powder
3 cups diced zucchini
1 cup canned crushed tomatoes

½ teaspoon each salt and basil
 leaves
¼ teaspoon oregano leaves
Dash freshly ground pepper
1 cup drained canned whole-kernel
 corn

In 12-inch skillet heat oil over medium heat; add onion and garlic (or garlic powder) and sauté until onion is soft. Stir in zucchini, tomatoes, and
seasonings; cover and cook until zucchini is tender, about 5 minutes. Stir
in corn and cook just until heated.

For Additional Servings Use

	3 servings	4 servings	6 servings
oil	2 T	2 T + 2 t	¼ c
onions	¾ c	1 c	1½ c
garlic	1 clove or ¼ t powder	2 cloves or ½ t powder	3 cloves or ¾ t powder
zucchini	4½ c	6 c	9 c
tomatoes	1½ c	2 c	3 c
salt and basil leaves	½ t each	1 t each	1½ t each
oregano leaves	¼ t	½ t	¾ t
pepper	dash	⅛ t	⅛ t, or to taste
corn	1½ c	2 c	3 c
skillet	12-inch	3-qt saucepan	5-qt saucepot or Dutch oven

Broccoli-Stuffed Potato

MAKES 2 SERVINGS

Potato can be stuffed early in the day, then wrapped and refrigerated until ready to bake; bake just prior to serving.

2 teaspoons margarine
2 tablespoons minced shallots or onion
½ cup cooked chopped fresh or frozen broccoli, pureed
¼ cup prepared instant chicken broth and seasoning mix (prepared according to packet directions)

1 baked potato (9 ounces), cut in half lengthwise
2 ounces Cheddar cheese, shredded
Dash each salt, pepper, and paprika

In small nonstick skillet heat margarine until bubbly and hot; add shallots (or onion) and sauté briefly, about 1 minute. Add broccoli and broth and stir to combine; remove from heat and set aside.

Preheat oven to 400°F. Scoop pulp from potato halves into small bowl, reserving shells; add broccoli mixture, cheese, and seasonings to bowl and mash until thoroughly blended. Divide mixture into reserved shells and bake until lightly browned, 20 to 25 minutes.

For Additional Servings Use

	4 servings	6 servings	8 servings
margarine	1 T + 1 t	2 T	2 T + 2 t
shallots or onions	¼ c	⅓ c + 2 t	½ c
broccoli	1 c	1½ c	2 c
broth	½ c	¾ c	1 c
potatoes	2 (9 oz each)	3 (9 oz each)	4 (9 oz each)
cheese	4 oz	6 oz	8 oz
salt, pepper, and paprika	⅛ t each	⅛ t each, or to taste	¼ t each
skillet	small	8-inch	9-inch

Parmesan-Topped Stuffed Potato

MAKES 2 SERVINGS

Stuffed potatoes lend themselves to advance preparation; see note on Broccoli-Stuffed Potato (page 278).

2 teaspoons margarine
2 tablespoons minced shallots or
  onion
1 baked potato (9 ounces), cut in
  half lengthwise

½ cup cooked fresh or frozen
  broccoli, pureed
¼ cup plain lowfat yogurt
Dash each salt and pepper
2 teaspoons grated Parmesan cheese

In small nonstick skillet heat margarine until bubbly and hot; add shallots (or onion) and sauté briefly, about 1 minute; remove from heat and set aside.

Preheat oven to 400°F. Scoop pulp from potato halves into small bowl, reserving shells; add sautéed shallots (or onion), broccoli, yogurt, salt, and pepper and mash until thoroughly blended. Divide mixture into reserved shells and sprinkle each with 1 teaspoon cheese; bake until lightly browned, 20 to 25 minutes.

For Additional Servings Use

	4 servings	6 servings	8 servings
margarine	1 T + 1 t	2 T	2 T + 2 t
shallots or onions	¼ c	⅓ c + 2 t	½ c
potatoes	2 (9 oz each)	3 (9 oz each)	4 (9 oz each)
broccoli	1 c	1½ c	2 c
yogurt	½ c	¾ c	1 c
salt and pepper	⅛ t each	⅛ t each, or to taste	¼ t each
cheese	1 T + 1 t	2 T	2 T + 2 t

Italian-Style Scalloped Potatoes

MAKES 2 SERVINGS

---

1 tablespoon olive oil
½ cup diced onion
2 garlic cloves, minced
1 cup canned crushed tomatoes
1 tablespoon chopped fresh basil or
    ½ teaspoon dried

1 teaspoon mashed drained canned
    anchovies
6 ounces pared potatoes, thinly
    sliced
1 ounce grated Parmesan cheese

In 9- or 10-inch nonstick skillet heat oil; add onion and garlic and sauté until onion is lightly browned. Add tomatoes, basil, and anchovies and cook, stirring occasionally, until mixture thickens slightly.

Preheat oven to 425°F. In shallow 1-quart casserole spread half of tomato mixture; arrange potato slices evenly over sauce and spoon remaining sauce over potatoes. Sprinkle evenly with cheese and bake until potatoes are cooked and cheese has melted and formed a crust, 30 to 35 minutes.

For Additional Servings Use

	3 servings	4 servings	6 servings
oil	1 T + 1½ t	2 T	3 T
onions	¾ c	1 c	1½ c
garlic	2 cloves	3 cloves	4 cloves
tomatoes	1½ c	2 c	3 c
basil	1 T fresh or ½ t dried	2 T fresh or 1 t dried	3 T fresh or 1½ t dried
anchovies	1½ t	2 t	1 T
potatoes	9 oz	12 oz	1 lb 2 oz
cheese	1½ oz	2 oz	3 oz
skillet	9- or 10-inch	10-inch	10-inch

Orange Rice

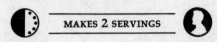

MAKES 2 SERVINGS

1 tablespoon margarine
½ cup diced celery
¼ cup diced onion
1 cup orange juice (no sugar added)

2 ounces uncooked converted rice
1 teaspoon grated orange peel
 (optional)
¼ teaspoon salt

In 1½-quart nonstick saucepan heat margarine over medium heat until bubbly and hot; add celery and onion and sauté, stirring occasionally, until vegetables are tender. Add remaining ingredients and bring to a boil. Reduce heat, cover, and let simmer until liquid is absorbed and rice is tender, 12 to 15 minutes.

For Additional Servings Use

	3 servings	*4 servings*	*6 servings*
margarine	1 T + 1½ t	2 T	3 T
celery	¾ c	1 c	1½ c
onions	⅓ c + 2 t	½ c	¾ c
orange juice	1½ c	2 c	3 c
rice	3 oz	4 oz	6 oz
orange peel (optional)	1½ t	2 t	1 T
salt	¼ t	½ t	¾ t

Mexican Corn Bread

MAKES 2 SERVINGS

¼ cup drained canned whole-kernel corn

3 tablespoons all-purpose flour

1 tablespoon uncooked yellow cornmeal

1½ teaspoons superfine sugar

¼ teaspoon each salt and double-acting baking powder

1 large egg, lightly beaten

2 tablespoons buttermilk (made from skim milk)

2 teaspoons margarine, melted

2 tablespoons each diced onion, chili pepper, and pimiento

Dash thyme leaves, crumbled

Preheat oven to 350°F. Spray 7⅜ x 3⅝ x 2¼-inch loaf pan with nonstick cooking spray and set aside.

In medium bowl combine corn, flour, cornmeal, sugar, salt, and baking powder. In small bowl combine egg, milk, and margarine; add to corn mixture and stir gently just to combine. Gently stir in remaining ingredients and pour mixture into sprayed pan; bake until firm and lightly browned, 20 to 25 minutes. Cut into squares and serve warm.

For Additional Servings Use

	4 servings	6 servings
corn	½ c	¾ c
flour	⅓ c + 2 t	½ c + 1 T
cornmeal	¾ oz (2 T)	1⅛ oz (3 T)
sugar	1 T	1 T + 1½ t
salt and baking powder	½ t each	¾ t each
eggs	2 large	3 large
buttermilk	¼ c	⅓ c + 2 t
margarine	1 T + 1 t	2 T
onions, chili peppers, and pimientos	¼ c each	⅓ c + 2 t each
thyme leaves	⅛ t	⅛ to ¼ t
pan	8 x 8 x 2-inch	8 x 8 x 2-inch
Method: bake for	30 to 35 minutes	40 to 45 minutes

Raisin Bread Pudding

MAKES 2 SERVINGS
---

1 tablespoon plus 1 teaspoon reduced-calorie margarine, divided

2 teaspoons granulated sugar, divided

1 large egg, separated

¼ cup each skim milk and orange juice (no sugar added)

½ teaspoon grated orange peel

2 slices raisin bread, cut into ½-inch cubes

1. In medium mixing bowl, using electric mixer on medium speed, beat together 1 tablespoon margarine and 1 teaspoon sugar until combined; add egg yolk and beat until fluffy. Add milk, juice, and peel and beat at low speed until combined (mixture will appear grainy). Stir in bread cubes and let stand for 15 minutes, then stir again.

2. Preheat oven to 350°F. Grease two 6-ounce custard cups with ½ teaspoon margarine each and set aside.

3. In separate mixing bowl, using clean beaters, beat egg white at high speed until soft peaks form; add remaining sugar and continue beating until stiff peaks form. Gently fold beaten white into bread mixture.

4. Turn bread mixture into greased cups and bake for 30 minutes (until pudding is puffed and browned); let stand for 5 minutes before serving.

For Additional Servings Use

	4 servings	*6 servings*	*8 servings*
margarine	2 T + 2 t	¼ c	⅓ c
sugar	1 T + 1 t	2 T	2 T + 2 t
eggs	2 large	3 large	4 large
milk and juice	½ c each	¾ c each	1 c each
orange peel	1 t	1½ t	2 t
bread	4 slices	6 slices	8 slices
Method: in Step 1 beat	2 T margarine with 2 t sugar	3 T margarine with 1 T sugar	¼ c margarine with 1 T + 1 t sugar

Good Lookin' Cookin'

Entrées
Chilled Poached Fish Salad with Louis Dressing
Pasta Salad
Tortilla Pie
Curried Papaya Chicken
Meat Loaf Wellington
Chicken Livers with Caper Sauce in Croustades

Side Dishes
Potato Soufflé
Skillet Broccoli Soufflé
Florets and Pasta in Parmesan Sauce
Vegetable-Pasta Medley in Onion-Cheddar Sauce

Accompaniments
Onion Popovers
Spicy Vegetable-Filled Biscuits

Desserts and Snacks
Orange "Cream" Crêpes
Lemon Meringue Pie
"Linzer Tart" Cookies
Rugalach (Raisin Crescents)
Fruited Chiffon Parfaits
Orange Spanish "Cream"
Strawberry Gelatin Cloud

"If it looks good, it tastes good" is a popular theory among chefs. It's true that we eat with our eyes as well as our mouths, and even a delicious dish may be spurned if it doesn't look appetizing.

The easiest way to bring a dish to life is to use garnishes. These are edible items added to a dish to decorate it, the way jewelry dresses up an outfit. Garnishes should be pleasing in shape, offer a contrast in color, and be compatible in taste with the dishes they are decorating. Fortunately, garnishes don't have to be difficult or complicated to be eye-catching. Often, the simplest ones, which can be prepared in just a few minutes, are the most effective, such as a parsley sprig or strips of orange peel. Once you realize how easy garnishing is and what a difference it can make, you won't feel that it is something to be reserved only for company. Try a few of our suggestions; then let your own creativity concoct others. (Remember to wash all vegetables before making garnishes.)

GARNISHES

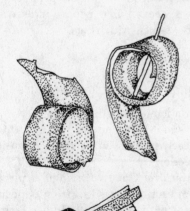

Carrot Curls

Pare carrot. Using vegetable peeler, shave off wafer-thin lengthwise strips. Twist each strip into a circle around your finger; secure with a toothpick. Place in bowl of ice water; refrigerate to set curls. Remove picks before using; curls will remain intact.

Carrot and Celery Sticks in Black Olive Rings

Pare celery and carrots; cut into ¼-inch-wide x 2½- to 3-inch-long sticks. Using pitted olives, cut each into 3 to 4 rings. Push 2 to 3 vegetable sticks through each ring.

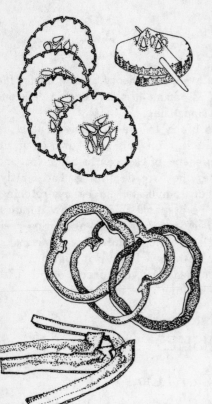

Fluted Cucumber Slices and Cucumber Cones

Slices: Using tines of a fork, score cucumber lengthwise. Cut crosswise into thin slices. Refrigerate on ice until ready to serve. Pat dry with paper towels before using.

Cones: Score and cut cucumber as directed above. Make one cut just to center of each fluted slice; twist into a cone and secure with a toothpick. Refrigerate as for slices.

Green and Red Bell Pepper Strips and Rings

Strips: Cut pepper in half lengthwise; remove seeds. Cut each half into ¼-inch-wide strips.

Rings: Cut stem end off pepper; remove seeds. Cut pepper crosswise into ¼-inch-wide rings.

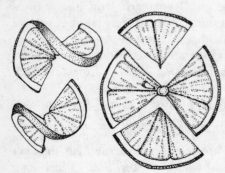

Lemon Twists and Butterflies

Cut a lemon into thin slices.

Twists: Make one cut just to center of each slice; twist halves in opposite directions.

Butterflies: Cut two triangular pieces from each lemon slice (from opposite sides) with points of triangles facing center of slice. The remaining shape will resemble a butterfly.

Radish Roses, Accordions, and Mushrooms

Roses: Select large radishes. Cut thin slice from both ends of radish. With a sharp paring knife, beginning at top and working downward, cut 4 to 6 thin slices around radish, as if paring (cutting almost to, but not through, base). This will form petals. Place in bowl of ice water and refrigerate until petals open; pat dry before using.

Accordions: Trim a thin slice from each end of radish. Cut parallel slashes, about ⅛ inch apart, along length of radish, cutting almost to, but not through, other side. Refrigerate as for roses.

Mushrooms: Cut off tip of radish. Using sharp paring knife, make ¼-inch-deep cut all around center of radish. Shape a mushroom stem by cutting away portions of radish from stem end to center cut.

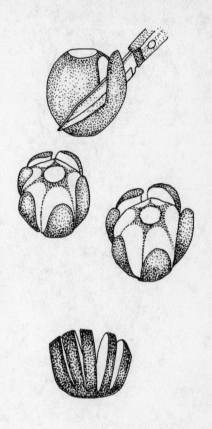

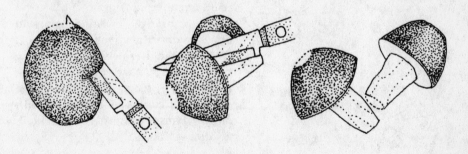

Fluted Mushrooms

Use medium mushrooms. With tip of sharp paring knife, mark center of mushroom cap. Holding knife at slight angle, make curved cut from center of cap to edge, about ⅛ inch deep. Repeat all around cap, making about ten evenly spaced cuts. Make a second curved cut just behind each original cut, slanting knife to create narrow strips that can be lifted out. If desired, trim stems level with caps.

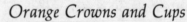

Orange Crowns and Cups

Crowns: Holding orange so that stem end is up, insert point of sharp paring knife at an angle in center of side of orange, making small, angular cut. Remove knife and insert again right next to original cut, angling knife in opposite direction. Repeat all around fruit, creating a zigzag cut around center of orange. Twisting halves in opposite directions, pull halves apart, creating orange crowns.

Cups: Using a serrated spoon or melon-baller, scoop pulp from orange crown. Fill cup as desired (e.g., with dietary frozen dessert, fruit cocktail, gelatin, seafood salad).

Pickle Fans

Starting from top, make several evenly spaced lengthwise slices through pickle to about ¼ inch from stem end. Spread slices to form a fan. The more slices, the wider the fan.

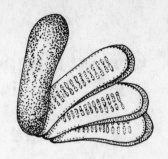

Scallion (Green Onion) Brushes

Trim off roots and top of scallion, leaving a piece 3 to 4 inches long, half white, half green. Using sharp paring knife and starting at either end, make several 1-inch long cuts in scallion. Cut other end in same manner. Place in bowl of ice water until ends curl; pat dry before using. (This also works well with celery. Use 2-inch lengths and proceed in same manner.)

Tomato Crowns

Using a firm tomato, cut as for orange crowns. Carefully pull tomato halves apart.

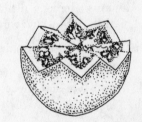

Other Garnishes

Chopped chives, chopped fresh basil and parsley, sprigs of basil, mint, parsley, or watercress, grated carrot, celery ribs, or lemon wedges, cinnamon sticks, ground cinnamon and nutmeg.

Chilled Poached Fish Salad with Louis Dressing

MAKES 2 SERVINGS

½ cup each diced onion, celery, and carrot
4 lemon slices
Dash each salt and pepper
1 cup water
10 ounces fish fillets (any firm white-meat fish)

2 tablespoons chopped scallion
1 tablespoon plus 1 teaspoon chili sauce
1 tablespoon each mayonnaise, plain lowfat yogurt, and lemon juice
8 chilled loose-leafed lettuce leaves

In 10-inch nonstick skillet combine onion, celery, carrot, lemon slices, salt, and pepper; add water and bring to a boil. Add fish and spoon some vegetables over fillets; return liquid to boil. Reduce heat, cover, and let simmer until fish flakes easily when tested with a fork but is still firm, about 5 minutes. Remove fish to a plate, discarding liquid and solids; let fish cool slightly, then cover and refrigerate until chilled.

In small bowl combine remaining ingredients except lettuce; mix well. Chill covered.

Cut fish into bite-size pieces and serve on lettuce leaves. Spoon sauce over fish.

For Additional Servings Use

	3 servings	4 servings	6 servings
onions, celery, and carrots	¾ c each	1 c each	1½ c each
lemon slices	6	8	12
salt and pepper	dash each	⅛ t each	⅛ t each
water	1½ c	2 c	3 c
fish	15 oz	1¼ lb	1 lb 14 oz
scallions	3 T	¼ c	⅓ c + 2 t
chili sauce	2 T	2 T + 2 t	¼ c
mayonnaise, yogurt, and lemon juice	1 T + 1½ t each	2 T each	3 T each
lettuce	12 leaves	16 leaves	24 leaves
skillet	10-inch	12-inch	5-qt saucepot or Dutch oven

Pasta Salad

MAKES 2 SERVINGS

A variety of shapes and colors gives this easy-to-prepare salad special eye-appeal.

1 cup grated zucchini
¾ cup cooked ditalini (small tube macaroni), chilled
4 ounces diced boiled ham
2 ounces Cheddar cheese, diced
6 cherry tomatoes, cut into halves
1 tablespoon diced onion
1 tablespoon each olive oil, wine vinegar, and lemon juice

½ teaspoon oregano leaves
¼ teaspoon each salt and garlic powder
Dash pepper
8 iceberg, romaine, or loose-leafed lettuce leaves

In large bowl combine all ingredients except lettuce and toss until well mixed; cover and refrigerate for at least 1 hour. Toss again just before serving and serve on bed of lettuce leaves.

For Additional Servings Use

	3 servings	4 servings	6 servings
zucchini	1½ c	2 c	3 c
ditalini	1 c + 2 T	1½ c	2¼ c
ham	6 oz	8 oz	12 oz
cheese	3 oz	4 oz	6 oz
cherry tomatoes	9	12	18
onions, oil, vinegar, and lemon juice	1 T + 1½ t each	2 T each	3 T each
oregano leaves	½ t	¾ t	1 t
salt and garlic powder	¼ t each	½ t each	½ t each
pepper	dash	⅛ t	⅛ t
lettuce	12 leaves	16 leaves	24 leaves

Tortilla Pie

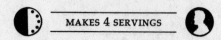

MAKES 4 SERVINGS

12 ounces drained canned red
  kidney beans
¼ cup (4-ounce can) drained
  canned whole green chili peppers,
  minced
¼ cup minced onion
1 tablespoon chili powder
½ teaspoon oregano leaves

¼ teaspoon salt
⅛ teaspoon hot sauce
Dash ground cumin
4 corn tortillas (6-inch diameter
  each)
4 ounces sharp Cheddar cheese,
  shredded

Preheat oven to 400°F. In medium bowl, using the back of a fork, mash kidney beans to a paste; add chili peppers, onion, and seasonings and mix well. Set aside.

Break each tortilla in half; on baking sheet or sheet of foil bake tortilla halves until crisp, about 2 minutes. Remove from oven but do not turn oven off.

Arrange baked halves, curved-side out and overlapping, around edge of 8-inch pie plate; spread kidney bean mixture evenly over tortillas, leaving a tortilla border all the way around. Sprinkle mixture with cheese and bake until cheese is melted and pie is hot, about 15 minutes.

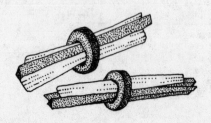

Curried Papaya Chicken

MAKES 2 SERVINGS

1½ pounds chicken parts, skinned
2½ teaspoons all-purpose flour, divided
¾ teaspoon curry powder, divided
¼ teaspoon salt
⅛ teaspoon pepper
2 teaspoons margarine, divided

¼ cup diced onion
½ packet instant chicken broth and seasoning mix, dissolved in ¾ cup hot water
2 tablespoons plain lowfat yogurt
½ medium papaya, pared, seeded, and cut into long strips

Pat chicken dry. On wax paper combine 1½ teaspoons flour, ¼ teaspoon curry powder, and salt and pepper; dredge chicken in mixture. In 10-inch skillet heat half the margarine until bubbly and hot; add chicken and brown on all sides. Remove from pan. In same skillet heat remaining margarine; add onion and sauté until softened, 1 to 2 minutes. Return chicken to skillet; add broth and bring to a boil. Reduce heat, cover and let simmer until chicken is tender, about 40 minutes. Remove chicken to platter; reserve pan juices.

In small bowl combine yogurt and remaining flour and curry powder, mixing well; add to pan juices along with papaya. Cook, stirring gently, until papaya is heated and sauce is thickened; serve over chicken.

For Additional Servings Use

	3 servings	4 servings	6 servings
chicken	2¼ lb	3 lb	4½ lb
flour	1 T + ¾ t	1 T + 2 t	2 T + 1½ t
curry powder	¾ t	1 to 1¼ t	1½ t
salt	¼ t	½ t	½ t
pepper	⅛ t	¼ t	¼ t
margarine	1 T	1 T + 1 t	2 T
onions	⅓ c + 2 t	½ c	¾ c
broth mix	¾ pkt (about ¾ t) in 1 c + 2 T water	1 pkt in 1½ c water	1½ pkt in 2¼ c water
yogurt	3 T	¼ c	⅓ c + 2 t
papayas	¾ medium	1 medium	1½ medium
skillet	10-inch	12-inch	5-qt saucepot or Dutch oven
Method: dredge in	2¼ t flour and ¼ t curry powder	1 T flour and ½ t curry powder	1 T + 1½ t flour and ¾ t curry powder

Meat Loaf Wellington

MAKES 2 SERVINGS

---

5 ounces ground beef
⅓ cup part-skim ricotta cheese
1 egg
3 tablespoons plain dried bread
  crumbs
2 tablespoons each minced celery
  and chopped fresh parsley
1 tablespoon water

2 teaspoons minced shallot or onion
1 teaspoon Worcestershire sauce
¼ teaspoon salt
Dash pepper
3 ounces peeled cooked potato
2 tablespoons skim milk
2 teaspoons each margarine and
  grated Parmesan cheese

In medium bowl combine first 10 ingredients; shape into a loaf. Transfer to rack in roasting pan and bake at 375°F. for 25 to 30 minutes.

In small mixing bowl combine potato, milk, margarine, and grated cheese and, using electric mixer, whip until smooth.

Transfer meat loaf to an 8 x 8-inch ovenproof serving dish; spread with potato mixture, coating entire loaf. Using a fork, make ridges in coating to form a design. Bake at 425°F. until lightly browned, about 15 minutes.

For Additional Servings Use

	4 servings	*6 servings*	*8 servings*
beef	10 oz	15 oz	1¼ lb
ricotta cheese	⅔ c	1 c	1⅓ c
eggs	2	3	4
bread crumbs	⅓ c + 2 t	½ c + 1 T	¾ c
celery and parsley	¼ c each	⅓ c each	½ c each
water	2 T	3 T	¼ c
shallots or onions	1 T + 1 t	2 T	2 T + 2 t
Worcestershire sauce	2 t	1 T	1 T + 1 t
salt	½ t	¾ t	1 t
pepper	⅛ t	⅛ t	¼ t
potatoes	6 oz	9 oz	12 oz
milk	¼ c	⅓ c + 2 t	½ c
margarine and Parmesan cheese	1 T + 1 t each	2 T each	2 T + 2 t each
Method: to prepare loaf, bake at 375°F. for	25 to 30 minutes	35 to 40 minutes	40 to 45 minutes

Chicken Livers with Caper Sauce in Croustades (Toast Cases)

MAKES 2 SERVINGS

2 slices white bread
10 ounces chicken livers, cut into halves
2 teaspoons all-purpose flour, divided
½ cup plain lowfat yogurt
2 teaspoons each Dijon-style or spicy brown mustard and margarine

½ cup chopped onion
1 tablespoon plus 1 teaspoon dry white wine or vermouth
2 teaspoons chopped capers
½ teaspoon Worcestershire sauce
⅛ teaspoon each salt and pepper
2 teaspoons chopped fresh parsley

Preheat oven to 400°F. Using a rolling pin, flatten each slice of bread; press each slice into a 6-ounce custard cup, forming bread into cup shape, and bake until lightly browned, about 7 minutes.

Sprinkle livers with half of the flour and set aside. In small bowl combine yogurt, mustard, and remaining flour and set aside. In 9-inch skillet heat margarine until bubbly and hot; add onion and sauté until soft, about 2 minutes. Add livers and sauté until browned, about 3 minutes; stir in wine (or vermouth) and bring to a boil. Add yogurt mixture, stirring to combine; add capers, Worcestershire, salt, and pepper and cook, stirring constantly, until thickened. Stir in parsley. Fill each croustade with an equal amount of liver mixture.

For Additional Servings Use

	3 servings	4 servings	6 servings
bread	3 slices	4 slices	6 slices
livers	15 oz	1¼ lb	1 lb 14 oz
flour	1 T	1 T + 1 t	2 T
yogurt	¾ c	1 c	1½ c
mustard and margarine	1 T each	1 T + 1 t each	2 T each
onions	¾ c	1 c	1½ c
wine or vermouth	2 T	2 T + 2 t	¼ c
capers	1 T	1 T + 1 t	2 T
Worcestershire sauce	¾ t	1 t	1½ t
salt and pepper	⅛ t each	¼ t each	¼ t each
parsley	1 T	1 T + 1 t	2 T
skillet	10-inch	12-inch	12-inch

Potato Soufflé

MAKES 2 SERVINGS

1 tablespoon plus 1 teaspoon
  margarine
½ cup each minced scallions (green
  onions) or onion and minced
  carrot
3 tablespoons all-purpose flour
½ cup each evaporated skimmed
  and skim milk

3 ounces peeled cooked potato,
  mashed
2 large eggs, separated (at room
  temperature)
½ teaspoon salt
Dash each white pepper and cream
  of tartar

Preheat oven to 350°F. In 1- or 1½-quart nonstick saucepan heat margarine until bubbly and hot; add scallions (or onion) and carrot and sauté until scallions soften, about 2 minutes (*do not brown*). Add flour and stir quickly to combine. Remove pan from heat and add evaporated skimmed and skim milk, stirring until well combined. Cook over low heat, stirring constantly, until thickened; add mashed potato and combine thoroughly. Remove pan from heat and quickly stir in egg yolks; season with salt and pepper and set aside.

In medium bowl, using electric mixer at high speed, beat egg whites until foamy; add cream of tartar and beat until stiff peaks form. Gently fold whites into potato mixture. Spray 1½-quart soufflé dish or casserole with nonstick cooking spray; turn potato mixture into dish and bake for 30 minutes (until puffed and golden brown). Serve immediately.

For Additional Servings Use

	3 servings	4 servings	6 servings
margarine	2 T	2 T + 2 t	¼ c
scallions (or onions) and carrots	¾ c each	1 c each	1½ c each
flour	¼ c + 1½ t	⅓ c + 2 t	½ c + 1 T
evaporated skimmed and skim milk	¾ c each	1 c each	1½ c each
potatoes	4½ oz	6 oz	9 oz
eggs	3 large	4 large	6 large
salt	¾ t	1 t	1½ t
white pepper and cream of tartar	dash each	⅛ t each	⅛ t each

Skillet Broccoli Soufflé

MAKES 2 SERVINGS

This can be used as an entrée as well as a side dish.

1 teaspoon olive or vegetable oil
2 garlic cloves, minced
1 cup well-drained cooked chopped broccoli (reserve 2 florets for garnish)
¼ teaspoon salt
⅔ cup part-skim ricotta cheese

2 eggs, separated (at room temperature)
1 tablespoon chopped fresh parsley
2 teaspoons grated Parmesan cheese
⅛ teaspoon freshly ground pepper
1 teaspoon margarine

In 8-inch skillet that has an ovenproof or removable handle heat oil over medium heat; add garlic and sauté briefly, about 30 seconds (*do not brown*). Add broccoli and salt and cook, stirring occasionally, for about 3 minutes to blend flavors. Remove broccoli to a plate and wipe skillet clean; set aside.

Preheat oven to 400°F. In 1-quart mixing bowl combine ricotta cheese, egg yolks, parsley, Parmesan cheese, and pepper; beat until smooth. In separate bowl, using clean beaters, beat egg whites until stiff peaks form; fold egg whites alternately with broccoli into cheese mixture.

In same skillet heat margarine until bubbly and hot; pour in broccoli mixture and, using spatula, gently smooth top. Remove skillet to oven and bake for 15 to 20 minutes (until puffed and lightly browned); serve immediately, garnished with reserved broccoli florets.

For Additional Servings Use _____

	3 servings	4 servings	6 servings
olive or vegetable oil	1½ t	2 t	1 T
garlic	3 cloves	4 cloves	6 cloves
broccoli	1½ c	2 c	3 c
salt	¼ t	½ t	¾ t
ricotta cheese	1 c	1⅓ c	2 c
eggs	3	4	6
parsley	1 T	2 T	3 T
Parmesan cheese	1 T	1 T + 1 t	2 T
pepper	⅛ t	¼ t	¼ t, or to taste
margarine	1½ t	2 t	1 T
skillet	9-inch	10-inch	12-inch

Florets and Pasta in Parmesan Sauce

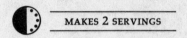 MAKES 2 SERVINGS

Let Béchamel thaw in refrigerator for several hours before using.

2 servings frozen Béchamel (see
    page 192), thawed
2 ounces grated Parmesan cheese
½ teaspoon oregano leaves
⅛ teaspoon garlic powder

2 cups each cooked broccoli and
    cauliflower florets
¾ cup cooked rotelle or ditalini
    (spiral or small tube macaroni)

In 2-quart nonstick saucepan combine Béchamel, cheese, oregano, and garlic powder; cook over low heat, stirring constantly, until cheese is melted and mixture is thoroughly blended. Add vegetables and pasta and cook, stirring gently, until vegetables and macaroni are thoroughly coated with sauce and heated.

For Additional Servings Use

	3 servings	4 servings	6 servings
Béchamel	3 servings	4 servings	6 servings
cheese	3 oz	4 oz	6 oz
oregano leaves	½ t	1 t	1 t
garlic powder	⅛ t	¼ t	¼ t
broccoli and cauliflower florets	3 c each	4 c each	6 c each
rotelle or ditalini	1 c + 2 T	1½ c	2¼ c

Vegetable-Pasta Medley in Onion-Cheddar Sauce

MAKES 2 SERVINGS

2 teaspoons margarine
¼ cup minced onion
1 tablespoon plus 1½ teaspoons all-purpose flour
1 cup skim milk (at room temperature)
2 ounces extra-sharp Cheddar cheese, shredded

¼ teaspoon Worcestershire sauce
Dash each salt and pepper
2 cups each cooked broccoli florets and diagonally sliced carrots (¼-inch-thick slices)
½ cup cooked rotelle (spiral macaroni) or shell macaroni

In 2-quart nonstick saucepan heat margarine over medium heat until bubbly and hot; add onion and cook until translucent, about 2 minutes. Add flour and, using wire whisk, stir until thoroughly combined; continue cooking and stirring for 1 minute longer.

Remove pan from heat and gradually stir in milk; return to medium heat and cook, stirring constantly, until mixture is smooth and thickened. Reduce heat to low and add cheese and seasonings; cook, stirring constantly, until cheese is melted and mixture is thoroughly blended. Add vegetables and macaroni and cook, stirring gently, until macaroni and vegetables are thoroughly coated with sauce and heated.

For Additional Servings Use

	3 servings	4 servings	6 servings
margarine	1 T	1 T + 1 t	2 T
onions	⅓ c + 2 t	½ c	¾ c
flour	2 T + ¾ t	3 T	¼ c + 1½ t
milk	1½ c	2 c	3 c
cheese	3 oz	4 oz	6 oz
Worcestershire sauce	¼ t	½ t	¾ t
salt and pepper	dash each	⅛ t each	⅛ t each
broccoli and carrots	3 c each	4 c each	6 c each
rotelle or shell macaroni	¾ c	1 c	1½ c

Onion Popovers

MAKES 2 SERVINGS, 1 POPOVER EACH

⅓ cup skim milk
1 egg
1½ teaspoons instant minced
    onion, reconstituted in 2
    tablespoons warm water

1 teaspoon vegetable oil
⅛ teaspoon salt
⅓ cup plus 2 teaspoons
    all-purpose flour

Preheat oven to 400°F. Spray two 6-ounce custard cups with nonstick cooking spray and set aside.

In small mixing bowl combine all ingredients except flour; add flour and, using electric mixer, beat until blended. Divide mixture into sprayed cups; place cups on baking sheet and bake until firm and golden brown, 40 to 45 minutes. Serve warm.

Variation: Cheese Popovers—Omit instant minced onion. Add 1½ teaspoons grated Parmesan cheese with the flour and proceed as directed.

For Additional Servings Use

	4 servings	6 servings	8 servings
milk	⅔ c	1 c	1⅓ c
eggs	2	3	4
instant minced onions	1 T reconstituted in ¼ c water	1 T + 1½ t reconstituted in ⅓ c water	2 T reconstituted in ½ c water
vegetable oil	2 t	1 T	1 T + 1 t
salt	¼ t	¼ t, or to taste	½ t
flour	¾ c	1 c + 2 T	1½ c
Variation: grated Parmesan cheese	1 T	1 T + 1½ t	2 T

Spicy Vegetable-Filled Biscuits

 MAKES 2 SERVINGS, 1 BISCUIT EACH

2 ready-to-bake refrigerated
    buttermilk flaky biscuits (1 ounce
    each)
1 teaspoon olive oil
2 tablespoons each minced onion,
    red bell pepper, and green bell
    pepper

⅛ teaspoon mashed fresh garlic
Dash each chili powder and hot
    sauce

Separate each biscuit into 2 halves and set aside. In small nonstick skillet heat oil; add vegetables and sauté until soft. Add seasonings and stir to combine; remove from heat.

Preheat oven to 400°F. In 7-inch round baking pan arrange 2 biscuit halves and spoon ¼ of vegetable mixture onto each; top each portion with 1 of the remaining biscuit halves and divide remaining vegetable mixture over each. Bake until browned, 10 to 12 minutes.

For Additional Servings Use

	3 servings	*4 servings*	*6 servings*
biscuits	3 (1 oz each)	4 (1 oz each)	6 (1 oz each)
oil	1½ t	2 t	1 T
onions and peppers	3 T each	¼ c each	⅓ c + 2 t each
garlic	⅛ t	½ clove	1 clove
chili powder	dash	dash	⅛ t
hot sauce	dash	2 drops	2 to 3 drops
Method: onto bottom half of each biscuit spoon	⅙ veg. mix.	⅛ veg. mix.	1⁄12 veg. mix.

Orange "Cream" Crêpes

 MAKES 2 SERVINGS, 2 CRÊPES EACH

Filling

1 cup part-skim ricotta cheese
2 teaspoons granulated sugar
1 teaspoon grated orange peel
¼ teaspoon ground cinnamon

Crêpes

4 frozen crêpes (see Basic Crêpes, page 182), thawed for about 15 minutes

Sauce

1 small orange
½ cup orange juice (no sugar added)
1 tablespoon plus 1 teaspoon reduced-calorie orange marmalade (16 calories per 2 teaspoons)
1 teaspoon grated orange peel

To Prepare Filling: In small bowl combine cheese, sugar, orange peel, and cinnamon, mixing well; cover and refrigerate until chilled.

To Prepare Sauce: Peel and section orange over small saucepan to catch juice, adding sections to pan; add orange juice, marmalade, and orange peel and bring to a boil. Reduce heat and let simmer, stirring occasionally, until sauce is syrupy and reduced to about ½ cup; let cool.

To Serve: Spoon an equal amount of chilled filling onto center of each crêpe and fold sides over filling to enclose; arrange crêpes, seam-side down, on serving platter and top with sauce.

For Additional Servings Use

	3 servings	*4 servings*	*6 servings*
cheese	1½ c	2 c	3 c
sugar	1 T	1 T + 1 t	2 T
orange peel (for filling)	1½ t	2 t	1 T
cinnamon	¼ t	½ t	¾ t
crêpes	6	8	12
oranges	1½ small	2 small	3 small
orange juice	¾ c	1 c	1½ c
marmalade	2 T	2 T + 2 t	¼ c
orange peel (for sauce)	1½ t	2 t	1 T
Method: reduce sauce to about	¾ c	1 c	1½ c

Lemon Meringue Pie

MAKES 8 SERVINGS

Crust

1 frozen pastry shell (in pie plate),
   see Basic Pastry Shell (page 180)

Filling

1 envelope (four ½-cup servings)
   lemon-flavored gelatin

1 cup each boiling water and ice
   cubes
½ cup thawed frozen dairy
   whipped topping

Meringue

2 egg whites (at room temperature)
1 teaspoon confectioners' sugar,
   sifted

Advance Preparation—About 2 hours before serving, prepare:
Crust: Preheat oven to 400°F. Using fork, prick bottom and sides of pastry shell in several places; bake until lightly browned, 30 to 35 minutes (if shell has not been frozen, bake 20 to 25 minutes). Remove from oven and let cool.

Filling: In 1-quart heatproof mixing bowl dissolve gelatin in boiling water; add ice cubes and stir until mixture thickens. Remove and discard any unmelted ice. Add whipped topping and, using wire whisk or electric mixer, blend thoroughly. Cover bowl and refrigerate until mixture mounds when dropped from a spoon, about 15 minutes (if mixture becomes too firm, whip slightly); pour into cooled pie crust, cover, and refrigerate until firm, about 1 hour.

Final Preparation—About 15 minutes before serving, prepare:
Meringue: In 1-quart mixing bowl, using electric mixer at high speed, beat egg whites until soft peaks form; add sugar and beat until stiff but not dry.

Pie: Spread meringue over chilled filling, making sure that meringue touches edges of crust (this will prevent meringue from shrinking). Broil until meringue is lightly browned, about 15 seconds; immediately remove from broiler. Let stand 5 to 10 minutes before cutting.

"Linzer Tart" Cookies

 MAKES 2 SERVINGS, 6 COOKIES EACH

⅓ cup plus 2 teaspoons
  all-purpose flour
¼ teaspoon double-acting baking
  powder
Dash salt
1 tablespoon plus 1 teaspoon
  margarine

1½ teaspoons granulated sugar
½ teaspoon vanilla extract
1 tablespoon ice water
2 teaspoons reduced-calorie apricot
  or red raspberry spread (16
  calories per 2 teaspoons)
½ teaspoon confectioners' sugar

Onto sheet of wax paper or paper plate sift together flour, baking powder, and salt; set aside. In small bowl cream margarine with granulated sugar; add vanilla and stir to combine. Mix in sifted dry ingredients; add water and mix to form dough (if mixture is dry and crumbly, add up to an additional teaspoon ice water to adjust consistency).

Preheat oven to 375°F. Between 2 sheets of wax paper roll dough to about ¼-inch thickness; remove paper and, using 2-inch round cookie cutter, cut out cookies. Roll scraps of dough and continue cutting until all dough has been used (should yield 12 cookies). Transfer cookies to non-stick baking sheet and bake for 10 minutes; remove cookies to wire rack and let cool.

Top center of each cookie with an equal amount of apricot or raspberry spread and sprinkle each with an equal amount of confectioners' sugar.

For Additional Servings Use

	4 servings	6 servings	8 servings
flour	¾ c	1 c + 2 T	1½ c
baking powder	½ t	¾ t	1 t
salt	⅛ t	⅛ t	¼ t
margarine	2 T + 2 t	¼ c	⅓ c
granulated sugar	1 T	1 T + 1½ t	2 T
vanilla	1 t	1½ t	2 t
ice water	2 T	3 T	¼ c
reduced-calorie spread	1 T + 1 t	2 T	2 T + 2 t
confectioners' sugar	1 t	1½ t	2 t
Method: form	24 cookies	36 cookies	48 cookies

Rugalach (Raisin Crescents)

MAKES 2 SERVINGS, 6 RUGALACH EACH

Chilled Pastry Dough (see page 181)
4 dried apricot halves, chopped
2 tablespoons raisins, chopped
2 teaspoons each granulated sugar
  and reduced-calorie apricot
  spread (16 calories per 2
  teaspoons)

1 teaspoon confectioners' sugar,
  sifted

Preheat oven to 400°F. Between 2 sheets of wax paper roll dough, forming a circle about ⅛ inch thick; cut into 12 equal wedges.

In small bowl combine remaining ingredients except confectioners' sugar. Spoon an equal amount of mixture onto each wedge near curved end; roll each from curved end toward point. Place crescents on nonstick baking sheet, point-side down, and bake until golden brown, about 20 minutes. Transfer rugalach to wire rack to cool; just before serving, sprinkle each crescent with an equal amount of confectioners' sugar.

For Additional Servings Use

	3 servings	4 servings	6 servings
dough	3 servings	4 servings	6 servings
apricots	6 halves	8 halves	12 halves
raisins	3 T	¼ c	⅓ c + 2 t
granulated sugar and apricot spread	1 T each	1 T + 1 t each	2 T each
confectioners' sugar	1½ t	2 t	1 T
Method: roll out	three ⅛-inch-thick circles	two ⅛-inch-thick circles	three ⅛-inch-thick circles
cut each circle into	6 equal wedges	12 equal wedges	12 equal wedges

Fruited Chiffon Parfaits

MAKES 4 SERVINGS

To toast graham cracker crumbs, spread crumbs on baking sheet or sheet of foil; toast in oven (or toaster-oven) at 350°F.

2 cups canned fruit cocktail (no sugar added)

1 envelope (four ½-cup servings) low-calorie lemon-flavored gelatin (8 calories per ½ cup)

2 cups ice cubes

½ cup thawed frozen dairy whipped topping

4 graham crackers (2½-inch squares), made into coarse crumbs and toasted

1 tablespoon plus 1 teaspoon shredded coconut

Drain juice from 2 cups fruit cocktail into a 1-cup measure and set fruit aside; add enough water to juice to measure 1 cup liquid. Pour mixture into small saucepan and bring to a boil. Pour hot juice mixture into heat-proof medium mixing bowl; add gelatin and stir until dissolved. Add ice cubes and stir until mixture thickens, 2 to 3 minutes; remove any un-melted ice. Add whipped topping and, using electric mixer or wire whisk, beat until combined; cover with plastic wrap and refrigerate until mixture mounds when dropped from a spoon, about 5 minutes.

Chill 4 parfait glasses. In small bowl combine cracker crumbs and coco-nut. Spoon ⅛ of gelatin mixture (about ½ cup) into each chilled glass and top each with ¼ of the reserved fruit cocktail; top each portion of fruit with ¼ of the remaining gelatin mixture. Sprinkle each parfait with ¼ of the crumb mixture, cover with plastic wrap, and refrigerate until chilled.

Orange Spanish "Cream"

MAKES 4 SERVINGS

1½ teaspoons unflavored gelatin
1 cup skim milk, divided
1 large egg, separated
1 tablespoon plus ½ teaspoon
  granulated sugar, divided
2 tablespoons thawed frozen
  concentrated orange juice (no
  sugar added)

½ teaspoon grated orange peel
1 small orange, peeled and
  sectioned

1. In blender container sprinkle gelatin over ¼ cup milk and let stand to soften, about 5 minutes.

2. In small saucepan heat remaining ¾ cup milk just to a boil; add to softened gelatin and process at low speed until gelatin is dissolved. Add egg yolk and 2½ teaspoons sugar and process until well combined; add juice and orange peel and process for 1 minute longer. Pour into a bowl, cover, and chill until mixture mounds slightly when dropped from a spoon, 20 to 30 minutes.

3. In separate bowl, using electric mixer at high speed, beat egg white until soft peaks form; add remaining sugar and continue beating until stiff but not dry.

4. Fold beaten white into chilled gelatin mixture; turn into a 1-quart glass serving bowl or divide into 4 dessert dishes. Cover and chill until set, 2 to 3 hours. Serve each portion garnished with ¼ of the orange sections.

Strawberry Gelatin Cloud

MAKES 4 SERVINGS

1 envelope (four ½-cup servings)
  low-calorie strawberry-flavored
  gelatin (8 calories per ½ cup)
1 cup boiling water
2 cups ice cubes

1 egg white (from large egg), at
  room temperature
¼ cup thawed frozen dairy
  whipped topping

In medium heatproof bowl dissolve gelatin in boiling water. Add ice cubes and stir until gelatin starts to thicken, 2 to 3 minutes; remove any un-melted ice. Spoon ⅓ cup of gelatin into each of 4 dessert glasses and set aside; reserve remaining gelatin.

  In small mixing bowl, using electric mixer at high speed, beat egg white just until peaks hold their shape. Add beaten white and whipped topping to reserved gelatin and beat until combined. Spoon ¼ of mixture over each portion of gelatin in dessert glasses; cover and refrigerate until firm, about 15 minutes.

Appendix

———◆◆◆———

VEGETABLE CONVERSIONS

Recipes usually specify cup measure for vegetables. Since vegetables are not purchased in this form, in order to give you an idea of approximately how much to buy, the chart below converts cup measures to weights. Figures for canned items are based on drained weights and measures; weights of fresh items are based on cleaned and trimmed vegetables.

Vegetables	*Volume*	*Approximate Weight*
Artichoke Hearts		
Frozen	2 cups	9-ounce package
Canned	1 cup	8 ounces
Asparagus		
Fresh (sliced)	1 cup	5 ounces
Frozen (cuts and tips)	2 cups	8-ounce package
Canned (cut spears)	1 cup	8 ounces
Bean Sprouts		
Fresh	1 cup	4 ounces
Canned	1 cup	4½ ounces
Beets		
Fresh (diced or sliced)	1 cup	5 ounces
Canned (whole, diced, sliced, or julienne-cut)	1 cup	6 ounces
Broccoli		
Fresh		
chopped	2 cups	8 ounces
florets	2 cups	6 ounces
Frozen		
chopped	2 cups	10-ounce package
spears	7 to 9	10-ounce package

Vegetables	Volume	Approximate Weight
Brussels Sprouts		
Fresh	2 cups	9 ounces
Frozen	2½ cups	10-ounce package
Cabbage (shredded or chopped)	2 cups	6 ounces
Carrots		
Fresh		
chopped, diced, or chunks	2 cups	10 ounces
sliced, shredded, or strips	2 cups	8 ounces
Frozen (sliced)	2 cups	10-ounce package
Canned (sliced, diced, or whole)	2 cups	11 ounces
Cauliflower		
Fresh		
sliced	2 cups	6 ounces
chopped	2 cups	8 ounces
florets	2 cups	7 ounces
Frozen	2 cups	10-ounce package
Celery		
sliced	2 cups	8 ounces
chopped, diced, chunks, or strips	2 cups	8½ ounces
minced	2 cups	9 ounces
Chilies, canned, chopped	1 cup	8 ounces
Chinese Pea Pods (Snow Peas)		
Fresh (stem ends and strings removed)	1 cup	4 ounces
Frozen	2 cups	6-ounce package
Cucumbers		
whole (unpared)	1 medium (yields about 24 slices)	8 ounces
diced (pared)	1 cup	5 ounces
Eggplant		
sliced (pared)	2 cups	6 ounces
sliced (unpared)	2 cups	8 ounces
diced (pared)	2 cups	9 ounces

Vegetables	Volume	Approximate Weight
Green and Wax Beans		
Fresh		
whole	2 cups (about 20)	5 ounces
cut	2 cups	8 ounces
Frozen		
whole	2½ cups	9-ounce package
French-style and cuts	2 cups	9-ounce package
Canned		
cut	2 cups	9½ ounces
French-style	2 cups	9 ounces
Green and Red Bell Peppers		
whole (unseeded)	1 medium	3½ ounces
diced or chopped	1 cup	5½ ounces
sliced	1 cup	3 ounces
Lettuce (shredded or chopped)	2 cups	4 ounces
Mushrooms		
Fresh		
chopped, diced, minced, or sliced	2 cups	6½ ounces
quartered	2 cups	8 ounces
Canned		
stems and pieces	2 cups	11 ounces
slices	2 cups	9 ounces
button	2 cups	14 ounces
Onions		
sliced or rings	1 cup	4 ounces
chopped, diced, or minced	1 cup	6 ounces
Parsley (chopped)	1 cup	1 ounce
Peas		
Fresh	1 cup	5 ounces
Frozen	2 cups	10-ounce package
Canned	1 cup	6 ounces
Pimientos (diced or strips)	1 cup	9 ounces
Radishes (sliced)	1 cup	4 ounces
Sauerkraut, canned	1 cup	8 ounces

Vegetables	Volume	Approximate Weight
Scallions		
finely chopped	1 cup	4½ ounces
sliced	1 cup	3½ ounces
Shallots		
minced or chopped	½ cup	3 ounces
thinly sliced	½ cup	2 ounces
Spinach		
Fresh		
leaves	2 cups	3½ ounces
chopped	2 cups	4 ounces
Frozen (leaf-style and chopped)	2 cups	10-ounce package
Tomatoes		
Fresh		
whole	1 medium	5 ounces
chopped (with skin and seeds)	1 cup	8 ounces
chopped (blanched, peeled, and seeded)	1 cup	7½ ounces
Canned		
whole	1 cup	7¾ ounces
chopped	1 cup	8½ ounces
crushed	1 cup	9¼ ounces
Zucchini		
sliced	1 cup	4½ ounces
diced or cubed	1 cup	6¼ ounces

HELPFUL HINTS

Pan Substitutions

Where possible, it is best to use the pan size that is recommended in a recipe; however, a substitution will usually work just as well. Depending on the size of the pan and the amount of food in it, you may need to adjust the cooking time by 5 to 10 minutes. If glass or glass-ceramic is substituted for metal, the oven temperature should be reduced by 25°F. Some common pan substitutions appear at top of page 315.

Recommended Size	Approximate Volume	Possible Substitutions
8 x 1½-inch round baking pan	1½ quarts	10 x 6 x 2-inch baking dish 9 x 1½-inch round baking pan 8 x 4 x 2-inch loaf pan 9-inch pie plate
8 x 8 x 2-inch baking pan	2 quarts	11 x 7 x 1½-inch baking pan 12 x 7½ x 2-inch baking pan 9 x 5 x 3-inch loaf pan two 8 x 1½-inch round baking pans
13 x 9 x 2-inch baking pan	3 quarts	14 x 11 x 2-inch baking dish two 8 x 1½-inch round baking pans two 9 x 1½-inch round baking pans

Pan and Casserole Sizes for Expanded Recipes

When increasing a recipe, it will be necessary to increase the pan size accordingly. The following chart can be used as a "rule of thumb" for saucepans and casseroles.

Size for Unexpanded Recipe	1½ × Recipe	2 × Recipe	3 × Recipe
Small (less than 1-quart)	1-quart	1- or 1½-quart	1½- or 2-quart
1-quart	1½-quart	2-quart	3-quart
1½-quart	3-quart	3-quart	5-quart saucepot or Dutch oven
2-quart	3-quart	4-quart	6-quart saucepot or Dutch oven
3-quart	5-quart saucepot or Dutch oven	6-quart saucepot or Dutch oven	9-quart Dutch oven or 14- x 10-inch baking pan
4-quart	6-quart saucepot or Dutch oven	8-quart saucepot or Dutch oven	

SUGAR SUBSTITUTES

The use of sugar substitutes on the Weight Watchers Food Plan has always been optional. Natural sweetness is available in the form of fruits and honey. You may also use white and brown sugar, fructose, molasses, and syrup. The use of sugar substitutes is completely optional, and we believe that the decision about using them should be made by you and your physician.

NUTRITION NOTES

Nutrition is defined as the process by which we utilize foods in order to maintain healthy bodily functions. Foods provide the nutrients necessary for energy, growth, and repair of body tissues, as well as for regulation and control of body processes. You need about forty different nutrients to stay healthy. These include proteins, fats, carbohydrates, vitamins, minerals, and water. It is the amount of proteins, carbohydrates, and fats in foods that determines their energy value or caloric content. The objective of daily menu planning is to provide yourself with basic nutrients while staying within your caloric limit.

Proteins are necessary for building and maintaining body tissues. Poultry, meat, fish, eggs, milk, and cheese are the best sources of protein. Fats and carbohydrates provide energy in addition to assisting other body functions. Fruits, vegetables, cereals, and grains are rich in carbohydrates. Margarine, vegetable oils, poultry, meat, and fish supply the fats we need.

Vitamins and minerals are also essential for the body's proper functioning. Sodium is especially important for maintaining body water balance and therefore has a significant effect on weight control. Sodium occurs naturally in some foods, and additional amounts are often added in processing prepared foods. Some of our recipes call for cooked rice or pasta; the sodium figures on these recipes are based on the assumption that these items have been cooked without additional salt.

Variety is the key to success. No single food supplies all the essential nutrients in the amounts needed. The greater the variety of food the less likely you are to develop either a deficiency or an excess of any single nutrient, and the more interesting and attractive your diet will be.

EXCHANGE INFORMATION AND NUTRITION INFORMATION

MAGIC IN MINUTES

Bacon-Flavored Corn Chowder

Each serving provides: 1 Bread Exchange; 1 Vegetable Exchange; 1 Fat Exchange; ¾ Milk Exchange; 25 calories Optional Exchange

Per serving: 234 calories; 11 g protein; 5 g fat; 40 g carbohydrate; 616 mg sodium; 4 mg cholesterol

Broiled Ham 'n' Cheese with Mustard Dressing

Each serving provides: 3 Protein Exchanges; 1 Bread Exchange; 1 Vegetable Exchange; 25 calories Optional Exchange

Per serving: 314 calories; 27 g protein; 14 g fat; 19 g carbohydrate; 897 mg sodium; 80 mg cholesterol

Broiled Mustard-Scrod with Wine Sauce

Each serving provides: 4 Protein Exchanges; 2 Fat Exchanges; 25 calories Optional Exchange

Per serving with scrod or cod: 212 calories; 25 g protein; 8 g fat; 4 g carbohydrate; 245 mg sodium; 75 mg cholesterol

With flounder: 213 calories; 24 g protein; 9 g fat; 4 g carbohydrate; 257 mg sodium; 75 mg cholesterol

With haddock: 213 calories; 26 g protein; 8 g fat; 4 g carbohydrate; 233 mg sodium; 89 mg cholesterol

Cheddar-Chicken Soup

Each serving provides: 3 Protein Exchanges; 1 Bread Exchange; 2 Vegetable Exchanges; 1 Fat Exchange; ¼ Milk Exchange; 15 calories Optional Exchange

Per serving: 418 calories; 32 g protein; 18 g fat; 32 g carbohydrate; 839 mg sodium; 81 mg cholesterol

Chicken Tacos

Each serving provides: 2½ Protein Exchanges; 1 Bread Exchange; 3 Vegetable Exchanges; 1 Fat Exchange

Per serving: 309 calories; 23 g protein; 16 g fat; 18 g carbohydrate; 504 mg sodium; 65 mg cholesterol

Glazed "Danish"

Each serving provides: 1 Bread Exchange; 25 calories Optional Exchange

Per serving: 95 calories; 2 g protein; 2 g fat; 17 g carbohydrate; 246 mg sodium; 0 mg cholesterol

Hot Fruit Compote with Coconut Topping

Each serving provides: 1 Bread Exchange; 1 Fat Exchange; 1 Fruit Exchange; 30 calories Optional Exchange

Per serving: 159 calories; 2 g protein; 6 g fat; 28 g carbohydrate; 142 mg sodium; 0 mg cholesterol

Hot Open-Face Roast Beef Sandwich

Each serving provides: 4 Protein Exchanges; 1 Bread Exchange; 1 Vegetable Exchange; 1 Fat Exchange; 15 calories Optional Exchange

Per serving: 341 calories; 39 g protein; 11 g fat; 20 g carbohydrate; 652 mg sodium; 103 mg cholesterol

Hot Open-Face Turkey Sandwich

Each serving provides: 4 Protein Exchanges; 1 Bread Exchange; 1 Vegetable Exchange; 1 Fat Exchange; 15 calories Optional Exchange

Per serving: 310 calories; 37 g protein; 10 g fat; 18 g carbohydrate; 688 mg sodium; 88 mg cholesterol

Hot Potato Salad

Each serving provides: 1½ Bread Exchanges; 1 Vegetable Exchange; 1 Fat Exchange; 15 calories Optional Exchange

Per serving: 164 calories; 4 g protein; 5 g fat; 27 g carbohydrate; 428 mg sodium; 0 mg cholesterol

Macaroni-Cheddar Salad

Each serving provides: 1 Protein Exchange; 1½ Bread Exchanges; 1⅔ Vegetable Exchanges; 1½ Fat Exchanges; 15 calories Optional Exchange

Per serving: 318 calories; 12 g protein; 17 g fat; 30 g carbohydrate; 724 mg sodium; 34 mg cholesterol

Orange-Ginger-Glazed Pork Chops

Each serving provides: 4 Protein Exchanges; 1 Fat Exchange; 1 Fruit Exchange; 25 calories Optional Exchange

Per serving: 450 calories; 35 g protein; 21 g fat; 30 g carbohydrate; 217 mg sodium; 10 mg cholesterol

Orange Loaf Bars

Each serving provides: ½ Protein Exchange; 1 Bread Exchange; 1 Fat Exchange; ½ Fruit Exchange; 35 calories Optional Exchange

Per serving: 228 calories; 6 g protein; 7 g fat; 34 g carbohydrate; 80 mg sodium; 137 mg cholesterol

Oriental Beef and Vegetable Stir-Fry

Each serving provides: 4 Protein Exchanges; 2 Bread Exchanges; ½ Vegetable Exchange; 40 calories Optional Exchange

Per serving: 563 calories; 38 g protein; 26 g fat; 41 g carbohydrate; 1,435 mg sodium; 107 mg cholesterol

Oriental Chicken Livers en Brochette

Each serving provides: 4 Protein Exchanges; 3 Vegetable Exchanges; 15 calories Optional Exchange

Per serving: 255 calories; 32 g protein; 5 g fat; 18 g carbohydrate; 687 mg sodium; 846 mg cholesterol

Oven-Fried Chicken with Orange-Teriyaki Sauce

Each serving provides: 4 Protein Exchanges; 1 Bread Exchange; ⅛ Vegetable Exchange; 1 Fat Exchange; ½ Fruit Exchange; 16 calories Optional Exchange

Per serving: 390 calories; 38 g protein; 9 g fat; 36 g carbohydrate; 999 mg sodium; 96 mg cholesterol

Pizza Pie

Each ½ pie provides: 1 Protein Exchange; 2 Bread Exchanges; 2 Vegetable Exchanges; 1 Fat Exchange; 20 calories Optional Exchange

Per serving: 340 calories; 12 g protein; 16 g fat; 38 g carbohydrate; 966 mg sodium; 24 mg cholesterol

Each ¼ pie provides: ½ Protein Exchange; 1 Bread Exchange; 1 Vegetable Exchange; ½ Fat Exchange; 10 calories Optional Exchange

Per serving: 170 calories; 6 g protein; 8 g fat; 19 g carbohydrate; 483 mg sodium; 12 mg cholesterol

Potato-Vegetable Casserole

Each serving provides: 2 Protein Exchanges; 1 Bread Exchange; 2¼ Vegetable Exchanges; ¾ Milk Exchange

Per serving: 356 calories; 22 g protein; 18 g fat; 29 g carbohydrate; 527 mg sodium; 56 mg cholesterol

Puffy Fruit Omelet

Each serving provides: 1 Protein Exchange; 1 Fat Exchange; 1 Fruit Exchange; 30 calories Optional Exchange

Per serving: 184 calories; 7 g protein; 10 g fat; 17 g carbohydrate; 182 mg sodium; 274 mg cholesterol

Puffy Pancake

Each ½ pancake provides: 1 Protein Exchange; 1 Bread Exchange; 2 Fat Exchanges; ¼ Milk Exchange; 40 calories Optional Exchange

Per serving: 292 calories; 12 g protein; 14 g fat; 30 g carbohydrate; 190 mg sodium; 276 mg cholesterol

Each ¼ pancake provides: ½ Protein Exchange; ½ Bread Exchange; 1 Fat Exchange; 30 calories Optional Exchange

Per serving: 146 calories; 6 g protein; 7 g fat; 15 g carbohydrate; 95 mg sodium; 138 mg cholesterol

Quick Minestrone

Each serving provides: 3 Protein Exchanges; ½ Bread Exchange; 2 Vegetable Exchanges; 1 Fat Exchange; 30 calories Optional Exchange

Per serving: 343 calories; 20 g protein; 12 g fat; 42 g carbohydrate; 1,763 mg sodium (estimated); 26 mg cholesterol

Sole (or Flounder) Véronique

Each serving provides: 4 Protein Exchanges; 1½ Fat Exchanges; 1 Fruit Exchange; 60 calories Optional Exchange

Per serving: 297 calories; 26 g protein; 9 g fat; 24 g carbohydrate; 467 mg sodium; 71 mg cholesterol

Spaghetti Carbonara

Each serving provides: 3 Protein Exchanges; 1½ Bread Exchanges; ½ Vegetable Exchange; 1 Fat Exchange; ¼ Milk Exchange; 20 calories Optional Exchange

Per serving: 410 calories; 25 g protein; 19 g fat; 33 g carbohydrate; 1,286 mg sodium; 312 mg cholesterol

Spicy Garbanzos

Each serving provides: 3 Protein Exchanges; 1½ Vegetable Exchanges; ½ Fat Exchange

Per serving: 265 calories; 14 g protein; 5 g fat; 43 g carbohydrate; 856 mg sodium (estimated); 0 mg cholesterol

---

SIMPLE SKILLET SPECIALTIES

Bacon-Corn Fritters

Each serving provides: ½ Protein Exchange; 1 Bread Exchange; 1 Fat Exchange; 15 calories Optional Exchange

Per serving: 174 calories; 6 g protein; 9 g fat; 19 g carbohydrate; 332 mg sodium; 137 mg cholesterol

Bacon-Liver Burgers

Each serving provides: 4 Protein Exchanges; 1 Bread Exchange; 1 Vegetable Exchange; 1½ Fat Exchanges; 45 calories Optional Exchange

Per serving: 378 calories; 35 g protein; 12 g fat; 33 g carbohydrate; 610 mg sodium; 846 mg cholesterol

Carrot-Asparagus Toss

Each serving provides: 2 Vegetable Exchanges; 1 Fat Exchange

Per serving: 92 calories; 3 g protein; 5 g fat; 11 g carbohydrate; 390 mg sodium; 0 mg cholesterol

Chicken Marsala

Each serving provides: 4 Protein Exchanges; 2 Fat Exchanges; ½ Fruit Exchange; 40 calories Optional Exchange

Per serving: 342 calories; 36 g protein; 13 g fat; 13 g carbohydrate; 585 mg sodium; 96 mg cholesterol

Chicken Velouté

Each serving provides: 4 Protein Exchanges; 1 Bread Exchange; ⅓ Vegetable Exchange; 1½ Fat Exchanges; 15 calories Optional Exchange

Per serving: 369 calories; 38 g protein; 11 g fat; 27 g carbohydrate; 880 mg sodium; 96 mg cholesterol

Chili-Cheese Corn Fritters

Each serving provides: 2 Protein Exchanges; 1 Bread Exchange; 1½ Fat Exchanges

Per serving: 349 calories; 16 g protein; 25 g fat; 17 g carbohydrate; 561 mg sodium; 182 mg cholesterol

Deviled Lamb

Each serving provides: 4 Protein Exchanges; 1½ Fat Exchanges; 20 calories Optional Exchange

Per serving: 217 calories; 20 g protein; 13 g fat; 5 g carbohydrate; 382 mg sodium; 114 mg cholesterol

Frankfurter-Vegetable Stir-Fry

Each serving provides: 3 Protein Exchanges; 2½ Vegetable Exchanges; 1 Fat Exchange; 5 calories Optional Exchange

Per serving: 370 calories; 12 g protein; 30 g fat; 15 g carbohydrate; 1,343 mg sodium; 43 mg cholesterol

Glazed Fruited Carrots

Each serving provides: 2 Vegetable Exchanges; 1 Fat Exchange; ½ Fruit Exchange; 25 calories Optional Exchange

Per serving: 150 calories; 2 g protein; 4 g fat; 25 g carbohydrate; 114 mg sodium; 0 mg cholesterol

If salt is used, increase sodium to 180 mg.

Grapes, Seeds, 'n' Sprouts

Each serving provides: 1 Vegetable Exchange; 1 Fat Exchange; 45 calories Optional Exchange

Per serving: 97 calories; 3 g protein; 5 g fat; 9 g carbohydrate; 119 mg sodium; 0 mg cholesterol

Kasha-Chicken Combo

Each serving provides: 3½ Protein Exchanges; 1 Bread Exchange; 1 Vegetable Exchange; ½ Fat Exchange; 5 calories Optional Exchange

Per serving: 339 calories; 32 g protein; 12 g fat; 27 g carbohydrate; 553 mg sodium; 213 mg cholesterol

Mexican Stir-Fry

Each serving provides: 3 Protein Exchanges; 1 Bread Exchange; 2⅔ Vegetable Exchanges; 1½ Fat Exchanges; 25 calories Optional Exchange

Per serving: 440 calories; 27 g protein; 14 g fat; 53 g carbohydrate; 957 mg sodium (estimated); 55 mg cholesterol

Oriental Vegetable Stir-Fry

Each serving provides: 2½ Vegetable Exchanges; ½ Fat Exchange; 15 calories Optional Exchange

Per serving: 95 calories; 3 g protein; 4 g fat; 15 g carbohydrate; 590 mg sodium; 0 mg cholesterol

"Pan-Fried" Spaghetti Squash

Each serving provides: 3½ Vegetable Exchanges; 1½ Fat Exchanges

Per serving: 121 calories; 3 g protein; 6 g fat; 16 g carbohydrate; 350 mg sodium; 0 mg cholesterol

Parmesan Chicken

Each serving provides: 3½ Protein Exchanges; 1 Bread Exchange; 2 Fat Exchanges; 20 calories Optional Exchange

Per serving: 396 calories; 36 g protein; 19 g fat; 19 g carbohydrate; 786 mg sodium; 86 mg cholesterol

Potato-Carrot Fritters

Each serving provides: ½ Protein Exchange; 1 Bread Exchange; ½ Vegetable Exchange; 1 Fat Exchange; 25 calories Optional Exchange

Per serving: 195 calories; 7 g protein; 8 g fat; 25 g carbohydrate; 342 mg sodium; 138 mg cholesterol

Potatoes O'Brien

Each serving provides: 1½ Bread Exchanges; ¾ Vegetable Exchange; 1 Fat Exchange

Per serving: 140 calories; 3 g protein; 5 g fat; 23 g carbohydrate; 305 mg sodium; 0 mg cholesterol

Quick Liver, Tomato, 'n' Onion Sauté

Each serving provides: 4 Protein Exchanges; ½ Bread Exchange; 3 Vegetable Exchanges; 2 Fat Exchanges

Per serving: 470 calories; 38 g protein; 23 g fat; 28 g carbohydrate; 773 mg sodium; 497 mg cholesterol

Shrimp Fandango

Each serving provides: 4 Protein Exchanges; 1 Bread Exchange (optional); 2 Vegetable Exchanges; 1½ Fat Exchanges; 25 Calories Optional Exchange

Per serving with carrot: 277 calories; 30 g protein; 8 g fat; 14 g carbohydrate; 245 mg sodium; 170 mg cholesterol

With carrot & rice: 391 calories; 32 g protein; 8 g fat; 39 g carbohydrate; 245 mg sodium; 170 mg cholesterol

With broccoli: 276 calories; 31 g protein; 8 g fat; 13 g carbohydrate; 239 mg sodium; 170 mg cholesterol

With broccoli & rice: 389 calories; 33 g protein; 8 g fat; 38 g carbohydrate; 239 mg sodium; 170 mg cholesterol

Skillet Chicken and Garbanzos

Each serving provides: 4 Protein Exchanges; 2¾ Vegetable Exchanges; 1 Fat Exchange; 15 calories Optional Exchange

Per serving: 333 calories; 28 g protein; 9 g fat; 36 g carbohydrate; 948 mg sodium (estimated); 48 mg cholesterol

Skillet Yams and Apples

Each serving provides: 1 Bread Exchange; ⅛ Vegetable Exchange; 1½ Fat Exchanges; 1 Fruit Exchange; 20 calories Optional Exchange

Per serving: 221 calories; 2 g protein; 6 g fat; 42 g carbohydrate; 379 mg sodium; 0 mg cholesterol

Sweet 'n' Sour Cabbage and Bacon Sauté

Each serving provides: 3 Protein Exchanges; 5 Vegetable Exchanges; 1 Fat Exchange; 15 calories Optional Exchange

Per serving: 314 calories; 21 g protein; 17 g fat; 21 g carbohydrate; 1,657 mg sodium; 51 mg cholesterol

---

COCKTAIL QUICKIES

Apple-Ale Punch

Each 1-cup serving provides: 1 Fruit Exchange; 10 calories Optional Exchange

Per serving: 62 calories; 1 g protein; 0.2 g fat; 18 g carbohydrate; 44 mg sodium; 0 mg cholesterol

Each ½-cup serving provides: ½ Fruit Exchange; 5 calories Optional Exchange

Per serving: 31 calories; 0.5 g protein; 0.1 g fat; 9 g carbohydrate; 22 mg sodium; 0 mg cholesterol

Apple Tonic

Each serving provides: 1 Fruit Exchange; 3 calories Optional Exchange

Per serving: 42 calories; 1 g protein; 0 g fat; 10 g carbohydrate; 1 mg sodium; 0 mg cholesterol

If club soda is substituted, omit Optional Exchange and reduce calories to 39.

Caramel Corn

Each serving provides: ½ Bread Exchange; 1 Fat Exchange; 25 calories Optional Exchange

Per serving: 87 calories; 1 g protein; 4 g fat; 12 g carbohydrate; 47 mg sodium; 0 mg cholesterol

Champagne Cocktail

Each serving provides: ½ Fruit Exchange; 60 calories Optional Exchange

Per serving: 91 calories; 1 g protein; 0.1 g fat; 12 g carbohydrate; 4 mg sodium; 0 mg cholesterol

Cheddar-Beer Crackers

Each serving provides: ½ Protein Exchange; 1 Bread Exchange; 1 Fat Exchange; 20 calories Optional Exchange

Per serving: 196 calories; 6 g protein; 9 g fat; 20 g carbohydrate; 251 mg sodium; 15 mg cholesterol

Cran-Orange Tonic

Each serving provides: 1 Fruit Exchange; 20 calories Optional Exchange

Per serving: 79 calories; 1 g protein; 0.1 g fat; 19 g carbohydrate; 4 mg sodium; 0 mg cholesterol

Crème de Champagne Cocktail

Each serving provides: 80 calories Optional Exchange

Per serving: 80 calories; 2 g protein; 1 g fat; 5 g carbohydrate; 28 mg sodium; 0 mg cholesterol

Crostini Appetizer

Each serving provides: 1 Bread Exchange; ⅓ Vegetable Exchange; ½ Fat Exchange; 10 calories Optional Exchange

Per serving: 121 calories; 4 g protein; 4 g fat; 18 g carbohydrate; 206 mg sodium; 3 mg cholesterol

Cucumber-Yogurt Dip

Each serving provides: 1 Vegetable Exchange; ½ Milk Exchange

Per serving: 46 calories; 4 g protein; 0.2 g fat; 8 g carbohydrate; 317 mg sodium; 1 mg cholesterol

Far East Broccoli

Each serving provides: 2 Vegetable Exchanges; 1½ Fat Exchanges

Per serving: 102 calories; 5 g protein; 7 g fat; 7 g carbohydrate; 268 mg sodium; 0 mg cholesterol

Glazed Popcorn Treat

Each serving provides: ½ Bread Exchange; 1 Fat Exchange; 1 Fruit Exchange; 30 calories Optional Exchange

Per serving: 137 calories; 2 g protein; 5 g fat; 23 g carbohydrate; 50 mg sodium; 0 mg cholesterol

Golden "Eggnog"

Each serving provides: ½ Fruit Exchange; ¾ Milk Exchange; 25 calories Optional Exchange

Per serving: 119 calories; 6 g protein; 2 g fat; 19 g carbohydrate; 99 mg sodium; 3 mg cholesterol

Herbed Romano Sticks

Each serving provides: 1 Bread Exchange; 2 Fat Exchanges; 20 calories Optional Exchange

Per serving: 171 calories; 4 g protein; 8 g fat; 20 g carbohydrate; 184 mg sodium; 2 mg cholesterol

If Parmesan cheese is substituted, increase calories to 172 and sodium to 196 mg.

"Mai Tai"

Each serving provides: 1 Fruit Exchange; 5 calories Optional Exchange

Per serving: 57 calories; 1 g protein; 0.1 g fat; 14 g carbohydrate; 1 mg sodium; 0 mg cholesterol

Marinated Roasted Peppers

Each serving provides: 4 Vegetable Exchanges; 5 calories Optional Exchange

Per serving: 51 calories; 3 g protein; 1 g fat; 10 g carbohydrate; 51 mg sodium; 2 mg cholesterol

"Martini"

Each serving provides: 55 calories Optional Exchange

Per serving: 55 calories; 0.2 g protein; 1 g fat; 3 g carbohydrate; 190 mg sodium; 0 mg cholesterol

If lemon strips are substituted, reduce Optional Exchange and calories to 50, protein to 0.1 g, and sodium to 97 mg.

Mimosa

Each serving provides: 65 calories Optional Exchange

Per serving: 65 calories; 0.3 g protein; trace fat; 6 g carbohydrate; 3 mg sodium; 0 mg cholesterol

Mocha-Almond Delight

Each serving provides: ½ Fruit Exchange; ¼ Milk Exchange; 15 calories Optional Exchange

Per serving: 67 calories; 2 g protein; 2 g fat; 11 g carbohydrate; 35 mg sodium; 1 mg cholesterol

"Orange-Crème" Stuffed Prunes

Each serving provides: 1½ Fruit Exchanges; 25 calories Optional Exchange

Per serving: 96 calories; 2 g protein; 1 g fat; 22 g carbohydrate; 15 mg sodium; 3 mg cholesterol

Orange Tonic

Each serving provides: 1 Fruit Exchange; 3 calories Optional Exchange

Per serving: 63 calories; 2 g protein; 0.1 g fat; 14 g carbohydrate; 1 mg sodium; 0 mg cholesterol

Peanut-Corn Crunch

Each serving provides: 1½ Protein Exchanges; 1½ Fat Exchanges; ½ Fruit Exchange; 35 calories Optional Exchange

Per serving: 195 calories; 8 g protein; 13 g fat; 15 g carbohydrate; 150 mg sodium; 0 mg cholesterol

Scallion-Cheese Rounds

Each serving provides: ½ Protein Exchange; 1 Bread Exchange; ⅛ Vegetable Exchange; 1 Fat Exchange; 10 calories Optional Exchange

Per serving: 156 calories; 8 g protein; 7 g fat; 16 g carbohydrate; 208 mg sodium; 10 mg cholesterol

Sesame Breadsticks

Each serving provides: 1 Bread Exchange; ½ Fat Exchange; 10 calories Optional Exchange

Per serving: 96 calories; 2 g protein; 4 g fat; 13 g carbohydrate; 268 mg sodium; 0 mg cholesterol

Spicy Blue Cheese Dip or Dressing

Each serving provides: 1 Protein Exchange; 10 calories Optional Exchange

Per serving: 99 calories; 9 g protein; 6 g fat; 3 g carbohydrate; 369 mg sodium; 16 mg cholesterol

Spicy Popcorn Snack

Each serving provides: 1 Bread Exchange; 10 calories Optional Exchange

Per serving: 74 calories; 2 g protein; 1 g fat; 14 g carbohydrate; 316 mg sodium; 0 mg cholesterol

Spinach-Stuffed Mushrooms

Each serving provides: 1 Protein Exchange; ½ Bread Exchange; 3¾ Vegetable Exchanges; 1½ Fat Exchanges; 2 calories Optional Exchange

Per serving with Fontina cheese: 273 calories; 15 g protein; 15 g fat; 22 g carbohydrate; 334 mg sodium; 33 mg cholesterol

With mozzarella cheese: 242 calories; 13 g protein; 13 g fat; 22 g carbohydrate; 440 mg sodium; 22 mg cholesterol

Spinach Turnovers

Each serving provides: 1 Bread Exchange; ⅓ Vegetable Exchange; ½ Fat Exchange; 15 calories Optional Exchange

Per serving: 116 calories; 4 g protein; 4 g fat; 15 g carbohydrate; 306 mg sodium; 2 mg cholesterol

Tropical Wine Punch

Each 1-cup serving provides: 1 Fruit Exchange; 50 calories Optional Exchange

Per serving: 102 calories; 0.8 g protein; 0.1 g fat; 18 g carbohydrate; 34 mg sodium; 0 mg cholesterol

Each ½-cup serving provides: ½ Fruit Exchange; 25 calories Optional Exchange

Per serving: 51 calories; 0.4 g protein; 0.05 g fat; 9 g carbohydrate; 17 mg sodium; 0 mg cholesterol

Zippy Parsley Dip

Each serving provides: ½ Protein Exchange; ⅛ Vegetable Exchange; 1 Fat Exchange; 5 calories Optional Exchange

Per serving: 87 calories; 6 g protein; 6 g fat; 4 g carbohydrate; 197 mg sodium; 9 mg cholesterol

---

GUESTS ARE COMING

Apple Dumplings

Each serving provides: 1 Bread Exchange; 1 Fat Exchange; 1 Fruit Exchange; 25 calories Optional Exchange

Per serving: 168 calories; 2 g protein; 4 g fat; 32 g carbohydrate; 261 mg sodium; 0 mg cholesterol

Apple-Raisin Turnovers

Each serving provides: 1 Bread Exchange; ½ Fat Exchange; 1 Fruit Exchange; 5 calories Optional Exchange

Per serving: 153 calories; 2 g protein; 4 g fat; 28 g carbohydrate; 269 mg sodium; 0 mg cholesterol

Asparagus Vinaigrette

Each serving provides: 1 Vegetable Exchange; ½ Fat Exchange; 10 calories Optional Exchange

Per serving: 54 calories; 2 g protein; 4 g fat; 4 g carbohydrate; 35 mg sodium; 0 mg cholesterol

Chicken Diane

Each serving provides: 4 Protein Exchanges; ¼ Vegetable Exchange; 2 Fat Exchanges; 20 calories Optional Exchange

Per serving: 300 calories; 36 g protein; 13 g fat; 5 g carbohydrate; 440 mg sodium; 96 mg cholesterol

Chicken-Mushroom Crêpes

Each serving provides: 3½ Protein Exchanges; 1½ Bread Exchanges; ¾ Vegetable Exchange; 1 Fat Exchange; ¼ Milk Exchange; 25 calories Optional Exchange

Per serving: 415 calories; 37 g protein; 14 g fat; 35 g carbohydrate; 997 mg sodium; 214 mg cholesterol

Creamy Pasta with Broccoli

Each serving provides: 1 Protein Exchange; 1½ Bread Exchanges; 1 Vegetable Exchange; 1 Fat Exchange; 50 calories Optional Exchange

Per serving: 305 calories; 17 g protein; 12 g fat; 33 g carbohydrate; 417 mg sodium; 27 mg cholesterol

Crispy Cinnamon-Chicken Bake

Each serving provides: 4 Protein Exchanges; ½ Bread Exchange; 1 Fat Exchange; 30 calories Optional Exchange

Per serving: 333 calories; 35 g protein; 13 g fat; 16 g carbohydrate; 532 mg sodium; 102 mg cholesterol

Fiesta Chicken

Each serving provides: 4 Protein Exchanges; 1 Bread Exchange; 2 Vegetable Exchanges; 1 Fat Exchange; 10 calories Optional Exchange

Per serving: 398 calories; 40 g protein; 11 g fat; 34 g carbohydrate; 1,101 mg sodium; 96 mg cholesterol

Haddock Provencale

Each serving provides: 4 Protein Exchanges; 1 Vegetable Exchange; 1½ Fat Exchanges; 25 calories Optional Exchange

Per serving: 218 calories; 27 g protein; 7 g fat; 8 g carbohydrate; 223 mg sodium; 85 mg cholesterol

Ham 'n' Cabbage Crêpes

Each serving provides: 3 Protein Exchanges; 1 Bread Exchange; 3 Vegetable Exchanges; 2½ Fat Exchanges; ¾ Milk Exchange; 30 calories Optional Exchange

Per serving: 485 calories; 33 g protein; 19 g fat; 45 g carbohydrate; 1,155 mg sodium; 203 mg cholesterol

Lamb and Bean Salad with Vinaigrette Dressing

Each serving provides: 3 Protein Exchanges; ¼ Vegetable Exchange; ½ Fat Exchange; 10 calories Optional Exchange

Per serving: 224 calories; 20 g protein; 10 g fat; 14 g carbohydrate; 362 mg sodium (estimated); 57 mg cholesterol

Orange Sauce

Each serving provides: 1 Fat Exchange; ½ Fruit Exchange; 5 calories Optional Exchange

Per serving: 76 calories; 1 g protein; 4 g fat; 10 g carbohydrate; 45 mg sodium; 0 mg cholesterol

Peanut Butter Brittle

Each serving provides: ½ Protein Exchange; ½ Fat Exchange; 30 calories Optional Exchange

Per serving: 74 calories; 2 g protein; 4 g fat; 8 g carbohydrate; 80 mg sodium; 0 mg cholesterol

Potato-Cheese Pie

Each serving provides: 2 Protein Exchanges; 1 Bread Exchange; ⅛ Vegetable Exchange

Per serving: 225 calories; 17 g protein; 9 g fat; 18 g carbohydrate; 1,449 mg sodium; 285 mg cholesterol

Quick Shortcakes

Each serving provides: 1 Bread Exchange; ½ Fat Exchange; 10 calories Optional Exchange

Serving Suggestion—Add ½ Fruit Exchange and increase Optional Exchange to 25 calories.

Per serving without topping and fruit: 97 calories; 2 g protein; 4 g fat; 14 g carbohydrate; 246 mg sodium; 0 mg cholesterol

With topping and blueberries: 129 calories; 2 g protein; 5 g fat; 20 g carbohydrate; 248 mg sodium; 0 mg cholesterol

With topping and raspberries: 126 calories; 2 g protein; 5 g fat; 19 g carbohydrate; 246 mg sodium; 0 mg cholesterol

With topping and strawberries: 132 calories; 3 g protein; 5 g fat; 20 g carbohydrate; 247 mg sodium; 0 mg cholesterol

Rolled Stuffed Flounder Fillets

Each serving provides: 4 Protein Exchanges; 1⅛ Vegetable Exchanges; 1½ Fat Exchanges; 10 calories Optional Exchange

Per serving: 194 calories; 26 g protein; 7 g fat; 5 g carbohydrate; 261 mg sodium; 75 mg cholesterol

Salad Niçoise

Each serving provides: 3 Protein Exchanges; 2 Vegetable Exchanges; 1½ Fat Exchanges; 15 calories Optional Exchange

Per serving: 303 calories; 22 g protein; 22 g fat; 7 g carbohydrate; 470 mg sodium; 290 mg cholesterol

Sautéed Chili-Shrimp

Each serving provides: 4 Protein Exchanges; 3 Vegetable Exchanges; 1½ Fat Exchanges; 15 calories Optional Exchange

Per serving: 279 calories; 32 g protein; 9 g fat; 20 g carbohydrate; 594 mg sodium; 213 mg cholesterol

Seafood Crêpes

Each serving provides: 3½ Protein Exchanges; 1 Bread Exchange; 1⅛ Vegetable Exchanges; 2½ Fat Exchanges; ¾ Milk Exchange; 25 calories Optional Exchange

Per serving: 410 calories; 32 g protein; 15 g fat; 37 g carbohydrate; 1,183 mg sodium; 247 mg cholesterol

Shrimp and Linguini with Basil-Caper Sauce

Each serving provides: 4 Protein Exchanges; 1½ Bread Exchanges; 2¾ Vegetable Exchanges; 1½ Fat Exchanges; 5 calories Optional Exchange

Per serving: 381 calories; 33 g protein; 10 g fat; 40 g carbohydrate; 721 mg sodium; 214 mg cholesterol

Sticky Raisin Buns

Each serving provides: 1 Bread Exchange; ½ Fat Exchange; ½ Fruit Exchange; 10 calories Optional Exchange

Per serving: 131 calories; 2 g protein; 4 g fat; 23 g carbohydrate; 271 mg sodium; 0 mg cholesterol

Strawberry Chiffon

Each serving provides: 1 Fruit Exchange; ¼ Milk Exchange; 65 calories Optional Exchange

Per serving: 122 calories; 4 g protein; 2 g fat; 25 g carbohydrate; 73 mg sodium; 1 mg cholesterol

Wine-Poached Pears

Each serving provides: 1 Fruit Exchange; 100 calories Optional Exchange

Per serving: 181 calories; 1 g protein; 1 g fat; 28 g carbohydrate; 8 mg sodium; 0 mg cholesterol

Yogurt-Caraway Quiche

Each serving (including pastry shell) provides: 2 Protein Exchanges; 1 Bread Exchange; ⅓ Vegetable Exchange; 2½ Fat Exchanges; ¼ Milk Exchange; 3 calories Optional Exchange

Per serving: 374 calories; 18 g protein; 22 g fat; 25 g carbohydrate; 527 mg sodium; 298 mg cholesterol

---

TREAT YOURSELF LIKE COMPANY

Apple Syrup

Each serving provides: 1 Fruit Exchange; 7 calories Optional Exchange

Per serving: 63 calories; 0.2 g protein; 0.3 g fat; 17 g carbohydrate; 0.1 mg sodium; 0 mg cholesterol

Asparagus with Sesame "Butter"

Each serving provides: 1 Vegetable Exchange; 1 Fat Exchange; 15 calories Optional Exchange

Per serving: 70 calories; 3 g protein; 5 g fat; 5 g carbohydrate; 584 mg sodium; 0 mg cholesterol

Blueberry Topping

Each serving provides: 1 Fruit Exchange; 25 calories Optional Exchange

Per serving: 59 calories; 0.4 g protein; 0.3 g fat; 15 g carbohydrate; 4 mg sodium; 0 mg cholesterol

Chicken Cordon Bleu

Each serving provides: 4 Protein Exchanges; 1 Fat Exchange; 20 calories Optional Exchange

Per serving: 280 calories; 35 g protein; 13 g fat; 4 g carbohydrate; 311 mg sodium; 98 mg cholesterol

Chicken with Hot Peanut Sauce

Each serving provides: 3½ Protein Exchanges; 1½ Bread Exchanges; 3 Fat Exchanges; 30 calories Optional Exchange

Per serving: 446 calories; 29 g protein; 21 g fat; 36 g carbohydrate; 1,322 mg sodium; 48 mg cholesterol

Chocolate Topping

Each serving provides: ½ Milk Exchange; 30 calories Optional Exchange

Per serving: 76 calories; 5 g protein; 0.5 g fat; 13 g carbohydrate; 74 mg sodium; 3 mg cholesterol

Cream of Asparagus Soup

Each serving provides: 1 Vegetable Exchange; 1 Fat Exchange; 1 Milk Exchange; 30 calories Optional Exchange

Per serving: 190 calories; 14 g protein; 4 g fat; 26 g carbohydrate; 1,076 mg sodium; 5 mg cholesterol

Curried Eggplant and Lamb Stew

Each serving provides: 4 Protein Exchanges; 3 Vegetable Exchanges; ½ Fat Exchange

Per serving: 317 calories; 33 g protein; 14 g fat; 14 g carbohydrate; 368 mg sodium; 113 mg cholesterol

Curried Livers in Wine Sauce

Each serving provides: 4 Protein Exchanges; 1½ Vegetable Exchanges; 1 Fat Exchange; 30 calories Optional Exchange

Per serving: 288 calories; 32 g protein; 10 g fat; 13 g carbohydrate; 352 mg sodium; 846 mg cholesterol

Glazed Coconut-Fruit Kabobs

Each serving provides: 1 Fruit Exchange; 20 calories Optional Exchange

Per serving: 90 calories; 1 g protein; 1 g fat; 22 g carbohydrate; 2 mg sodium; 0 mg cholesterol

Huevos Rancheros (South-of-the-Border Ranch-Style Eggs)

Each serving (including Salsa) provides: 2 Protein Exchanges; 1 Bread Exchange; 1½ Vegetable Exchanges; 1 Fat Exchange

Variation—Reduce Protein to 1 Exchange and add 10 calories Optional Exchange.

Per serving with Cheddar cheese: 316 calories; 16 g protein; 20 g fat; 18 g carbohydrate; 536 mg sodium; 304 mg cholesterol

With Parmesan cheese: 209 calories; 10 g protein; 11 g fat; 18 g carbohydrate; 391 mg sodium; 275 mg cholesterol

Lamb Patty in Mustard Gravy

Each serving provides: 4 Protein Exchanges; ½ Vegetable Exchange; 1 Fat Exchange; 5 calories Optional Exchange

Per serving: 303 calories; 31 g protein; 16 g fat; 5 g carbohydrate; 416 mg sodium; 113 mg cholesterol

"Lemon-Butter"-Baked Sole

Each serving provides: 4 Protein Exchanges; ½ Bread Exchange; 1½ Fat Exchanges

Per serving: 210 calories; 25 g protein; 7 g fat; 10 g carbohydrate; 458 mg sodium; 71 mg cholesterol

Mexican Liver

Each serving provides: 4 Protein Exchanges; ½ Bread Exchange; ¾ Vegetable Exchange; 1 Fat Exchange; 20 calories Optional Exchange

Per serving: 385 calories; 33 g protein; 18 g fat; 24 g carbohydrate; 951 mg sodium; 497 mg cholesterol

Monte Cristo Sandwich

Each serving provides: 3 Protein Exchanges; 2 Bread Exchanges; 1 Fat Exchange; ¼ Milk Exchange; 10 calories Optional Exchange

Per serving: 426 calories; 28 g protein; 22 g fat; 28 g carbohydrate; 741 mg sodium; 329 mg cholesterol

Oriental Salad

Each serving provides: 3 Protein Exchanges; 1 Bread Exchange; 1⅔ Vegetable Exchanges; 1½ Fat Exchanges; 10 calories Optional Exchange

Per serving with beef: 406 calories; 27 g protein; 16 g fat; 34 g carbohydrate; 758 mg sodium; 326 mg cholesterol

With pork: 437 calories; 25 g protein; 21 g fat; 34 g carbohydrate; 752 mg sodium; 324 mg cholesterol

With chicken: 396 calories; 27 g protein; 15 g fat; 34 g carbohydrate; 758 mg sodium; 322 mg cholesterol

Pineapple Topping

Each serving provides: ½ Fruit Exchange; 15 calories Optional Exchange

Per serving: 48 calories; 0.3 g protein; 0.1 g fat; 12 g carbohydrate; 1 mg sodium; 0 mg cholesterol

Pineapple-Yogurt Broil

Each serving provides: 1 Fruit Exchange; ½ Milk Exchange; 10 calories Optional Exchange

Per serving: 123 calories; 4 g protein; 0.2 g fat; 26 g carbohydrate; 45 mg sodium; 1 mg cholesterol

Scampi Supreme

Each serving provides: 4 Protein Exchanges; 1½ Fat Exchanges

Per serving: 189 calories; 26 g protein; 8 g fat; 3 g carbohydrate; 362 mg sodium; 213 mg cholesterol

Spiced Vegetable-Egg Bake

Each serving provides: 2 Protein Exchanges; 1 Vegetable Exchange; 1 Fat Exchange; ½ Milk Exchange; 10 calories Optional Exchange

Per serving: 310 calories; 22 g protein; 19 g fat; 14 g carbohydrate; 567 mg sodium; 308 mg cholesterol

"Waldorf" Chicken Salad

Each serving provides: 4 Protein Exchanges; ½ Vegetable Exchange; 1½ Fat Exchanges; 1 Fruit Exchange; ¼ Milk Exchange; 25 calories Optional Exchange

Per serving: 350 calories; 38 g protein; 12 g fat; 20 g carbohydrate; 605 mg sodium; 101 mg cholesterol

---

APPLIANCE APPEAL

Artichoke-Cheese Pie

Each serving provides: 2 Protein Exchanges; ¾ Vegetable Exchange; ½ Fat Exchange; 30 calories Optional Exchange

Per serving: 247 calories; 16 g protein; 16 g fat; 9 g carbohydrate; 368 mg sodium; 300 mg cholesterol

Brown Sugar Custard

Each serving provides: ½ Protein Exchange; ½ Milk Exchange; 30 calories Optional Exchange

Per serving: 118 calories; 7 g protein; 3 g fat; 13 g carbohydrate; 101 mg sodium; 139 mg cholesterol

Buttermilk-Cheese Dressing

Each serving provides: 30 calories Optional Exchange

Per serving: 30 calories; 3 g protein; 1 g fat; 3 g carbohydrate; 211 mg sodium; 4 mg cholesterol

Cauliflower Provençale

Each serving provides: 2⅔ Vegetable Exchanges; ½ Fat Exchange; 20 calories Optional Exchange

Per serving: 102 calories; 5 g protein; 6 g fat; 11 g carbohydrate; 362 mg sodium; 0 mg cholesterol

Chicken Rosé

Each serving provides: 4 Protein Exchanges; 2¾ Vegetable Exchanges; 1 Fat Exchange; 35 calories Optional Exchange

Per serving: 337 calories; 36 g protein; 14 g fat; 12 g carbohydrate; 729 mg sodium; 101 mg cholesterol

Cream of Celery Soup

Each serving provides: 2½ Vegetable Exchanges; 1 Fat Exchange; ½ Milk Exchange; 25 calories Optional Exchange

Per serving: 141 calories; 7 g protein; 4 g fat; 20 g carbohydrate; 637 mg sodium; 2 mg cholesterol

Creamy Cauliflower Soup

Each serving provides: 2⅛ Vegetable Exchanges; 1 Fat Exchange; 15 calories Optional Exchange

Per serving with fresh cauliflower: 79 calories; 4 g protein; 4 g fat; 9 g carbohydrate; 475 mg sodium; 0 mg cholesterol

With frozen cauliflower: 92 calories; 5 g protein; 4 g fat; 11 g carbohydrate; 481 mg sodium; 0 mg cholesterol

Easy Vegetable-Barley Soup

Each serving provides: ½ Bread Exchange; 2¼ Vegetable Exchanges; 1 Fat Exchange; 10 calories Optional Exchange

Per serving: 124 calories; 4 g protein; 4 g fat; 19 g carbohydrate; 711 mg sodium; 0 mg cholesterol

Honeydew Squash

Each serving provides: 1 Fruit Exchange

Per serving: 57 calories; 1 g protein; 0.1 g fat; 14 g carbohydrate; 9 mg sodium; 0 mg cholesterol

Marinated Cod Teriyaki

Each serving provides: 4 Protein Exchanges; 10 calories Optional Exchange

Per serving: 134 calories; 26 g protein; 0.4 g fat; 5 g carbohydrate; 766 mg sodium; 71 mg cholesterol

Potato-Vegetable Puree

Each serving provides: 1 Bread Exchange; 2½ Vegetable Exchanges; 1 Fat Exchange; 5 calories Optional Exchange

Per serving: 152 calories; 4 g protein; 4 g fat; 26 g carbohydrate; 849 mg sodium; 0 mg cholesterol

Rabbit Stew in White Wine Sauce

Each serving provides: 4 Protein Exchanges; 2¾ Vegetable Exchanges; 1 Fat Exchange; 35 calories Optional Exchange

Per serving: 361 calories; 36 g protein; 17 g fat; 12 g carbohydrate; 402 mg sodium; 103 mg cholesterol

Salmon Loaf

Each serving provides: 3½ Protein Exchanges; ½ Bread Exchange; ¼ Vegetable Exchange; ½ Fat Exchange; ¼ Milk Exchange; 10 calories Optional Exchange

Per serving: 246 calories; 24 g protein; 11 g fat; 11 g carbohydrate; 572 mg sodium; 168 mg cholesterol

Southern Stew

Each serving provides: 4 Protein Exchanges; 1 Bread Exchange; 1¾ Vegetable Exchanges; ½ Fat Exchange

Per serving: 370 calories; 43 g protein; 12 g fat; 22 g carbohydrate; 953 mg sodium (estimated); 103 mg cholesterol

Spiced Lamb Pilaf

Each serving provides: 4 Protein Exchanges; 1 Bread Exchange; ¾ Vegetable Exchange; 1 Fat Exchange; ½ Fruit Exchange; 10 calories Optional Exchange

Per serving: 400 calories; 36 g protein; 13 g fat; 35 g carbohydrate; 1,000 mg sodium; 113 mg cholesterol

Strawberry Milk Shake

Each serving provides: 1½ Fruit Exchanges; 1 Milk Exchange; 20 calories Optional Exchange

Per serving: 183 calories; 9 g protein; 1 g fat; 35 g carbohydrate; 136 mg sodium; 4 mg cholesterol

Stuffed Apple

Each serving provides: 3 Protein Exchanges; ⅛ Vegetable Exchange; 1 Fat Exchange; 1 Fruit Exchange

Per serving: 312 calories; 23 g protein; 17 g fat; 18 g carbohydrate; 661 mg sodium; 79 mg cholesterol

Veal Patties in Parsley Sauce

Each serving provides: 3½ Protein Exchanges; ½ Bread Exchange; ¼ Vegetable Exchange; 1½ Fat Exchanges; ½ Milk Exchange; 10 calories Optional Exchange

Per serving: 391 calories; 34 g protein; 20 g fat; 17 g carbohydrate; 963 mg sodium; 226 mg cholesterol

Vegetable Risotto

Each serving provides: 1 Bread Exchange; 3⅛ Vegetable Exchanges; 1 Fat Exchange; 5 calories Optional Exchange

Per serving: 192 calories; 5 g protein; 5 g fat; 32 g carbohydrate; 431 mg sodium; 0 mg cholesterol

Wine Custard

Each serving provides: ½ Protein Exchange; ½ Milk Exchange; 55 calories Optional Exchange

Per serving: 140 calories; 8 g protein; 3 g fat; 17 g carbohydrate; 100 mg sodium; 139 mg cholesterol

Yogurt Hollandaise

Each serving provides: ½ Protein Exchange; 1 Fat Exchange; ½ Milk Exchange; 15 calories Optional Exchange

Per serving: 120 calories; 7 g protein; 7 g fat; 8 g carbohydrate; 265 mg sodium; 138 mg cholesterol

---

FREEZE FOR THE FUTURE

Basic Crêpes

Each serving provides: ½ Protein Exchange; 1 Bread Exchange; ¼ Milk Exchange

Per serving: 149 calories; 8 g protein; 3 g fat; 22 g carbohydrate; 137 mg sodium; 138 mg cholesterol

Basic Pastry Shell

Each ¼ shell provides: 1 Bread Exchange; 2 Fat Exchanges; 10 calories Optional Exchange

Per serving: 162 calories; 4 g protein; 8 g fat; 18 g carbohydrate; 234 mg sodium; 0.2 mg cholesterol

Each ⅛ shell provides: ½ Bread Exchange; 1 Fat Exchange; 5 calories Optional Exchange

Per serving: 81 calories; 2 g protein; 4 g fat; 9 g carbohydrate; 117 mg sodium; 0.1 mg cholesterol

Basic Pot Pie Dough

Each serving provides: 1 Bread Exchange; 2 Fat Exchanges; 10 calories Optional Exchange

Per serving: 164 calories; 3 g protein; 8 g fat; 20 g carbohydrate; 164 mg sodium; 0.3 mg cholesterol

Variations: Cheddar Dough—Add ½ Protein Exchange.

Per serving: 221 calories; 7 g protein; 13 g fat; 20 g carbohydrate; 252 mg sodium; 15 mg cholesterol

Pastry Dough

Per serving: 164 calories; 3 g protein; 8 g fat; 20 g carbohydrate; 100 mg sodium; 0.3 mg cholesterol

Béchamel (White Sauce)

Each serving provides: 1½ Fat Exchanges; ½ Milk Exchange; 20 calories Optional Exchange

Per serving: 116 calories; 5 g protein; 6 g fat; 11 g carbohydrate; 201 mg sodium; 2 mg cholesterol

Beef Pot Pie

Each serving (including Cheddar Dough) provides: 3½ Protein Exchanges; 1 Bread Exchange; 2 Vegetable Exchanges; 2½ Fat Exchanges; 20 calories Optional Exchange

Per serving: 482 calories; 35 g protein; 23 g fat; 32 g carbohydrate; 750 mg sodium; 93 mg cholesterol

Chicken-Mushroom Crêpe Filling

Each serving provides: 3 Protein Exchanges; ½ Bread Exchange; ¾ Vegetable Exchange; 1 Fat Exchange; 25 calories Optional Exchange

Per serving: 266 calories; 29 g protein; 10 g fat; 13 g carbohydrate; 859 mg sodium; 76 mg cholesterol

Freezer French Toast

Each serving provides: 1 Protein Exchange; 1 Bread Exchange; ½ Fat Exchange; 5 calories Optional Exchange

Per serving: 177 calories; 9 g protein; 9 g fat; 13 g carbohydrate; 195 mg sodium; 275 mg cholesterol

Serving Suggestions:

1. Add 1 Fruit Exchange and increase Optional Exchange to 12 calories; increase calories to 240 and carbohydrate to 39 g.

2. Increase Optional Exchange to 21 calories; increase calories to 193 and carbohydrate to 17 g.

3. Increase Optional Exchange to 19 calories; increase calories to 191 and carbohydrate to 17 g.

Fresh Tomato Sauce

Each ¼-cup serving provides: 1 Vegetable Exchange

Per serving: 17 calories; 0.8 g protein; 0.2 g fat; 4 g carbohydrate; 137 mg sodium; 0 mg cholesterol

Ham 'n' Cabbage Crêpe Filling

Each serving provides: 2½ Protein Exchanges; 3 Vegetable Exchanges; 1 Fat Exchange

Per serving: 217 calories; 20 g protein; 10 g fat; 11 g carbohydrate; 721 mg sodium; 62 mg cholesterol

Italian Bread Four Ways

Each serving provides: With Onion Spread—1 Bread Exchange; ⅛ Vegetable Exchange; 1 Fat Exchange

With Cheese Spread—1 Bread Exchange; 1 Fat Exchange; 15 calories Optional Exchange

With Garlic-Herb "Butter"—1 Bread Exchange; 1 Fat Exchange

With Anchovy "Butter"—1 Bread Exchange; 1 Fat Exchange; 5 calories Optional Exchange

Per serving with Onion Spread: 116 calories; 3 g protein; 4 g fat; 17 g carbohydrate; 211 mg sodium; 0.3 mg cholesterol

With Cheese Spread: 128 calories; 4 g protein; 5 g fat; 16 g carbohydrate; 258 mg sodium; 2 mg cholesterol

With Garlic-Herb "Butter": 113 calories; 3 g protein; 4 g fat; 16 g carbohydrate; 226 mg sodium; 0.3 mg cholesterol

With Anchovy "Butter": 118 calories; 3 g protein; 4 g fat; 16 g carbohydrate; 235 mg sodium; 2 mg cholesterol

Lace Cookie Cones

Each serving provides: 1 Fat Exchange; 50 calories Optional Exchange

Per serving: 85 calories; 1 g protein; 4 g fat; 12 g carbohydrate; 48 mg sodium; 0 mg cholesterol

Serving Suggestions:

1. Increase Optional Exchange to 75 calories.

Per serving: 110 calories; 2 g protein; 4 g fat; 17 g carbohydrate; 66 mg sodium; 0.5 mg cholesterol

2. Add 1 Fruit Exchange and increase Optional Exchange to 65 calories.

Per serving: 137 calories; 1 g protein; 5 g fat; 23 g carbohydrate; 53 mg sodium; 0 mg cholesterol

3. Increase Optional Exchange to 66 calories.

Per serving: 101 calories; 1 g protein; 5 g fat; 14 g carbohydrate; 50 mg sodium; 100 mg cholesterol

Mango Sherbet

Each serving provides: 1 Fruit Exchange; ¼ Milk Exchange; 20 calories Optional Exchange

Per serving: 92 calories; 3 g protein; 0.3 g fat; 21 g carbohydrate; 39 mg sodium; 1 mg cholesterol

Peanut Butter Muffins

Each serving provides: 1 Protein Exchange; ½ Bread Exchange; 1 Fat Exchange; 20 calories Optional Exchange

Per serving: 160 calories; 7 g protein; 8 g fat; 15 g carbohydrate; 110 mg sodium; 69 mg cholesterol

Serving Suggestion—Increase Optional Exchange to 28 calories and calories to 168.

Pineapple Upside-Down Cake

Each serving provides: 1 Bread Exchange; 1 Fat Exchange; ½ Fruit Exchange; 55 calories Optional Exchange

Per serving: 186 calories; 4 g protein; 5 g fat; 31 g carbohydrate; 248 mg sodium; 69 mg cholesterol

Raisin Biscuits

Each serving provides: 1 Bread Exchange; ½ Fat Exchange; 45 calories Optional Exchange

Per serving: 135 calories; 3 g protein; 3 g fat; 25 g carbohydrate; 251 mg sodium; 0.3 mg cholesterol

Serving Suggestion—Increase Optional Exchange to 50 calories and calories to 140.

Rum-Raisin "Ice Cream"

Each serving provides: 1½ Fruit Exchanges; ½ Milk Exchange

Per serving: 130 calories; 4 g protein; 1 g fat; 26 g carbohydrate; 71 mg sodium; 2 mg cholesterol

Serving Suggestions:

1. Add 10 calories Optional Exchange.

Per serving: 140 calories; 5 g protein; 2 g fat; 28 g carbohydrate; 75 mg sodium; 2 mg cholesterol

2. Add 15 calories Optional Exchange.

Per serving: 145 calories; 4 g protein; 2 g fat; 28 g carbohydrate; 71 mg sodium; 2 mg cholesterol

Seafood Crêpe Filling

Each serving provides: 3 Protein Exchanges; 1⅛ Vegetable Exchanges; 1 Fat Exchange; 5 calories Optional Exchange

Per serving: 145 calories; 19 g protein; 5 g fat; 5 g carbohydrate; 845 mg sodium; 107 mg cholesterol

Tortoni

Each serving provides: 60 calories Optional Exchange

Per serving: 60 calories; 1 g protein; 1 g fat; 8 g carbohydrate; 68 mg sodium; 0 mg cholesterol

Tropical Muffins

Each serving provides: 1 Bread Exchange; 1½ Fat Exchanges; 35 calories Optional Exchange

Per serving: 175 calories; 3 g protein; 6 g fat; 27 g carbohydrate; 103 mg sodium; 0 mg cholesterol

Tuna Pot Pie

Each serving (including Basic Pot Pie Dough) provides: 3½ Protein Exchanges; 1 Bread Exchange; 1¾ Vegetable Exchanges; 2½ Fat Exchanges; ¼ Milk Exchange; 50 calories Optional Exchange

Per serving: 524 calories; 33 g protein; 25 g fat; 34 g carbohydrate; 1,014 mg sodium; 39 mg cholesterol

Turkey Pot Pie

Each serving (including Basic Pot Pie Dough) provides: 4 Protein Exchanges; 1½ Bread Exchanges; 1 Vegetable Exchange; 2 Fat Exchanges; 25 calories Optional Exchange

Per serving: 422 calories; 40 g protein; 13 g fat; 33 g carbohydrate; 741 mg sodium; 88 mg cholesterol

Vanilla Fudge Swirl

Each serving provides: 1 Fruit Exchange; ½ Milk Exchange; 30 calories Optional Exchange

Per serving: 128 calories; 4 g protein; 2 g fat; 24 g carbohydrate; 70 mg sodium; 2 mg cholesterol

Veal Chili Pot Pie

Each serving (including Basic Pot Pie Dough) provides: 4 Protein Exchanges; 1½ Bread Exchanges; 1½ Vegetable Exchanges; 2½ Fat Exchanges; 40 calories Optional Exchange

Per serving: 557 calories; 41 g protein; 26 g fat; 41 g carbohydrate; 625 mg sodium (estimated); 115 mg cholesterol

---

REFRIGERATOR READY

Bacon and Egg Salad

Each serving provides: 3 Protein Exchanges; 1⅔ Vegetable Exchanges; 1½ Fat Exchanges

Per serving: 306 calories; 22 g protein; 21 g fat; 5 g carbohydrate; 1,738 mg sodium; 325 mg cholesterol

Buttermilk-Herb Dressing

Each serving provides: 1½ Fat Exchanges; ½ Milk Exchange; 5 calories Optional Exchange

Per serving: 109 calories; 4 g protein; 7 g fat; 8 g carbohydrate; 724 mg sodium; 9 mg cholesterol

Chocolate Fudge

Each 4-piece serving provides: 2 Fat Exchanges; ½ Fruit Exchange; ½ Milk Exchange; 20 calories Optional Exchange

Per serving: 150 calories; 4 g protein; 8 g fat; 16 g carbohydrate; 90 mg sodium; 0 mg cholesterol

Each 2-piece serving provides: 1 Fat Exchange; ¼ Milk Exchange; 20 calories Optional Exchange

Per serving: 75 calories; 2 g protein; 4 g fat; 8 g carbohydrate; 45 mg sodium; 0 mg cholesterol

Confetti Rice Salad

Each serving provides: 1 Bread Exchange; ⅔ Vegetable Exchange; ½ Fat Exchange

Per serving: 112 calories; 2 g protein; 3 g fat; 20 g carbohydrate; 293 mg sodium; 0 mg cholesterol

Curried Rice Salad

Each serving provides: 4 Protein Exchanges; 1 Bread Exchange; ¾ Vegetable Exchange; 1½ Fat Exchanges; ½ Milk Exchange; 10 calories Optional Exchange

Per serving: 438 calories; 40 g protein; 15 g fat; 33 g carbohydrate; 542 mg sodium; 110 mg cholesterol

Fresh Mushroom Salad

Each serving provides: 2¾ Vegetable Exchanges; 1½ Fat Exchanges

Per serving: 93 calories; 2 g protein; 7 g fat; 6 g carbohydrate; 282 mg sodium; 0 mg cholesterol

Jellied Apple

Each serving provides: ½ Bread Exchange; 1 Fruit Exchange; 25 calories Optional Exchange

Per serving: 114 calories; 0.1 g protein; 2 g fat; 26 g carbohydrate; 47 mg sodium; 0 mg cholesterol

Macaroni Salad

Each serving provides: 1½ Bread Exchanges; ¾ Vegetable Exchange; 1½ Fat Exchanges; 15 calories Optional Exchange

Per serving: 202 calories; 5 g protein; 6 g fat; 31 g carbohydrate; 372 mg sodium; 5 mg cholesterol

Melon Mélange

Each serving provides: 1 Fruit Exchange; 30 calories Optional Exchange

Per serving: 89 calories; 1 g protein; 0.5 g fat; 17 g carbohydrate; 7 mg sodium; 0 mg cholesterol

Mixed Fruit Chutney

Each serving provides: ⅛ Vegetable Exchange; 1 Fruit Exchange; 15 calories Optional Exchange

Per serving: 62 calories; 1 g protein; 0.1 g fat; 16 g carbohydrate; 68 mg sodium; 0 mg cholesterol

Oriental Ginger Slaw

Each serving provides: 2½ Vegetable Exchanges; 1½ Fat Exchanges; 20 calories Optional Exchange

Per serving: 113 calories; 2 g protein; 7 g fat; 12 g carbohydrate; 252 mg sodium; 0 mg cholesterol

Pepper Relish

Each 6-tablespoon serving provides: 1¼ Vegetable Exchanges; 5 calories Optional Exchange

Per serving: 34 calories; 2 g protein; 0.2 g fat; 8 g carbohydrate; 280 mg sodium; 0 mg cholesterol

Each 3-tablespoon serving provides: ⅔ Vegetable Exchange; 3 calories Optional Exchange

Per serving: 17 calories; 1 g protein; 0.1 g fat; 4 g carbohydrate; 140 mg sodium; 0 mg cholesterol

Pineapple Cheesecake

Each serving provides: 1 Protein Exchange; 1 Bread Exchange; 1 Fat Exchange; ½ Fruit Exchange; ¼ Milk Exchange; 30 calories Optional Exchange

Per serving: 264 calories; 12 g protein; 11 g fat; 30 g carbohydrate; 234 mg sodium; 151 mg cholesterol

Serving Suggestion—Increase Optional Exchange to 45 calories.

Per serving: 276 calories; 12 g protein; 12 g fat; 31 g carbohydrate; 234 mg sodium; 151 mg cholesterol

Potato-Egg Salad

Each serving provides: ½ Protein Exchange; 1 Bread Exchange; ⅓ Vegetable Exchange; 1½ Fat Exchanges; 10 calories Optional Exchange

Per serving: 159 calories; 6 g protein; 9 g fat; 15 g carbohydrate; 376 mg sodium; 141 mg cholesterol

Salsa

Each serving provides: 1½ Vegetable Exchanges; 1 Fat Exchange

Per serving: 81 calories; 2 g protein; 5 g fat; 8 g carbohydrate; 291 mg sodium; 0 mg cholesterol

Seasoned Bean 'n' Egg Salad

Each serving provides: 2½ Protein Exchanges; 2 Vegetable Exchanges; ½ Fat Exchange; 10 calories Optional Exchange

Per serving: 235 calories; 14 g protein; 10 g fat; 24 g carbohydrate; 492 mg sodium (estimated); 274 mg cholesterol

Spaghetti Squash Slaw

Each serving provides: 2 Vegetable Exchanges; 1½ Fat Exchanges

Per serving: 104 calories; 2 g protein; 8 g fat; 9 g carbohydrate; 541 mg sodium; 0 mg cholesterol

Sweet and Sour Barbecue Sauce

Each serving provides: ½ Fruit Exchange; 20 calories Optional Exchange

Per serving: 43 calories; 0.5 g protein; trace fat; 11 g carbohydrate; 154 mg sodium; 0 mg cholesterol

Sweet Herb Vinaigrette

Each serving provides: 1½ Fat Exchanges; 5 calories Optional Exchange

Per serving: 68 calories; 0.1 g protein; 7 g fat; 1 g carbohydrate; 103 mg sodium; 0 mg cholesterol

Tomato-Onion Salad with Basil Dressing

Each serving provides: 2½ Vegetable Exchanges; 1½ Fat Exchanges

Per serving: 110 calories; 2 g protein; 7 g fat; 11 g carbohydrate; 149 mg sodium; 0 mg cholesterol

Tuna-Macaroni Salad

Each serving (including Buttermilk-Herb Dressing) provides: 3 Protein Exchanges; 1½ Bread Exchanges; 3⅓ Vegetable Exchanges; 1½ Fat Exchanges; ½ Milk Exchange; 15 calories Optional Exchange

Per serving: 505 calories; 34 g protein; 22 g fat; 47 g carbohydrate; 1,162 mg sodium; 298 mg cholesterol

---

NO-COOK CREATIONS

Banana Split Breakfast

Each serving provides: 1 Protein Exchange; 1 Fruit Exchange; 25 calories Optional Exchange

Per serving: 154 calories; 10 g protein; 4 g fat; 20 g carbohydrate; 301 mg sodium; 11 mg cholesterol

Cheese-Filled Pears

Each serving provides: 1 Protein Exchange; 1½ Fat Exchanges; 1 Fruit Exchange; 10 calories Optional Exchange

Per serving: 250 calories; 8 g protein; 15 g fat; 23 g carbohydrate; 468 mg sodium, 21 mg cholesterol

Coconut-Berry Parfait

Each serving provides: 1 Bread Exchange; 1 Fruit Exchange; ½ Milk Exchange; 20 calories Optional Exchange

Per serving: 177 calories; 6 g protein; 1 g fat; 36 g carbohydrate; 226 mg sodium; 1 mg cholesterol

Coffee Cream

Each serving provides: ½ Milk Exchange; 35 calories Optional Exchange

Per serving: 75 calories; 4 g protein; 1 g fat; 12 g carbohydrate; 67 mg sodium; 2 mg cholesterol

Cran-Orange Relish

Each serving provides: ½ Fruit Exchange; 25 calories Optional Exchange

Per serving: 53 calories; 0.4 g protein; 0.2 g fat; 13 g carbohydrate; 2 mg sodium; 0 mg cholesterol

"Crème Fraîche"

Each 3-tablespoon serving provides: ¼ Milk Exchange; 15 calories Optional Exchange

Per serving: 30 calories; 2 g protein; 1 g fat; 4 g carbohydrate; 22 mg sodium; 0.4 mg cholesterol

Each 1½-tablespoon serving provides: 15 calories Optional Exchange

Per serving: 15 calories; 1 g protein; 0.5 g fat; 2 g carbohydrate; 11 mg sodium; 0.2 mg cholesterol

Fruited Coleslaw

Each serving provides: 2½ Vegetable Exchanges; 1 Fat Exchange; 1½ Fruit Exchanges; 25 calories Optional Exchange

Per serving: 170 calories; 2 g protein; 6 g fat; 32 g carbohydrate; 188 mg sodium; 3 mg cholesterol

Ginger "Ice Cream"

Each serving provides: 1 Fruit Exchange; ½ Milk Exchange

Per serving: 101 calories; 4 g protein; 1 g fat; 19 g carbohydrate; 70 mg sodium; 2 mg cholesterol

Honeyed Fruit and Carrot Salad

Each serving provides: 2 Vegetable Exchanges; 1 Fruit Exchange; 15 calories Optional Exchange

Per serving: 121 calories; 2 g protein; 1 g fat; 28 g carbohydrate; 57 mg sodium; 0 mg cholesterol

Italian Tomato-Cheese Salad

Each serving provides: ½ Protein Exchange; 1¼ Vegetable Exchanges; ½ Fat Exchange; 10 calories Optional Exchange

Per serving: 86 calories; 4 g protein; 7 g fat; 4 g carbohydrate; 413 mg sodium; 11 mg cholesterol

Lime-Dressed Melon Delight

Each serving provides: ½ Vegetable Exchange; 1 Fat Exchange; 2 Fruit Exchanges

Per serving: 141 calories; 3 g protein; 6 g fat; 24 g carbohydrate; 297 mg sodium; 0 mg cholesterol

Lox 'n' Horseradish Sauce Appetizer

Each serving provides: 1 Protein Exchange; ½ Vegetable Exchange; 15 calories Optional Exchange

Per serving: 71 calories; 7 g protein; 4 g fat; 3 g carbohydrate; 1,816 mg sodium; 11 mg cholesterol

Mixed Fruit Ambrosia

Each serving provides: 1 Fruit Exchange; 20 calories Optional Exchange

Per serving: 84 calories; 1 g protein; 1 g fat; 20 g carbohydrate; 3 mg sodium; 0 mg cholesterol

Peanut Butter Bonbons

Each serving provides: 1½ Protein Exchanges; ½ Bread Exchange; 1½ Fat Exchanges; ½ Fruit Exchange; 5 calories Optional Exchange

Per serving: 212 calories; 8 g protein; 12 g fat; 21 g carbohydrate; 281 mg sodium; 0 mg cholesterol

Quick Liverwurst Pâté

Each serving provides: 1½ Protein Exchanges; 1 Bread Exchange; ¼ Vegetable Exchange; ½ Fat Exchange; 20 calories Optional Exchange

Per serving: 249 calories; 8 g protein; 17 g fat; 16 g carbohydrate; 714 mg sodium; 69 mg cholesterol

Spiced Orange Salad

Each serving provides: ¼ Vegetable Exchange; 1½ Fat Exchanges; 1 Fruit Exchange; 10 calories Optional Exchange

Per serving: 146 calories; 1 g protein; 9 g fat; 19 g carbohydrate; 322 mg sodium; 0 mg cholesterol

Strawberry Fizz

Each serving provides: 1 Fruit Exchange; ½ Milk Exchange; 15 calories Optional Exchange

Per serving: 121 calories; 5 g protein; 1 g fat; 22 g carbohydrate; 68 mg sodium; 2 mg cholesterol

Sweet and Sour Corn Salad

Each serving provides: 1 Bread Exchange; 1⅔ Vegetable Exchanges; 1½ Fat Exchanges; 3 calories Optional Exchange

Per serving: 141 calories; 3 g protein; 6 g fat; 21 g carbohydrate; 547 mg sodium; 4 mg cholesterol

Tabouli

Each serving provides: 1 Bread Exchange; 4 Vegetable Exchanges; 1½ Fat Exchanges

Per serving: 231 calories; 6 g protein; 8 g fat; 38 g carbohydrate; 556 mg sodium; 0 mg cholesterol

Tomato-Cucumber Salad with Parsley Dressing

Each serving provides: 1½ Vegetable Exchanges; 1 Fat Exchange

Per serving: 68 calories; 1 g protein; 5 g fat; 6 g carbohydrate; 247 mg sodium; 0 mg cholesterol

Tossed Green Salad with Herb Dressing

Each serving provides: 2½ Vegetable Exchanges; ½ Fat Exchange

Per serving: 33 calories; 1 g protein; 3 g fat; 2 g carbohydrate; 73 mg sodium; 0 mg cholesterol

Tutti-"Fruiti" Milk Shake

Each serving provides: 1 Fruit Exchange; ½ Milk Exchange; 20 calories Optional Exchange

Per serving: 139 calories; 5 g protein; 1 g fat; 27 g carbohydrate; 131 mg sodium; 5 mg cholesterol

Zucchini-Pepper Slaw

Each serving (including Buttermilk-Cheese Dressing) provides: 2⅔ Vegetable Exchanges; 30 calories Optional Exchange

Per serving: 69 calories; 6 g protein; 1 g fat; 10 g carbohydrate; 357 mg sodium; 4 mg cholesterol

---

MEAL MATES

Braised Sweet and Sour Red Cabbage

Each serving provides: 2¼ Vegetable Exchanges; 1 Fat Exchange; 1 Fruit Exchange; 35 calories Optional Exchange

Per serving: 159 calories; 2 g protein; 4 g fat; 26 g carbohydrate; 388 mg sodium; 0 mg cholesterol

Broccoli-Stuffed Potato

Each serving provides: 1 Protein Exchange; 1½ Bread Exchanges; ⅔ Vegetable Exchange; 1 Fat Exchange; 2 calories Optional Exchange

Per serving: 288 calories; 12 g protein; 13 g fat; 31 g carbohydrate; 435 mg sodium; 30 mg cholesterol

Carrots au Gratin

Each serving provides: 1 Protein Exchange; ½ Bread Exchange; 2 Vegetable Exchanges; 1½ Fat Exchanges; ¼ Milk Exchange

Per serving: 271 calories; 12 g protein; 16 g fat; 21 g carbohydrate; 376 mg sodium; 31 mg cholesterol

Cauliflower-Carrot Stir-Fry

Each serving provides: 1½ Vegetable Exchanges; 1 Fat Exchange

Per serving: 67 calories; 2 g protein; 5 g fat; 5 g carbohydrate; 20 mg sodium; 0 mg cholesterol

Cauliflower Polonaise

Each serving provides: ½ Protein Exchange; ½ Bread Exchange; 4 Vegetable Exchanges; 1½ Fat Exchanges

Per serving: 205 calories; 12 g protein; 9 g fat; 22 g carbohydrate; 479 mg sodium; 137 mg cholesterol

Cream of Artichoke Soup

Each serving provides: 1 Vegetable Exchange; 1 Fat Exchange; ¼ Milk Exchange; 25 calories Optional Exchange

Per serving: 106 calories; 5 g protein; 4 g fat; 13 g carbohydrate; 585 mg sodium; 1 mg cholesterol

Creamy Tomato-Vegetable Soup

Each serving provides: 1 Vegetable Exchange; 1 Fat Exchange; ½ Milk Exchange; 50 calories Optional Exchange

Per serving: 147 calories; 8 g protein; 4 g fat; 22 g carbohydrate; 828 mg sodium; 3 mg cholesterol

Eggplant Provençale

Each serving provides: 3¼ Vegetable Exchanges; 1 Fat Exchange; 10 calories Optional Exchange

Per serving: 98 calories; 2 g protein; 6 g fat; 11 g carbohydrate; 297 mg sodium; 0 mg cholesterol

Elegant Mushroom Sauté

Each serving provides: 4¼ Vegetable Exchanges; 1½ Fat Exchanges; 5 calories Optional Exchange

Per serving: 103 calories; 4 g protein; 6 g fat; 8 g carbohydrate; 358 mg sodium; 0 mg cholesterol

Honeyed Pineapple Carrots

Each serving provides: 4 Vegetable Exchanges; 1½ Fat Exchanges; ½ Fruit Exchange; 15 calories Optional Exchange

Per serving: 198 calories; 3 g protein; 6 g fat; 36 g carbohydrate; 313 mg sodium; 0 mg cholesterol

House Special Soup

Each serving provides: 1 Protein Exchange; ½ Bread Exchange; ¾ Vegetable Exchange; 10 calories Optional Exchange

Per serving with shrimp: 88 calories; 9 g protein; 1 g fat; 12 g carbohydrate; 767 mg sodium; 43 mg cholesterol

With pork: 125 calories; 10 g protein; 4 g fat; 12 g carbohydrate; 746 mg sodium; 25 mg cholesterol

With chicken: 109 calories; 11 g protein; 2 g fat; 12 g carbohydrate; 752 mg sodium; 25 mg cholesterol

Italian-Style Scalloped Potatoes

Each serving provides: ½ Protein Exchange; 1 Bread Exchange; 1½ Vegetable Exchanges; 1½ Fat Exchanges; 5 calories Optional Exchange

Per serving: 243 calories; 10 g protein; 12 g fat; 25 g carbohydrate; 452 mg sodium; 13 mg cholesterol

Kidney Bean 'n' Ham Soup

Each serving provides: 2 Protein Exchanges; 1 Bread Exchange; 1¾ Vegetable Exchanges; 1 Fat Exchange; 3 calories Optional Exchange

Per serving: 204 calories; 18 g protein; 9 g fat; 13 g carbohydrate; 1,210 mg sodium (estimated); 50 mg cholesterol

Mexican Corn Bread

Each serving provides: ½ Protein Exchange; 1 Bread Exchange; ⅓ Vegetable Exchange; 1 Fat Exchange; 20 calories Optional Exchange

Per serving: 180 calories; 6 g protein; 7 g fat; 24 g carbohydrate; 469 mg sodium; 138 mg cholesterol

Orange Rice

Each serving provides: 1 Bread Exchange; ¾ Vegetable Exchange; 1½ Fat Exchanges; 1 Fruit Exchange

Per serving: 224 calories; 4 g protein; 6 g fat; 39 g carbohydrate; 379 mg sodium; 0 mg cholesterol

Orzo 'n' Vegetable Salad Italienne

Each serving provides: 1 Bread Exchange; 2 Vegetable Exchanges; 1½ Fat Exchanges; 20 calories Optional Exchange

Per serving: 196 calories; 5 g protein; 10 g fat; 24 g carbohydrate; 407 mg sodium; 1 mg cholesterol

Parmesan-Topped Stuffed Potato

Each serving provides: 1½ Bread Exchanges; ⅔ Vegetable Exchange; 1 Fat Exchange; ¼ Milk Exchange; 10 calories Optional Exchange

Per serving: 195 calories; 7 g protein; 5 g fat; 33 g carbohydrate; 175 mg sodium; 2 mg cholesterol

Raisin Bread Pudding

Each serving provides: ½ Protein Exchange; 1 Bread Exchange; 1 Fat Exchange; 45 calories Optional Exchange

Per serving: 182 calories; 6 g protein; 7 g fat; 23 g carbohydrate; 236 mg sodium; 138 mg cholesterol

Sautéed Tomatoes

Each serving provides: ½ Bread Exchange; 3 Vegetable Exchanges; 1½ Fat Exchanges

Per serving: 130 calories; 3 g protein; 6 g fat; 17 g carbohydrate; 342 mg sodium; 0 mg cholesterol

Sesame Three-Bean Salad

Each serving provides: 1 Protein Exchange; 2⅛ Vegetable Exchanges; ½ Fat Exchange; 10 calories Optional Exchange

Per serving with fresh or frozen green beans: 134 calories; 7 g protein; 4 g fat; 21 g carbohydrate; 474 mg sodium (estimated); 0 mg cholesterol

With canned green beans: 133 calories; 7 g protein; 4 g fat; 21 g carbohydrate; 778 mg sodium (estimated); 0 mg cholesterol

Sweet and Sour Spinach-Mushroom Salad

Each serving provides: 2¾ Vegetable Exchanges; ½ Fat Exchange; 10 calories Optional Exchange

Per serving: 56 calories; 3 g protein; 3 g fat; 7 g carbohydrate; 185 mg sodium; 0 mg cholesterol

If bacon bits are used, increase calories to 58 and sodium to 209 mg.

Vegetable-Cheddar Salad

Each serving provides: 1 Protein Exchange; 3 Vegetable Exchanges; 1½ Fat Exchanges; 20 calories Optional Exchange

Per serving: 266 calories; 15 g protein; 19 g fat; 14 g carbohydrate; 356 mg sodium; 30 mg cholesterol

Zucchini-Apple Sauté

Each serving provides: 4½ Vegetable Exchanges; 2 Fat Exchanges; 1 Fruit Exchange

Per serving: 183 calories; 4 g protein; 8 g fat; 28 g carbohydrate; 364 mg sodium; 0 mg cholesterol

Zucchini-Corn Sauté

Each serving provides: 1 Bread Exchange; 4½ Vegetable Exchanges; 2 Fat Exchanges

Per serving: 230 calories; 6 g protein; 11 g fat; 33 g carbohydrate; 898 mg sodium; 0 mg cholesterol

---

GOOD LOOKIN' COOKIN'

Chicken Livers with Caper Sauce in Croustades (Toast Cases)

Each serving provides: 4 Protein Exchanges; 1 Bread Exchange; ½ Vegetable Exchange; 1 Fat Exchange; ½ Milk Exchange; 20 calories Optional Exchange

Per serving: 356 calories; 36 g protein; 10 g fat; 27 g carbohydrate; 640 mg sodium; 848 mg cholesterol

Chilled Poached Fish Salad with Louis Dressing

Each serving provides: 4 Protein Exchanges; 1⅛ Vegetable Exchanges; 1½ Fat Exchanges; 15 calories Optional Exchange

Per serving: 223 calories; 26 g protein; 7 g fat; 15 g carbohydrate; 434 mg sodium; 75 mg cholesterol

Curried Papaya Chicken

Each serving provides: 4 Protein Exchanges; ¼ Vegetable Exchange; 1 Fat Exchange; ½ Fruit Exchange; 25 calories Optional Exchange

Per serving: 313 calories; 35 g protein; 12 g fat; 14 g carbohydrate; 634 mg sodium; 101 mg cholesterol

Florets and Pasta in Parmesan Sauce

Each serving (including Béchamel) provides: 1 Protein Exchange; 1 Bread Exchange; 4 Vegetable Exchanges; 1½ Fat Exchanges; ½ Milk Exchange

Per serving: 383 calories; 27 g protein; 16 g fat; 38 g carbohydrate; 769 mg sodium; 25 mg cholesterol

Fruited Chiffon Parfaits

Each serving provides: 1 Fruit Exchange; ½ Bread Exchange; 45 calories Optional Exchange

Per serving: 105 calories; 3 g protein; 3 g fat; 18 g carbohydrate; 57 mg sodium; 0 mg cholesterol

Lemon Meringue Pie

Each serving (including pastry shell) provides: ½ Bread Exchange; 1 Fat Exchange; 75 calories Optional Exchange

Per serving: 134 calories; 3 g protein; 5 g fat; 20 g carbohydrate; 159 mg sodium; 0.1 mg cholesterol

"Linzer Tart" Cookies

Each serving provides: 1 Bread Exchange; 2 Fat Exchanges; 30 calories Optional Exchange

Per serving: 183 calories; 3 g protein; 8 g fat; 24 g carbohydrate; 205 mg sodium; 0 mg cholesterol

Meat Loaf Wellington

Each serving provides: 3 Protein Exchanges; 1 Bread Exchange; ⅛ Vegetable Exchange; 1 Fat Exchange; 35 calories Optional Exchange

Per serving: 352 calories; 23 g protein; 20 g fat; 18 g carbohydrate; 598 mg sodium; 191 mg cholesterol

Onion Popovers

Each serving provides: ½ Protein Exchange; 1 Bread Exchange; ½ Fat Exchange; 15 calories Optional Exchange

Per serving: 165 calories; 7 g protein; 5 g fat; 21 g carbohydrate; 196 mg sodium; 138 mg cholesterol

Variation—Cheese Popovers—Increase Optional Exchange to 20 calories

Per serving: 170 calories; 7 g protein; 6 g fat; 21 g carbohydrate; 220 mg sodium; 139 mg cholesterol

Orange "Cream" Crêpes

Each serving (including crêpes) provides: 2½ Protein Exchanges; 1 Bread Exchange; 1 Fruit Exchange; ¼ Milk Exchange; 35 calories Optional Exchange

Per serving: 413 calories; 23 g protein; 13 g fat; 51 g carbohydrate; 293 mg sodium; 177 mg cholesterol

Orange Spanish "Cream"

Each serving provides: ½ Fruit Exchange; ¼ Milk Exchange; 40 calories Optional Exchange

Per serving: 88 calories; 5 g protein; 2 g fat; 14 g carbohydrate; 51 mg sodium; 70 mg cholesterol

Pasta Salad

Each serving provides: 3 Protein Exchanges; ½ Bread Exchange; 2½ Vegetable Exchanges; 1½ Fat Exchanges; 20 calories Optional Exchange

Per serving: 373 calories; 25 g protein; 22 g fat; 19 g carbohydrate; 965 mg sodium; 80 mg cholesterol

Potato Soufflé

Each serving provides: 1 Protein Exchange; 1 Bread Exchange; 1 Vegetable Exchange; 2 Fat Exchanges; ¾ Milk Exchange

Per serving: 314 calories; 16 g protein; 14 g fat; 32 g carbohydrate; 816 mg sodium; 278 mg cholesterol

Rugalach (Raisin Crescents)

Each serving (including Pastry Dough) provides: 1 Bread Exchange; 2 Fat Exchanges; 1 Fruit Exchange; 50 calories Optional Exchange

Per serving: 236 calories; 4 g protein; 8 g fat; 39 g carbohydrate; 102 mg sodium; 0.3 mg cholesterol

Skillet Broccoli Soufflé

Each serving provides: 2 Protein Exchanges; 1 Vegetable Exchange; 1 Fat Exchange; 50 calories Optional Exchange

Per serving: 266 calories; 19 g protein; 17 g fat; 10 g carbohydrate; 510 mg sodium; 301 mg cholesterol

Spicy Vegetable-Filled Biscuits

Each serving provides: 1 Bread Exchange; ⅓ Vegetable Exchange; ½ Fat Exchange

Per serving: 109 calories; 3 g protein; 4 g fat; 15 g carbohydrate; 251 mg sodium; 0 mg cholesterol

Strawberry Gelatin Cloud

Each serving provides: 25 calories Optional Exchange

Per serving: 25 calories; 2 g protein; 1 g fat; 1 g carbohydrate; 17 mg sodium; 0 mg cholesterol

Tortilla Pie

Each serving provides: 2½ Protein Exchanges; 1 Bread Exchange; ¼ Vegetable Exchange

Per serving: 266 calories; 15 g protein; 11 g fat; 30 g carbohydrate; 620 mg sodium (estimated); 30 mg cholesterol

Vegetable-Pasta Medley in Onion-Cheddar Sauce

Each serving provides: 1 Protein Exchange; ½ Bread Exchange; 4¼ Vegetable Exchanges; 1 Fat Exchange; ½ Milk Exchange; 20 calories Optional Exchange

Per serving: 355 calories; 20 g protein; 14 g fat; 40 g carbohydrate; 427 mg sodium; 32 mg cholesterol

Index